ANTON RAPHAEL MENGS 1728-1779
AND HIS BRITISH PATRONS

Steffi Roettgen

Anton Raphael Mengs 1728-1779 and his British Patrons

ZWEMMER
English Heritage

First published 1993 by
A. Zwemmer Ltd
26 Litchfield Street
London WC2H 9NJ

In association with
English Heritage
Keysign House
429 Oxford Street
London W1R 2HD

ISBN 0 302 00624 9

Designed by Alan Bartram
Translated from German by Eileen Martin
Edited by Alex Bell
Produced by Philip Wilson Publishers Ltd
Typeset by August Filmsetting, St Helens, England
Printed and bound by Snoeck, Ducaju & Zoon, NV
Ghent, Belgium

FRONT COVER:
A. R. Mengs, *Self-Portrait*

BACK COVER:
A. R. Mengs, *Portrait of Arabella Swimmer*

Contents

Foreword

Mengs was described by his German contemporary Winckelmann as 'the greatest artist of his time and perhaps of succeeding times, reborn like the phoenix, from the ashes of the first Raphael, to teach the world beauty in art, and to achieve the greatest flight committed to human powers in the same'. In his own lifetime, he was an international phenomenon, arguably the most famous and influential living artist in Europe.

Named after Antonio Correggio and after Raphael, he was predestined by his ambitious father for greatness. By his late teens he was Court Painter to the Elector of Saxony at Dresden. Moving to Rome, he became the only serious rival to Pompeo Batoni in the very particular field of Grand Tour portraiture, offering a more intellectual and restrained, though no less glamorous likeness for the richest patrons. In Madrid, as Court Painter to King Charles III, he took charge of the decorations of the Palacio Real where Tiepolo and his sons were also working. A generation of artists studied in his studios in Dresden, Rome and Madrid and his published ideas on art theory were translated into Italian, French, German, Spanish and English. And yet, within a decade of his death in Rome in 1779, Reynolds was attributing Mengs's success (and that of Batoni) to mere prejudice in favour of 'the Roman School' and accurately predicting his rapid descent into relative oblivion.

This book, published to accompany the first ever major exhibition on the artist in this country, re-evaluates the reputation of Mengs through examining his commissions from British patrons. It illustrates the variety of his talent, from grand religious pieces to an exquisite pastel, from designs for elaborate ceiling frescos to intimate, searching portraits of his friends and colleagues, and dazzling Grand Tour portraits of the British aristocracy.

Dr Steffi Roettgen's study serves as a companion not only to the exhibition at Kenwood but also to her catalogue raisonné on Mengs. I am most grateful to her for developing this project over several years and to John Jacob, formerly Curator of Kenwood, for initiating what is, in effect, a sequel to the Kenwood Batoni exhibition of 1982. Ian Dejardin, Senior Curator of Collections in English Heritage's Historic Properties (London), is to be congratulated for managing every aspect of the exhibition with engaging humour and contagious enthusiasm. Among other staff to whom thanks are due I would like to acknowledge the dedication of Christine Higgs, Sebastian Edwards, John Uden, Paul Highnam, Adrian Moore, Peter Cross, Martin Greenwood and the Kenwood custodians. Particular thanks are due to Eileen Martin for her heroic work translating the text into English.

English Heritage is greatly indebted to the many lenders who so generously agreed to contribute to the exhibition at the time of year when their houses and galleries most need to look their best. We are particularly grateful to His Grace the Duke of Wellington; The Earl and Countess of Rosebery; Lord Montagu of Beaulieu; Sir Brinsley Ford; Count Andrew Ciechanowiecki; The Hon. Christopher Lennox-Boyd; Marcello Violante; Ralph Holland; the National Gallery, Prague; the National Museum, Warsaw; the Boymans-van Beuningen Museum, Rotterdam; St John's College, Cambridge; as well as to those lenders who wish to remain anonymous. The National Museums and Galleries on Merseyside kindly agreed to the reproduction of their painting in the publicity material. Finally, I would like to thank the staff of Philip Wilson Publishers for producing such a handsome publication. As part of Kenwood's forty-year tradition of studies in British art history both book and exhibition provide a rich international context in which to enjoy the masterpieces of The Iveagh Bequest afresh.

JULIUS BRYANT
Head of Museums Division
English Heritage

Acknowledgements

This exhibition would not have been possible without the contributions of very many people. Of the many scholars who have paved the way and done so much to shed light on Mengs, I have made special mention in my introductory essay, and repeat my thanks to them here. Special thanks must go to Hugh Belsey, Mungo Campbell, Ann Hepper, Olivier Michel, Stella Rudolph, Julien Stock, and Marcello Violante. At Kenwood, my chief thanks are due to Ian Dejardin, to whom has fallen the chief responsibility for the day-to-day organisation of the exhibition, the co-editing of the text, and the planning of the display. I am grateful to all the Kenwood staff who helped him in his task, particularly Christine Higgs, whose administrative support, particularly in gathering together the photographic material, was invaluable. Many others have been generous with their time and assistance, notably David Alexander, Ann Bukantas, Timothy Clifford, James Holloway, Richard Knight, Candy Kuhl, Alastair Laing, Freda Matassa, Christine Mathez, Gayle Mault, Sarah MacDonald, Ian Mclure, David NcNeff, James Miller, Margaret Richardson, Joanna Rickards, Francis Russell, Nick Savage, Guy Shaw, Helen Valentine, Jonathon Voak and Clare Wilkins.

STEFFI ROETTGEN

Lenders to the Exhibition

The Warden and Fellows of All Souls College, Oxford 30
The Visitors of the Ashmolean Museum, Oxford 8, 36
The Trustees of the British Museum 32, 37, 46
Museum Boymans-van Beuningen, Rotterdam 34, 38
The Duke of Buccleuch KT 2, 40
Chaucer Fine Arts, London 19, 21, 22, 45
The Governing Body of Christ Church, Oxford 16
Count A. S. Ciechanowiecki 13
P & D Colnaghi & Co Ltd 12
The Courtauld Institute Galleries, London (Witt Collection) 35
Ferens Art Gallery: Hull City Museums and Art Galleries 31
Sir Brinsley Ford CBE Hon FRA FSA 10, 42
Ralph Holland 39
The Hon Christopher Lennox-Boyd 47, 48
Manchester City Art Galleries 20
Lord Montagu of Beaulieu 3
The Trustees of the National Gallery 25
The National Gallery of Ireland 33
The National Gallery of Scotland 41, 44
The National Museum of Wales, Cardiff 18
The National Museum in Warsaw 17
The National Trust: Dunham Massey, The Stamford Collection 9
The National Trust: Mount Stewart, The Londonderry Collection 14
The National Trust, Stourhead, the Wiltshire Record Office 52, 53, 54
Prague, National Gallery 4
The Earl of Rosebery, Dalmeny House, West Lothian 15
Royal Academy of Arts, London 56, 57, 61
Master and Fellows of St John's College, Cambridge 27
Trustees of Sir John Soane's Museum 49, 50
The Board of Trustees of The Victoria and Albert Museum 24, 43, 55
The Board of Trustees of the National Museums & Galleries on Merseyside, Walker Art Gallery 1
The Duke of Wellington 5, 28, 29
West Yorkshire Archive Service 51
Trustees of the Weston Park Foundation 26
Yale Center for British Art, Paul Mellon Collection 7
Private Collections 6, 11, 23, 58, 59, 60

Introduction

Anton Raphael Mengs never visited Britain, but his contacts and relations with British collectors, artists and connoisseurs were so extensive and evident that they offer rich material for study.

The decisive factor in Mengs's many contacts with Great Britain from 1751 until his death was evidently the Grand Tour. This had become obligatory for the British aristocracy in the eighteenth century, and it provided one of the most important channels of communication between the British Isles and the continent throughout that period.

The British love of travel was the result of growing wealth, and it continued astonishingly independently of political alliances and conditions.[1] However, political developments helped to further British interest in the continent – the Treaties of Utrecht and Rastatt of 1714, for example, which ended Anglo-French hostilities until 1731, and the 'renversement des alliances', which made Britain an ally of Prussia in the Seven Years' War.

The accession of the Protestant House of Hanover fuelled general interest in northern central Europe after 1714. Cultural contacts between the countries of Europe were greatly encouraged by the growth in diplomatic activity, which was one of the most striking developments of the eighteenth century. It created the basis for cross-relations and cultural symbioses which were new in this form, and again, the Grand Tour played an important part, as the activities of the diplomats and the interests and personal contacts of the travellers frequently coincided, opening up important and far-reaching prospects.

The British aristocrat on the Grand Tour was not only eager to see the art treasures and the variety of landscapes and peoples on the continent, he was also able, thanks to his generally comfortable financial situation, to take some of these treasures home with him. Italian art of the Counter-Reformation, later to be despised by John Ruskin's generation for its 'catholicity of taste',[2] and antique sculpture were particularly eagerly sought.[3] This preference may at first seem surprising, but its origins were political, religious and philosophical. A secret leaning to Catholicism played a considerable part, particularly among the Scots with their support for the Jacobites, who had found refuge in Rome, for astonishingly it was the monumental religious paintings, with their theatrical and rhetorical style, that exercised a strong fascination for many of the British tourists.[4]

However, British art theory in the early eighteenth century, which was also widely echoed in Germany, reflected a preference for the Italian seventeenth-century schools,[5] and this also influenced the itineraries of many travellers. The galleries in Düsseldorf and Dresden, which had rich collections of Italian and Flemish art, drew those British travellers who extended their Grand Tour to northern and eastern Europe, while in Italy the Uffizi and the collections in the private palaces of Genoa and Venice were the main focus of interest, creating and stimulating a love of Italian Baroque painting in their British visitors.

British purchasers and patrons promoted and determined the artistic direction of Europe in the second half of the eighteenth century in a further, unprecedented way. The British preference for an academic style, adorned with rhetorical effects but classically moderated, encouraged the emergence of an ideal of taste which was in many respects identical with what is now called Neo-Classicism. It is therefore not surprising that Pompeo Batoni, Anton Raphael Mengs, his pupil Anton von Maron and Angelika Kauffmann, the outstanding representatives of that style in Rome, enjoyed especial esteem in Great Britain during their lifetimes. In the case of Kauffmann, this reputation has been maintained up to the present, while Batoni's lavish and excellent portraits, like his pleasing historical paintings, have regained the appreciation they deserve in recent decades – we only need recall the exhibition at Kenwood in 1982.[6] However, the part played by Mengs in the development of a particular aspect of British taste and in the context of Anglo-German and Anglo-Italian artistic relations in the second half of the century has not so far been fully explored in all its complexity.[7] It is true that his role and his significance for British art and culture in the late eighteenth century are less obvious than those of other German-speaking painters, who, like Kauffmann, settled in London. These include Fuseli and Zoffany, both of whom were in direct contact with Mengs. Zoffany was his pupil, while Fuseli, whose father had published Mengs's essay 'Gedanken über die Schönheit und den Geschmack in der Mahlerey' ('Thoughts on Beauty and Taste in Painting') in 1762, felt he had outshone Mengs.

The relations between Mengs and British culture are largely a result of the cosmopolitanism of the second half of the eighteenth century, and if only on account of the places in which he lived and worked, Mengs must be seen as typical of the internationalism of the late Enlightenment. He was part of the culture of the Dresden court and of the Roman Settecento, but he was also involved with Tiepolo and Goya, in the fields of decorative painting and portraiture at the royal court of Madrid. His great range as a painter, his theoretical and academic ambitions, and the high offices he held as Senior Court Painter to two of the most cultured courts in Europe explain why his work is so difficult to grasp.

The contacts between Mengs and Great Britain which form the subject of this exhibition should be seen as one strand in a much more complex and far-reaching network in which his influence was felt.[8] Focussing on Mengs's British connections will show how greatly the Neo-Classical movement in taste was dependent on the unique constellation that had arisen in Rome from the meeting of very different interests, inclinations and talents.

This survey draws on a number of earlier works of research which have provided valuable material for our reconstruction. The following are the most important; they can only be briefly mentioned here, but are gratefully acknowledged.

Of fundamental importance was the work of Cooper on Richard Wilson's portraiture (1948), that of Sparrow on the altarpiece *Noli me tangere* in Oxford (1960) and the article by Kenneth Woodbridge on Henry Hoare's Stourhead (1965). Further research by Anthony M. Clark on Batoni and Roman painting in the eighteenth century has yielded much valuable information on Batoni's rival Mengs. In a number of articles, and above all in his work on Robert Adam, John Fleming has published hitherto unknown information from British private archives, which illuminates the scene in Rome as experienced by the travellers and collectors. This great stock of documents was also the source for the work by Leslie Lewis in 1961 on the Roman entourage of Cardinal Albani, and this has helped us to reconstruct the commission for the Northumberland copies.

Finally, it must be seen as fortunate that Sir Brinsley Ford in 1974 decided to publish part of the impressive stock of material which he had accumulated from many scattered and hitherto unknown sources. This provides an authentic and complete picture of the realities of Roman and British art life in the second half of the eighteenth century. The richness and density of the mosaic he assembled make this fascinatingly élitist and yet colourfully mixed culture come alive for the first time. It was also Brinsley Ford who, a few years later, decided to place important data at Francis Russell's disposal for his survey of the British portraits painted by Mengs.

This study aims to present Mengs's work for British patrons, the importance of which Brinsley Ford's pioneering work was primarily responsible for revealing, to a wider public.

Sir Charles Hanbury Williams

Mengs's first personal acquaintance with a British art lover was a brief encounter with Sir Charles Hanbury Williams (1709-59) in Dresden. By then, Mengs was already a successful artist, holding the office of Principal Court Painter in Saxony, although he was still very young; nevertheless, the meeting led to other important contacts which were to have a formative influence on his career.

Sir Charles's contemporaries saw him as a great eccentric. He first came to the court at Dresden on a diplomatic mission in 1746, then went to the court of the Margrave of Ansbach-Bayreuth in 1749 and to Berlin in 1750, returning to Dresden in February 1751. He remained there until 1753, and after a disagreement with the powerful Count Brühl left for St Petersburg in 1754, where he died in 1759 of the consequences of his licentious and dissipated habits. Sir Charles and Mengs must therefore have met between February and September 1751, a few months before the painter left Dresden for the third and last time for Italy. Mengs's biographer Gian Ludovico Bianconi, who had entered the service of the Elector Prince of Saxony as his private physician in 1751, tells us that Sir Charles Hanbury Williams took a great liking to Mengs, but that his attentions were rather a nuisance to the artist, who was very much in demand. Sir Charles made tempting offers to entice Mengs to England, but Mengs declined out of loyalty to his King.[9]

Nevertheless, during the few months of their acquaintance, and although he had plenty of work, Mengs painted Sir Charles's portrait. There are several versions in existence (cat.no.17). The original was in the possession of the Earl of Essex in 1752, and presumably he brought it back from his journey to the continent in 1751.[10] Joshua Reynolds owned a copy in 1757. The painting was praised especially for its vivid, lifelike quality, to which those who knew the sitter could testify. This is also confirmed by Bianconi: 'Those who knew this Englishman and have seen his portrait will say whether a better likeness could ever be painted'. An Irishman named Hupton, who visited Mengs in his studio in Rome, is said to have been startled by the likeness, as he was on hostile terms with the sitter.[11]

The encounter with Sir Charles Hanbury Williams, who was well known in England as a satirist and diplomat,[12] benefited Mengs, although it was only apparent later to what extent, for the picture made him known in England as a portrait painter.

When Mengs departed for Italy, Sir Charles gave him a letter of introduction to Sir Horace Mann, the British Ambassador in Florence. We know that Mengs presented the letter personally in April 1752, for the recipient men-

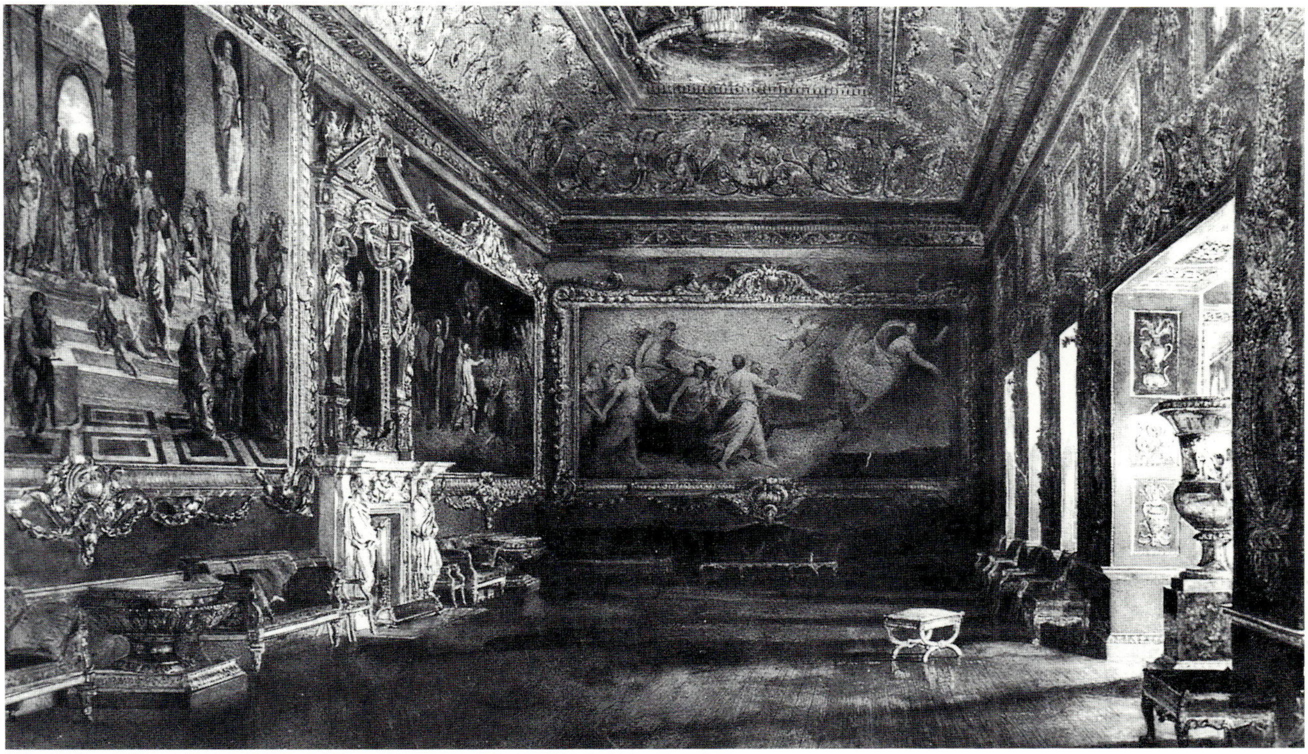

1. View of the Picture Gallery in Northumberland House (destroyed 1874). Photograph London Residuary Body, Record Office

tions this in a letter to Sir Charles on 25 April of that year.[13] On that occasion the Ambassador, who had little knowledge of art, asked Mengs for his opinion of a painting attributed to Titian. Mengs did not believe it was from Titian's hand, and provoked the wrathful reaction from the owner of the painting: 'He must be the most damned ignorant fellow in the world'.[14] Nevertheless, Mann gave the Principal Court Painter from Saxony a letter of recommendation to his main correspondent in Rome, Cardinal Alessandro Albani, who was to become one of Mengs's most important patrons in that city.

The Raphael Copy for Northumberland House

As a direct result of his acquaintance with Horace Mann, and the recommendation to Albani, Mengs was asked a few months later to make a copy, almost full-size, of Raphael's *School of Athens* for the picture gallery in Northumberland House at Charing Cross in London, which had been completed in 1749.

The commission is unusually well documented in the correspondence between Horace Mann and Cardinal Albani.[15] The following facts are known: Percy, Earl of Northumberland, had approached Horace Mann in Florence in 1752, requesting him to help him acquire full-size copies of a number of celebrated Roman Renaissance paintings. The copies were for the picture gallery in Northumberland House. The commissions went to the best known history painters in Rome of the time, through the mediation of Cardinal Albani, who also played a decisive part in the selection of the works to be copied. His choice was as follows: Agostino Masucci for Guido Reni's *Aurora* in the Casino Rospigliosi, Pompeo Batoni for Raphael's *Feast of the Gods* and *Council of the Gods* in the Villa Farnesina, Placido Costanzi for Carracci's *Triumph of Bacchus and Ariadne* in the Galleria Farnese and Mengs for Raphael's *School of Athens* in the Vatican.

The programmatic character of the selection made by the Cardinal is evident when seen against its theoretical background. Raphael, Guido Reni and the Carraccis were the formative models for the classical ideal in the seventeenth-century doctrine of art, which was strongly supported by British art theoreticians, among them Horace Walpole.[16] Mengs followed the same basic theoretical concept, that is, he believed the study of proven models was the necessary condition for quality in his own work. He was therefore probably the only painter commissioned by Northumberland who tackled his copy with serious interest and great care. He did not, for instance, trace the original, although he could probably have obtained permission to do so. His copy was the centrepiece dominating the picture gallery in Northumberland House, where the long wall measured 106 feet and was entirely devoted to Raphael. To fit the space allotted for the copy, the artist had to make some changes, but these were carried out so skilfully and unobtrusively that they do not detract from the faithfulness to the original.

The painstaking changes, which are hardly visible at first glance, are combined with an extremely correct rendering of the drawing and the formal elements. What aids and preliminary work the painter used for his copy can only be surmised, as virtually nothing has survived of his direct studies. There is some evidence to suggest that for the heads he was able to use copies he had made of the originals some years before. These copies are to be seen in the engravings made by Giovanni Volpato for the painter's heirs in 1785 and published under the title 'Le cinquantadue Teste della celebre Scuola di Atene'.

The gallery at Northumberland House was pulled down in 1874, but a photograph shows how the paintings were arranged (fig.1). With the exception of Mengs's copy, which has been on display for some years in the Cast Court of the Victoria and Albert Museum (fig.2), the other copies are now in the Palazzo Labia in Venice.[17] The work on the copies went on for several years and it was not until the spring of 1757 that the gallery was officially opened.

Horace Walpole wrote to Mann: 'It is a sumptuous chamber which might have been in a better taste... and as you was not the painter you will allow me not to be so profuse of applauses. Mengs' School of Athens pleased me, Pompeo's two are black and hard, Masucci's Apollo is faded and without beauty, Costanzi's piece is abominable'.[18] Justified and understandable as this criticism was in view of the mediocre quality of the other copies, the idea and scope of the project were entirely in keeping with the spirit of the age. It followed the artistic tendencies which predominated not only in England, but also in France and Italy. Good copies of Renaissance masterpieces in the original size were expected to improve contemporary painting, which was wallowing in Baroque extravagance. The disciplined study of an art that had fallen into neglect was seen by theoreticians and artists as a suitable way of regaining good taste. It was also believed that no contemporary artist could paint anything of comparable worth to these works, so copying was seen even by such arbitrary and cosmopolitan spirits as Francesco Algarotti, who was also highly esteemed in London, as a proven means of giving the arts a new direction. The reproduction of acknowledged examples of good taste was to stimulate the artist's own output as well as set new standards of judgement.

Horace Walpole was not the only critic to find Mengs's copy alone acceptable. Thomas Robinson, of whom more later, praised it for its quality and faithfulness to the original, and for the artist's handling of colour. James Barry, in a letter to Burke from Rome in 1766, reported a conversation he had had on art with several Englishmen, but did not give their names. In the course of the conversation Mengs's copy was mentioned, and one of those present said 'that Mengs' copy was not well relished at first by the people at home, which was not to be wondered at, as it required some time to form the taste of a nation, and that he was sorry that Mengs was not in England to teach'.[19] Barry, of course, did not hold the view that the existence of a good copy in a country would achieve anything, and to prove his point he argued that Raphael's tapestry cartoons had been in England for more than a hundred years but had not had the slightest influence on English art.

In later years the copy was cited to underline the widespread negative view of Mengs, formed particularly by Richard Cumberland as well as Reynolds and Fuseli. In his English translation of the works of Mengs, Cumberland wrote in 1796: 'Mengs has done but few pictures for England except copies'.

Richard Wilson, Thomas Jenkins, Daniel Webb and other Britons in Rome

On his third journey to Rome Mengs spent several months in Venice before reaching Florence in spring 1752, presumably from the end of October. Here he seems to have made two acquaintances who were to be formative influences on his future. Partly at the same time as Mengs, that is, from November 1750 to the end of 1751, Richard Wilson and the painter and later art dealer Thomas Jenkins were also in Venice. They set off for Rome in 1752 with the future collector William Locke, who was later to commission a paint-

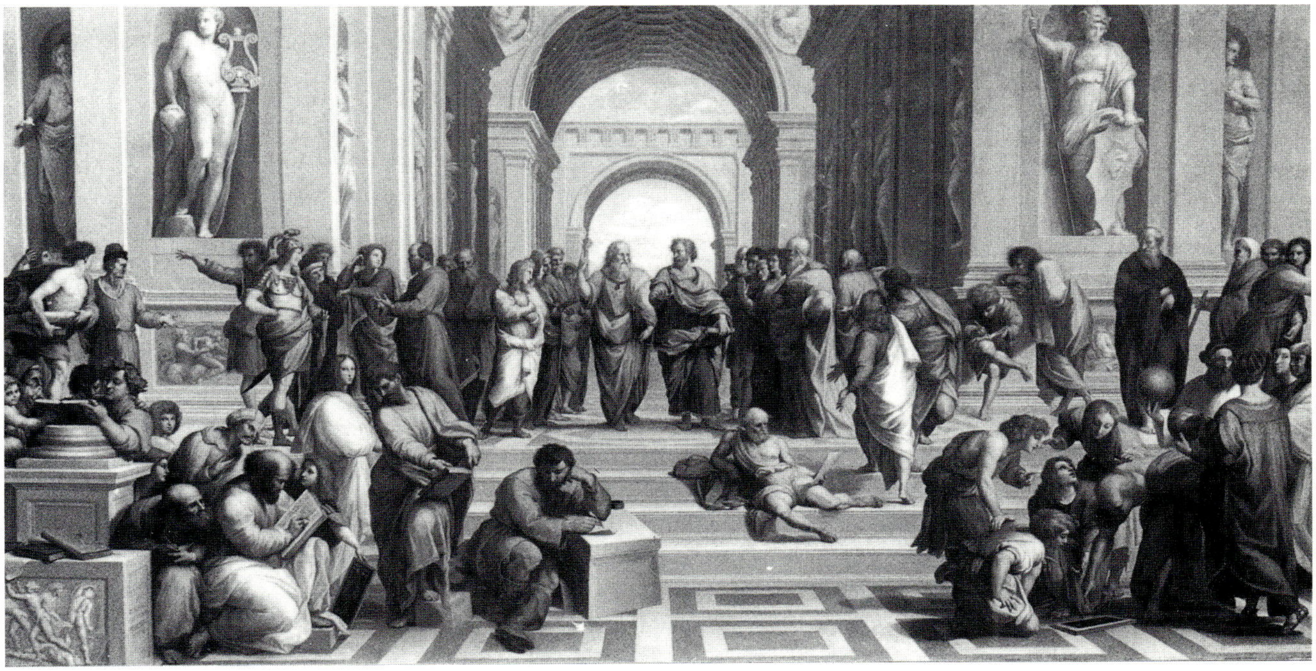

2. A.R. Mengs, *School of Athens*, copy after Raphael (Rome, Vatican), 1752-5, London, Victoria & Albert Museum

ing from Mengs. The fact that Mengs was already painting Wilson's portrait in 1752 (cat.no.18) suggests either that the two had already met in Venice or that they met as soon as they both arrived in Rome. In any case a good friendship certainly developed between them soon.

Wilson lived in Rome in 1753 at the same address as Thomas Jenkins, on the Piazza di Spagna 'verso Propaganda fide', while Mengs lived above the Spanish Steps, in what is now the Via Sistina, opposite the house of the painter Federico Zuccari, where Winckelmann was to live in 1755. Farington records in his diary that Mengs had particularly close contacts with Wilson in the first years of his stay in Rome, when he had clearly not yet had much contact with other British visitors to the city.[20] In 1752 Wilson applied in vain for membership of the Accademia di San Luca, but Mengs became a member on 20 August 1752, and he also taught as professor at the Accademia del Nudo in 1758. Mengs is said to have painted Wilson's portrait in exchange for a landscape by Wilson.[21] The other Briton with whom Mengs was friendly, according to Farington, was James Stuart. He was generally known as 'Athenian Stuart', on account of his interest in Greek antiquity, which had taken him to Greece in 1753 with Nicolas Revett.

Nicolas Guibal and Adolf Friedrich Harper, later Stuttgart court painters, were also close associates of Winckelmann and Mengs. They had come to Rome together from Paris and they brought many other Frenchmen to Mengs's studio, like Pêcheux and Clérisseau. Harper became a pupil of Richard Wilson in Rome, and the two Danish painters, Johan Mandelberg and Johan Wiedewelt, who were close to Mengs, almost pupils, and later friends of Winckelmann, also maintained close contact with Wilson, who gave them his drawings to copy.[22]

Thomas Jenkins, as we have already mentioned, was one of the circle of friends around Mengs and Wilson in Rome. He had been born in Rome, and in the first years after his return to the city he devoted himself principally to painting.[23] The few works of his which are known show the undeniable influence of Mengs, who moved increasingly closer to the style of Bolognese seventeenth-century painting after 1752.

This is particularly evident in the only two known subject paintings by Jenkins, who became a full member of the Roman Accademia di San Luca in 1761. The portrait of

Margherita Mengs as Diligentia, now in Pavlovsk, was painted for Jenkins.[24]. A copy was made by Nikolaus Mosmann and, like the Sibyl (cat.no.23), it represents the 'neo-Seicento' ideal of taste. Jenkins's paintings have come down to us in copies by Mosmann, and clearly they were among the works to be included in the reference book of 250 paintings by Italian masters planned by Lord Exeter (figs.3,4).[25] Mosmann was a pupil of Mengs in Rome and he must have been in close contact with Jenkins later. For a commission from Lord Exeter, while Mengs was in Spain, he made drawings of many paintings by Italian masters, some of which were owned by Jenkins, and they also include a large number of paintings and drawings by his teacher Mengs (cat.no.46).[26] Presumably he had access to Mengs's studio through Anton von Maron in Mengs's absence.

Jenkins was soon to become one of the most important channels for contacts between Mengs and British travellers and connoisseurs in Rome. He had studied in England under the portrait painter Thomas Hudson, who was one of the most consistent in his endeavours to move closer to the style and manner of Antony van Dyck's portraiture at this time,[27] and it may have been Jenkins who induced Mengs to orient his style towards van Dyck's in his portraits of British travellers. Certainly, one of the few portraits by Jenkins of this period that have survived, of Jenkins's friend Thomas Brand (fig.5), shows a tendency towards the style of van Dyck that is very close to the approach used by Mengs.

The stylistic relationship is so close that it is actually possible that a third portrait of Lord Brudenell (cat.no.3), hitherto attributed to Mengs, is by Jenkins. Jenkins introduced Lord Brudenell to Batoni and to Mengs, and he also acted as agent for the art purchases made by Lord Brudenell at this time.[28] From 1758 Jenkins lived on the Via del Corso with the landscape painter John Plimmer. Plimmer also acted as agent in Rome, and he mediated between Mengs and Hoare over the commission for the painting of *Augustus and Cleopatra* in Stourhead (fig.24).[29]

When Mengs went to Madrid in 1761 Jenkins bought a number of paintings and drawings from him, which he sold in the next few years to interested British travellers. They included the painting of the *Holy Family*, which Mengs had executed in 1749 for the King of Poland, but which owing to a technical defect had remained in his studio to serve as model for a second version. This early work was acquired from Jenkins around 1766 by William Weddell, whose portrait was painted by Batoni, and must therefore have been in Newby Hall for a time together with the collection of antiques which had also been acquired through Jenkins

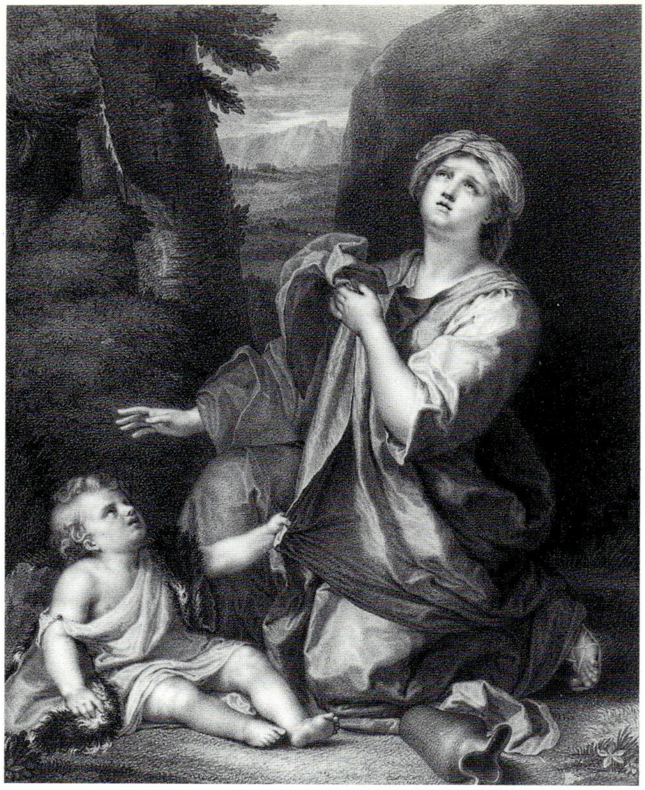

3. Nikolaus Mosmann, *Hagar and Ishmael in the Desert*, Mosmann, London, British Museum, after a lost painting by Thomas Jenkins, painted *c.*1755-60

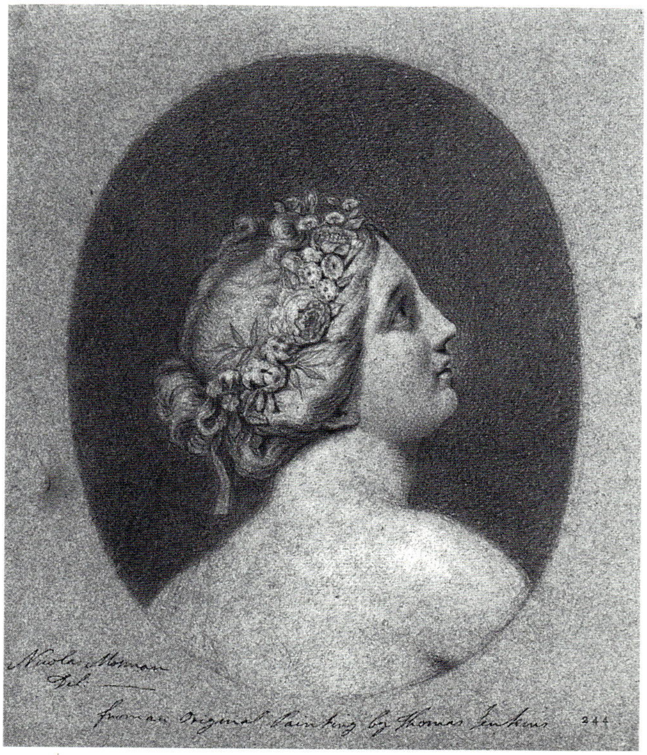

4. Nikolaus Mosmann, *Bust of Flora in Profile*, London, British Museum, drawing after a lost painting by Thomas Jenkins, painted *c.*1755

(cat.no.19). Although virtually nothing is known of any later contact between Mengs and Jenkins, it can be assumed that they maintained their relationship, which was based on common interests. In the years after 1770 Jenkins became one of the leading art dealers in Rome and he enjoyed excellent relations with Pope Clement XIV, who in 1771 commissioned Mengs to decorate the Stanza dei Papiri in the Vatican library.[30]

After Mengs's death Jenkins purchased thirteen drawings from his estate, mostly apparently life drawings. He subsequently offered them to British travellers at very high prices.[31]

From 1752 to 1761 Mengs's Roman studio was a great centre of attraction for young artists of all nationalities. He was not only very hospitable, keeping an opulent table, but he also gave many foreign artists access to his studio and to his collection of casts of antique statues, which was by then considerable, allowing them to draw from these. The visitors between 1752 and 1757 included Johann Zoffany, who 'placed himself under Mengs, and remained with him seven years', according to Farington's diary.[32]

Mengs also took some artists as lodgers: two painters from Viterbo, Domenico Corvi and Francesco Strigeri, lodged with him in 1753, as did Anton Maron, Mengs's most loyal student, in 1755. The longest staying house guest was Giovanni Casanova, brother of Giacomo Casanova, who went to Dresden as director of the Academy in 1764. In the new residence which Mengs took in 1758, in what is now Via Vittoria 54, he provided lodgings for three Englishmen, Colin Morison, Richard Brompton and James Nevay. The last two lived there for two years, 1758 and 1759, while Morison is only mentioned in the parish registers for 1758. He had come to Rome in 1755 with Robert Adam and placed himself under Mengs's wing.[33] With his good knowledge of classical literature he earned his living from 1763 as a guide to British visitors to Rome. Richard Brompton returned to London in 1763 and later went to Russia as court painter.[34] James Nevay remained in Rome, where he worked as a painter and copyist.[35]

We have a few reports of the working atmosphere and the discussions on art in Mengs's house. For a time, from 1755 to 1757, Winckelmann also joined in these discussions. He was particularly friendly with Colin Morison, who, like himself, was interested in Greek culture and literature.[36] He also maintained contact with Jenkins, again stimulated by their common interest in the art of antiquity.[37] Morison and Byres organised guided tours of Roman antiquities for English travellers from 1763. These

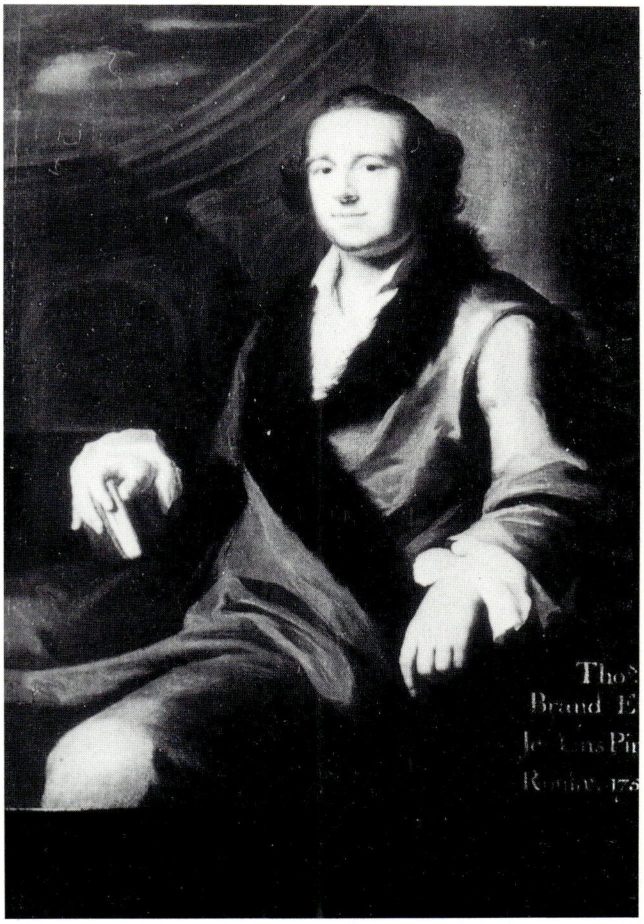

5. Thomas Jenkins, *Portrait of Thomas Brand Hollis*, 1753, sold at Sotheby's, London, 18 June 1976

lasted several weeks and were structured like private tuition courses. The tuition was clearly of superior quality, and it may have been inspired by the guided tours organised by Winckelmann from about 1758 for German-speaking travellers to Rome who had been recommended to him. Occasionally British visitors to the city were also privileged to be guided by him, like Edward Wortley Montagu in 1762. Winckelmann's walks through Rome, which were distinctly didactic in character, were clearly influenced by Mengs, for it was Mengs who had opened Winckelmann's eyes to Roman art, especially that of antiquity, after his arrival in the Eternal City. A description of one of these private tours has survived under the title 'Short Notes on a

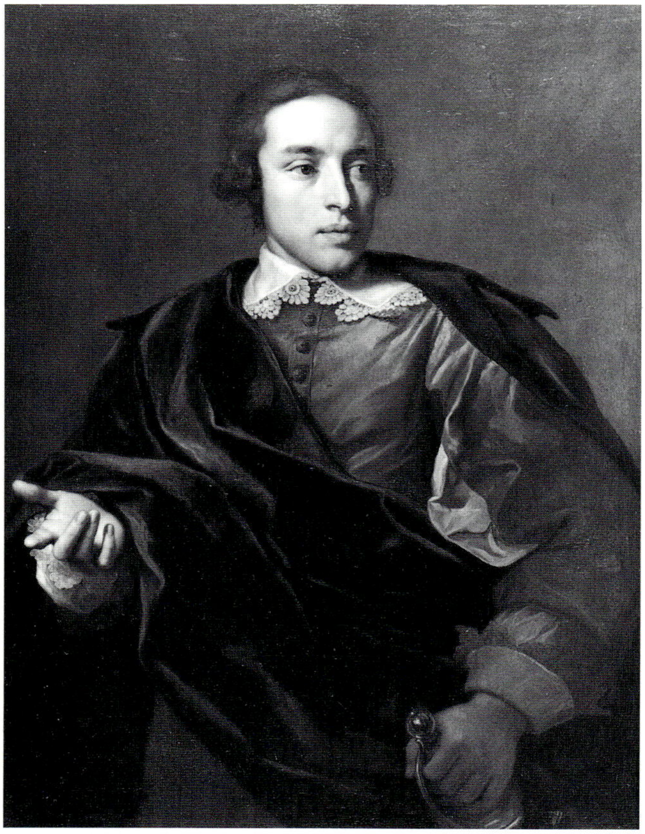

6. Thomas Jenkins (?), formerly attributed to P. Batoni and A. R. Mengs, *Portrait of Lord Brudenell*, Collection Lord Montagu of Beaulieu

Course of Antiquities at Rome in Company with Messrs. Apthorp, Morgan & Palmer begun May 21, 1764 under Mr. Byre, Antiquarian', and it would be interesting to compare its contents with Winckelmann's accounts.[38]

The Scottish architect James Byres lived in the same area as Mengs and Piranesi from 1756 to 1758. In the following decades he was to emerge as one of the leading British art agents in Rome besides Jenkins and Gavin Hamilton, as Brinsley Ford was able to show in his extremely detailed research.[39] Byres later described himself as a pupil of Mengs and maintained that he studied under him for five years. He certainly had direct access to Mengs's studio during the years when Mengs was painting the fresco in the church of Sant'Eusebio (cat.no.20), and he later maintained that during that time he assisted Maron, who in turn was assisting Mengs in the work on the ceiling fresco.[40] Byres later also became one of the main mediators for the numerous portraits painted of British visitors to Rome by Maron, with whom he was friendly. Like Jenkins, he was portrayed by Maron for the collection of portaits in the Accademia di San Luca in Rome.

Byres remained a good friend of Mengs in later years as well,[41] and he built up important contacts with British collectors. This is proven by the painting of *Perseus and Andromeda*, which Watkin Williams-Wynn commissioned from Mengs in 1768 together with a painting by Batoni. Mengs's later contact with the sculptor Christopher Hewetson, who made a portrait bust of him in 1779, (fig.25) was probably through Byres. Byres finally also mediated between Mengs and the commissioners of *Noli me tangere* for All Souls College, Oxford (cat.no.30).

Many celebrated British visitors to Rome between 1755 and 1758 sought out Mengs and came into contact with him. Besides Robert Wood and James Stuart they included Robert Adam, who arrived in Rome in February 1755,[42] and who had been recommended to Cardinal Alessandro Albani by Horace Mann.[43] He had travelled with the future collector Charles Hope, whose portrait Mengs then painted while he was in Rome. It is evident that Mengs knew Adam fairly well from a number of details. For instance, Mengs was present at the meeting of the Accademia di San Luca at which Adam was appointed a member.[44] Adam shared a lodging on the Piazza di Spagna with Clérisseau, with whom he had formed a close friendship, and who in turn had close relations with Winckelmann and Mengs. Robert Wood and the Duke of Bridgewater lived in the same house as Adam, and the Duke commissioned a picture from Mengs at this time. Central figures in this circle, whose social contacts mainly took the form of the many 'conversazioni', were Cardinal Alessandro Albani and his mistress Francesca Cheroffini. Adam's portrait was painted by Laurent Pècheux, who was a pupil of Mengs at the time, and this commission may have been executed in friendly rivalry with the portrait of Adam painted by Allan Ramsay, who was in Rome at the same time.[45] It is evident that Ramsay knew Mengs from the fact that Robert Wood, who was friendly with Ramsay, was portrayed by both painters in the same year, 1755. Ramsay clearly also discussed practical questions of painting with Mengs, however, for he noted a remark by Mengs in a manuscript of his containing observations on paints.[46] Mengs was still famous in the nineteenth century for his profound knowledge of paint. In 1820 Sir Thomas Lawrence gave George Field samples of

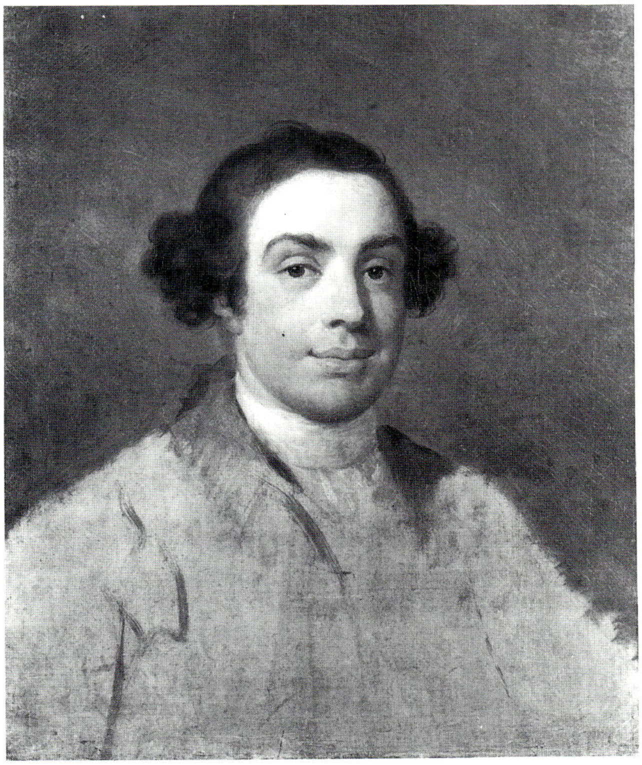

7. William Hogarth, *Portrait of James Caulfield, 1st Earl of Charlemont*, after 1759, Smith College Museum of Art, Northampton, MA. Gift of Mr and Mrs R. Keith Kane (Amanda Stewart Bryan '27), 1959.

pigments which he had taken from Mengs's paint box when in Rome, for chemical analysis.[47]

Other contacts, like those with Lord Charlemont (cat.no.4) and the Irish banker La Touche, can only be deduced from the fact that Mengs portrayed both of them. However, the relation to Lord Charlemont must be seen as particularly important, on account of the very programmatic nature of his portrait, which is an allegory on architecture. Charlemont was the main driving force in the foundation of a British Academy in Rome,[48] which was established in May 1752 on the initiative of sixteen British artists. The director was the painter and tutor John Parker, who later acted as agent for Lord Charlemont in the controversy with Piranesi. Mengs had similar academic ambitions, and a few years later (1755) he began to work for the establishment of a German academy in Rome, again to be on the model of the Académie de France. Thus in many respects he found a kindred spirit in Lord Charlemont, with his wide-ranging interests. Winckelmann also appears to have associated with Lord Charlemont, as he sent his regards to him in 1758.[49]

If one looks for a common thread in the many cross-relations and contacts between the throng of artists, art dealers, tutors and tourists who lodged or settled within or around the Piazza di Spagna after 1751, it must have been love of the greatness and beauty of Rome and its art treasures, although these were then somewhat dilapidated. However, they greatly stimulated the artists, and in the wealthy travellers they aroused the desire to own items from this veritable 'treasure chest'. Many of the contacts which laid the basis for future associations of an artistic or political nature came through recommendations, chance re-encounters with old acquaintances, the easy social life in the cafés around the Piazza di Spagna where the foreign visitors gathered, and on walks around the city.

About the time Mengs arrived in Rome Sir Joshua Reynolds left the city, so presumably the two painters never met.[50] Reynolds's caricature of the *School of Athens*, which he made in 1751-2 in Rome, does however include some of the personalities whom Mengs was soon to meet there, among them Lord Charlemont (cat.no.4). As nothing is known of any contact later between the two artists, we can only quote the annihilating prophecy on Mengs's future fame which Reynolds made in 1788 in his fourteenth Discourse to the students of the Royal Academy: 'I will venture to prophecy that two of the last distinguished painters of that country, I mean Pompeo Battoni and Raffaele Mengs, however great their names sound in our ears, will very soon fall into the rank of Imperiale, Sebastian Concha, Placido Constanza, Massuccio and the rest of their immediate predecessors'.[51] We only have one later comment from Mengs, on Reynolds as a teacher. It is also critical, but it does not come from an authentic source.[52]

Had the two painters met in Rome, or had Mengs in fact accepted another offer made to him while he was in Spain (p.29) and gone to England, this would presumably have had consequences of some significance for both men. If we pursue this rather idle speculation for a moment, we can imagine that a personal encounter might have opened up all kinds of interesting prospects, as for all their differences the affinity of their aims and views is undeniable. The two painters were pursuing such similar objectives that they would certainly always have been close rivals.

An episode concerning the self-portraits which both painted for the Uffizi would appear to confirm this. The self-portrait which Reynolds donated to the Uffizi in 1775 was hung directly beside Mengs's self-portrait. Both the Florentine director of the gallery, Siries, and Reynolds's pupil, James Northcote, found the proximity disadvantageous to Mengs.[53] As both portraits were in the grand manner, using means whose significance would be very evident to contemporaries, they were indeed a bad match.

Another leading painter of the eighteenth century hardly appears to have played any part in Mengs's career. This was Gavin Hamilton, who lived only in Rome after 1748, with a few intervals, and was a highly respected painter, archaeologist and art dealer there for decades. Mengs and Hamilton had friends and acquaintances in common, such as the aforementioned James Stuart and Robert Adam, but there is nothing to suggest that they met personally and certainly not that they were friends. Perhaps the reason was that their styles in history painting were basically very similar. We have a very apt characterisation of this from Heinrich Meyer.[54] The silence does however indicate mutual respect, and this is evident simply from the fact that they moved in the same circles. A certain parallel can be drawn to Batoni here: there was mutual tolerance and respect, but the artists avoided coming too close to each other. At any rate, Sir Ellis Waterhouse was not giving a very realistic picture when he said that Hamilton and Mengs were rivals for the same objective, which he saw as the birth of Neo-Classicism.[55]

Probably the most obscure of Mengs's British contacts is his relationship with Daniel Webb, who was in Rome in 1755 or 1756, and with whom Mengs struck up a friendship based on their shared interest in art theory. Mengs painted a portrait of Webb and according to Winckelmann, who must be seen as a reliable source, gave him the manuscript of his work 'Gedanken 'ber die Schönheit' ('Thoughts on Beauty)', which he was just composing, and the 'Riflessioni sopra i tre gran pittori' (Reflections on the Greatest Painters) which only appeared after Mengs's death. When a treatise by Webb, 'Inquiry into the Beauties of Painting and into the Merit of the most celebrated Painters Ancient and Modern' was published in 1760 in London, taking up many of Mengs's ideas, Winckelmann, who was easily roused, accused Webb of plagiarism.[55] Many of Webb's remarks on the selection the artist should make from the models of the past can indeed be found in Mengs's work, which was published only after Webb's. The two are also largely identical in their assessments of Raphael, Titian and Correggio and in their judgements on ancient art. On the other hand, their views on taste, for instance, and on the role of the passions in art, diverge widely.[57] Algarotti saw the advantage of Webb's work precisely in the fact that he expressed ideas which were largely in agreement with those of Mengs, whom he regarded as the 'più dotto pittore della presente età'.[58] Diderot also came to know Mengs's and Winckelmann's ideas through Webb, whose work became known throughout Europe and thus did indeed help to spread a knowledge of Mengs's views. One of the three German editions appeared in 1771, published by Johann Kaspar Füssli & Orell in Zurich, in one volume with Mengs's treatise.

Artistically Mengs's most important encounter with an English-speaking artist in Rome was with Benjamin West. West was of great importance for the development of history painting in Great Britain, and in many respects he can be regarded as Mengs's heir. During his brief stay in Rome, from summer 1760 to autumn 1761, West not only met Cardinal Albani and Winckelmann, but also, more importantly, enjoyed so intense an artistic interchange with Mengs that West actually called the German artist his 'favourite master'.[59] West became friendly with Thomas Robinson soon after he arrived in Rome, and apparently it was Robinson who introduced him to Cardinal Albani.[60] It could be that his meeting with Mengs also came about through Robinson, whose portrait had been painted by Mengs in the same year. West followed Mengs's style in portraiture so closely that a portrait of Robinson by West was believed to be by Mengs by Thomas Jenkins and Nathaniel Dance. Dance actually thought the painting 'much better coloured than those usually painted by Mengs'[61] and Mengs himself is then said to have had earnest discussions with West on the latter's further studies in Italy. West did follow Mengs's advice, for example by copying the *Madonna with St Jerome* by Correggio in Parma. After Mengs's departure from Rome in August 1761 West copied two of his paintings for English patrons (cat.no.31). One was *The Holy Family* for Lord Fordwich, later Earl of Cowper, who gave him permission to copy the work (fig.23).

Portraits of British Sitters

The first Englishman to have his portrait painted by Mengs in Rome was the rich merchant Anthony Langley Swymmer. He had come to Rome in 1752 with his young wife Arabella, and in addition to the portraits from Mengs he also commissioned two pastels, which cannot now be traced,[62] before leaving the city again on 21 April 1753. While the portrait of his wife has survived (cat.no.15), we only know that of Swymmer himself from a detailed

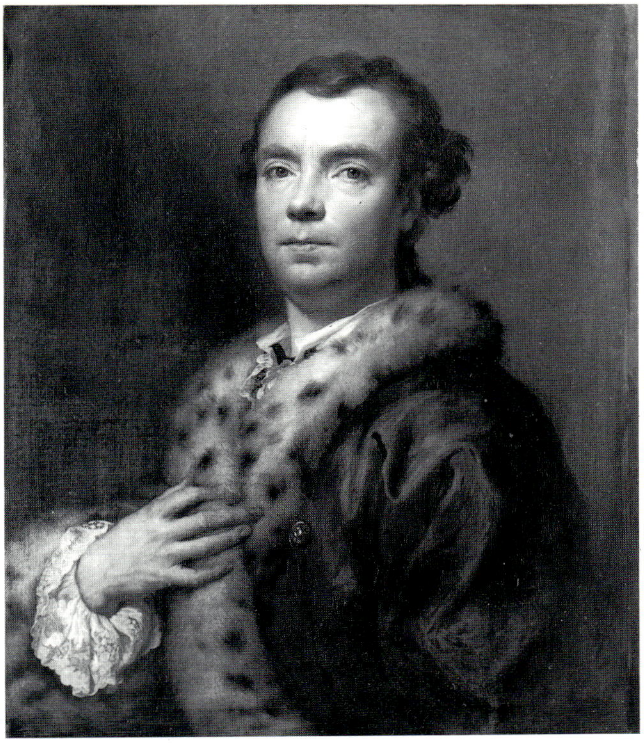

8. A. R. Mengs, *Portrait of Robert Wood*, painted 1755 for the Duke of Bridgewater. Private Collection

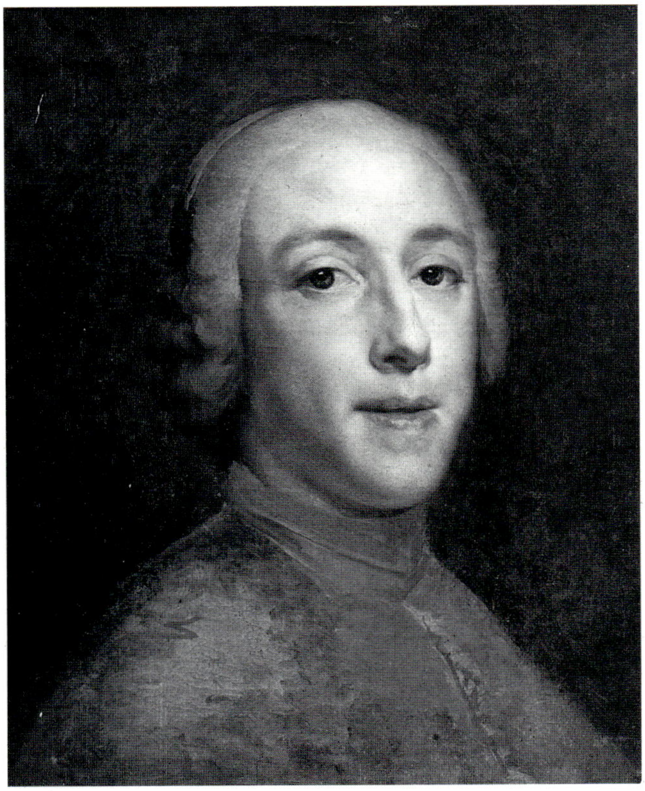

9. A. R. Mengs, *Portrait of Henry Benedict Marie Clement Edward Stuart, Cardinal York*, c.1756-8, Montpellier, Musée Fabre

description, which suggests that it was not marked by the taste for van Dyck that was to become characteristic of Mengs's later British work. From the description one can imagine the painting of Swymmer as similar to that of Richard Wilson – with power and depth, and lively colouring, perhaps also rather courtly, like the matching portrait of his wife, and also that of Sir Charles Hanbury Williams. Some of the famous Dresden pastels of 1744/5 that were so admired by British visitors to the gallery there[63] show that Mengs painted non-aristocratic sitters in the courtly manner in this early phase of his work.

The first portrait in which he moved away completely from this courtly style is that of Robert Wood, an archaeologist and expert on ancient Greece (fig.8). The picture was painted in 1755 for the Duke of Bridgewater, in whose company Wood had been travelling through France and Italy since 1753. They both arrived in Rome in January 1755. The encounter between Mengs and Wood probably came through James Stuart, who had met Wood and Revett in Athens in 1751. Apart from Wilson, 'Athenian Stuart' is said to have been the only Briton with whom Mengs was friendly in the first few years of his stay in Rome.

The portrait of Wood, like that of Wilson, is one of a small group of works of outstanding quality in which the personal relationship between the painter and his sitter has clearly influenced the creation of the work. The liveliness of the expression and the intensity and spontaneity of the painting derive from an individual and highly personal experience; in externals, the portrait may differ only slightly from the conventional portrait embellished with fashionable attributes, but inwardly it is far removed.

The portrait which Mengs painted of Henry Benedict Marie Clement Edward Stuart around 1755, on the other hand, must be placed in the category of official portraits. Stuart was the younger brother of the Pretender to the British throne, Charles Edward, who had been made a cardinal in 1747. The commission probably came through the close connections between the Stuarts and the Albani family. Only the study made from life for the portrait has survived, and it is an expressive and highly individualised likeness of great vividness and immediacy (fig.9). It is comparable with the study for the portrait of Clement XIII (cat.no.5), and of all the images of the cardinal that have survived, this is by far the most individual and spontaneous.[64] The naturalness with which Mengs endowed portraits of friends or persons whom he knew well also flowed into his portraits of an official nature, although in the execution of the finished work this first stage of free and spontaneous observation was overlaid by the addition of clothing accessories and the interior setting.

The study which Mengs made for the portrait of Henry Lyte shows the disparity between the drawing from life and the execution of the finished portrait particularly clearly (cat.nos.10 and 11). The creative spontaneity of the first sitting with the model is even more evident in an oil study which Mengs made in 1756 of Count Orsini-Rosenberg, who was in Rome on his *Kavaliersreise*, the continental equivalent of the British Grand Tour. The oil study (cat.no.12), as the inscription notes, was completed in a two-hour portrait sitting. The portrait was probably intended to be half-length or three-quarter-length, but, like some others, it was never executed. Grasping the sitter's individuality, his unmistakeable expression, as was possible in the study from life, interested Mengs more than the execution of the finished work, which was labour-intensive and, given the technical demands which Mengs made of himself in the way of highly finished and delicate workmanship, protracted and wearisome.

It was possibly the unavoidable process of putting the technical finishing touches which gave him a certain dislike of portraiture, and pastels, which can be executed in a single sitting with the model, might have suited him better. They would have offered him a more appropriate medium with which to capture the character of a sitter, as we see from the work of his contemporaries Liotard and Maurice Quentin la Tour, and it is no coincidence that Mengs achieved his first major successes in portraiture in this medium, where he needed no more than two hours to complete the work. However, Mengs drew a distinction between a spontaneous picture of a friend and a state portrait of a monarch.[65] Moreover, the liveliness and freshness which lent even his official portraits a particular and unusual touch, in fact brought him those clients who were particularly concerned to avoid stereotypical portraits, namely statesmen and leading churchmen.

As a highly paid court painter Mengs did not, during the first years of his stay in Rome, really need to take on commissions of this nature. The portraits of tourists actually belong in the same category, as most of them were persons whom the painter would only see for the duration of one sitting. Mengs painted about thirty portraits of British sitters in the course of his career, and the great majority of them were painted only between 1756 and 1760. The reason for this unequal distribution of Grand Tour portraits in his active life was probably simply economic necessity. Even a few months before the outbreak of the Seven Years' War in August 1756, salaries were no longer being paid in Saxony. As the painter had become accustomed to an expensive lifestyle in Rome and also had a large family to support, he was forced to earn his living with private commissions. Portraits were not particularly highly paid, but the fees were earned relatively quickly and easily. Moreover, the number of Britons visiting Rome increased markedly after 1755 and during the Seven Years' War it reached record levels, probably because Paris, which had until then been the main attraction of the Grand Tour, drew fewer visitors in the war years. Jenkins was able to intensify his work as agent for art purchases and portrait commissions at this time, and he frequently brought the collectors who sought his advice to the studios of Mengs and Batoni, thus helping the painters to obtain portrait commissions.[66]

His portrait commissions and many contacts with highly regarded Britons made Mengs's studio an essential stop for British travellers on their tour of Rome. From 1758 it was located at the foot of the Spanish Steps, not far from where Batoni, the older artist who had been in Rome for longer, resided in the Via Bocca di Leone. This, and the lower prices (by English standards) which Mengs charged for portraits[67] occasionally caused visitors to sit for both artists, as was the case with William Fermor, Lord Brudenell, the Duke of Richmond and the Third Earl of Goodnestone.

The difference in the approach of the two painters was also an attraction here, and the prospect of two different views of the same person particularly appealed to the British. They were still accustomed to the domestic portrait style of the period before 1760, when likenesses were still largely standardised, but they also had a well-trained eye and a marked ability to judge portraits, which came from the high regard in which portraiture had been held in Britain, unlike Italy, since Holbein.[68] Most important was a credible relationship between the individual expression and the social role of the sitter, and the matching of current taste and character. The quality of the painter was judged by his ability to meet these aesthetic and artistic requirements as well as to achieve a likeness. Nobody expressed this as clearly as Jonathan Richardson, who judged a good portrait by whether it gave a nobler idea of the beauty, character and other good qualities of the sitter than the sitter himself, without one being able to say, when seeing the picture, it differed from the original.[69] As Francis Haskell has said, it was ultimately the artistic interest which the model was able to arouse in the painter that would

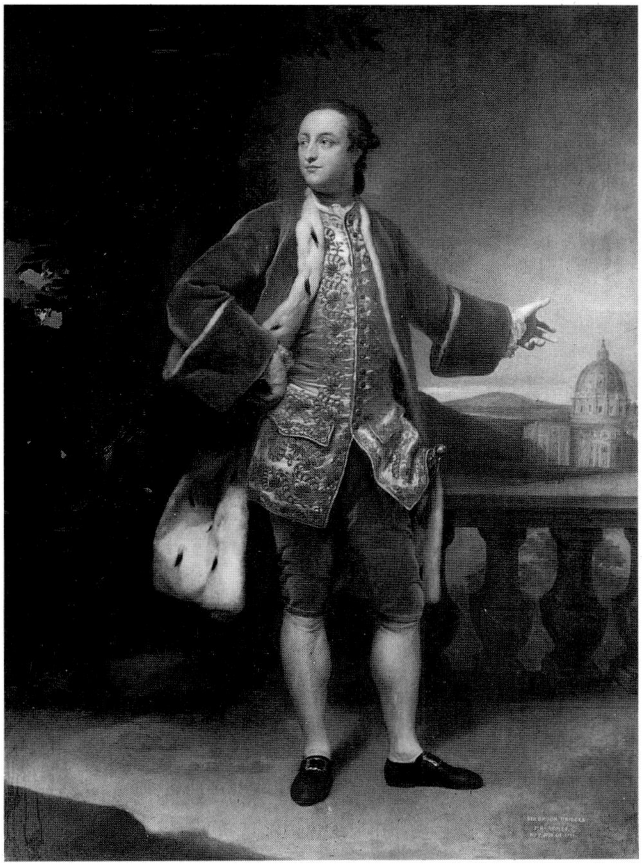

10. A. R. Mengs, *Portrait of Sir Brook Bridges, 3rd Baronet of Goodnestone*, 1758, Private Collection

secure lasting success for the portrait.[70] A fashionable portrait, perhaps extravagant and standardised, with which the sitter would hardly be able to identify in later years, would not, in the long term, have the resonance of a portrait in which the sitter would be able to recognise his character and his features in old age as well.

In Rome Batoni offered a style of portraiture for many decades in which the picture was embellished with Roman attributes, depending on the sitter's wishes and purse. The portraits were generally in brilliant and lavish colours, and with the foppish elegance of the pose the work would be a fitting and lasting memory of the Grand Tour. The costume *à l'italienne*, in colourful and expensive materials, did much to give these portraits character. The Roman attributes, costume and style of painting all combined to form an image that reflected a certain status and social class rather than an individual person. The portraits of young lords that Batoni painted against a background of Roman antiquities, tastefully arranged and with recognisable references, idealised their stay in Rome for them and created pictures whose romantically exaggerated settings still do much to form our idea of the young aristocrat on the Grand Tour today.[71]

This does not apply to any of Mengs's portraits of Britons, and that is partly due to the fact that he preferred a simpler setting, probably because it was more suitable to the outward appearance of his clients. Generally he uses a greenish background with a slight lightening around the head, creating an indistinct but flattering backdrop from which the head stands out effectively. Many of his portraits are also limited to half-length, which may have been a matter of cost, for apparently Mengs asked higher prices for his portraits than Batoni, although this has not been fully clarified. In the case of the portraits of Arabella Swymmer and her husband we know that Mengs asked 300 scudi for both, and got it (cat.no.15). However, the sitter thought the price too high, for at the same time Batoni was asking 50 scudi for a half-length portrait.[72] It is conceivable that Mengs later adapted his prices to Batoni's, when he needed to earn his living from the commissions. At first, his higher prices probably discouraged clients, which may have been his intention.

Altogether, only three full-length portraits of British sitters by Mengs are known. Of these, the portrait of Lord Brudenell (cat.no.2) comes closest to the new type of portrait in an interior evolved by Batoni, while Sir Brook Bridges, shown standing (fig.10), and the Fourth Duke of Manchester, painted in 1758 (Kimbolton Castle, Huntingdon), have a dignity and official poise closer to the court style of which Mengs was such a master. Some of his portraits show the sitters in costumes which, with their white lace collars and lustrous dark coats, look back to the fashions of the seventeenth century; other sitters are shown in sombre-coloured velvet coats with fur trimmings, or in dark jackets with gold borders. The simpler dress in which Mengs portrayed his sitters can be seen as an inheritance from the Northern tradition of portraiture in which he had been trained. His father had taught him to copy the portraits of van Dyck from an early age, and Mengs shared the view that van Dyck was one of the best portrait painters who had ever lived with the French masters of official portraiture, Rigaud and Largillière; this was also the view of William Hogarth.[73] To paint a portrait in the manner of

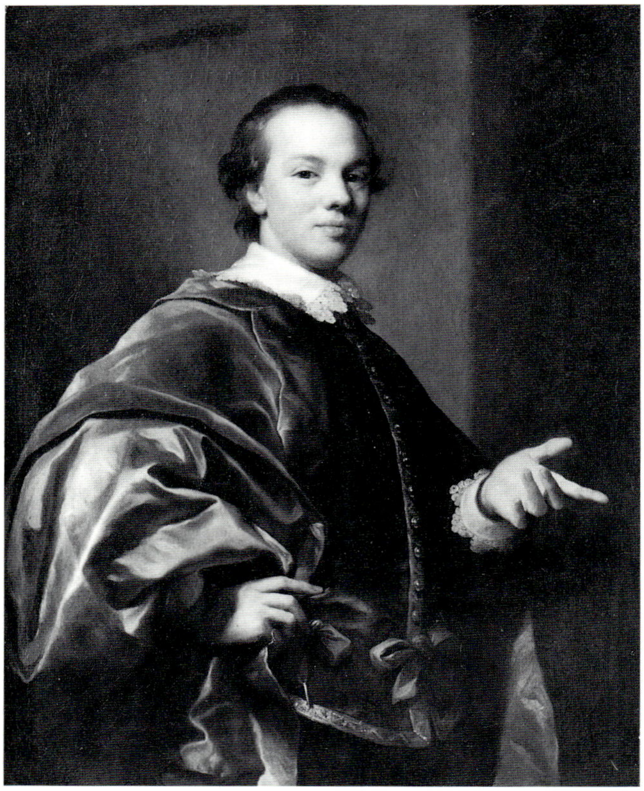

11 A. R. Mengs, *Portrait of John, Viscount Garlies, later 7th Earl of Galloway*, 1758, Private Collection

van Dyck was regarded as a sign of a painter's ability. The portrait of Viscount Garlies of 1758 (fig.11) depends directly on Van Dyck's portrait of Peters Stevens in the 'Iconographia'. However, simply using a 'vandyke' costume was a declaration of intent, and, of course, a costume in the seventeenth-century style was also a status symbol, which the British aristocracy were still using around 1750, as portraits by Hogarth, Thomas Hudson, Reynolds and the young Benjamin West show.[74]

Mengs's portraits cannot be regarded as aristocratic status symbols, nor were they purely private portraits. In their seventeenth-century garments his sitters represent a new type of personality, with a definite and critical individuality, who can proclaim their modernity and enlightenment by recourse to tradition. In the simplicity of their outer appearance we see a new attitude, which was no doubt also a moral one, and which was a deliberate renunciation of the fashionable trend. Winckelmann, who since the end of 1755 had been a frequent guest in Mengs's house, where he presumably met many of the people whom his friend painted, commented on the relationship between Mengs's style and the costumes of his sitters: 'One may mention here the portraits in van Dyck dress, a costume still beloved of the British, and very much more advantageous to the artist and the subject than the present formal dress.'[75] Other visitors to Mengs's studio in these years noted the large number of portraits with subjects clothed in the fashion of van Dyck.[76]

It can generally be said that the British sitters whom Mengs portrayed were for the most part of high intellectual standing. They therefore had different requirements for their portraits than the rich young lords who wanted to be depicted in fashionable garb in the Italian mode.

The differences in the approach to portraiture between Mengs and Batoni were also perceived and reflected by their potential clients. Most striking is the verdict by Thomas Robinson, who explained these differences using as examples the portraits of Pope Clement XIII, whom both Mengs and Batoni had painted in 1760 (cat.no.5). Robinson himself preferred Mengs and commissioned his own portrait only from him, not from Batoni. The painting (fig.12) shows clearly that he was concerned not with flattering external details but with 'force and dignity', qualities which he regarded as the most important in Mengs's work.

There are however, exceptions to this rule. In the portrait of Lord Brudenell (cat.no.2), for instance, whom both Batoni and Mengs painted in 1758, the characteristics of the two painters are, so to speak, reversed. In paintings where Mengs decided to use Roman attributes, as he did in the full-length picture of Sir Brook Bridges (fig.10) and the portrait of Tom Conolly (fig.13), the choice of motifs seems less fortuitous than with Batoni. In the first case the dome of St Peter's indicates a visit to Rome, and in the second the sarcophagus of the Muses from the Borghese collection, now in Paris, is probably a reference to the sitter's artistic interests. In the background of the portrait of the Duke of Richmond (fig.14), appears the same bust of Athena that Batoni often used to indicate the intellectual ambitions of the sitter. A frequent attribute in his British portraits is an open book, as in the brilliantly painted picture in Providence (fig.15). I have suggested that the sitter is William Willoughby, later Fifth Lord of Middleton, who was painted by Batoni in 1754.[77] Some of the portraits by Mengs have no attributes at all, or show only a bust without hands, like the portrait of a young man now in St

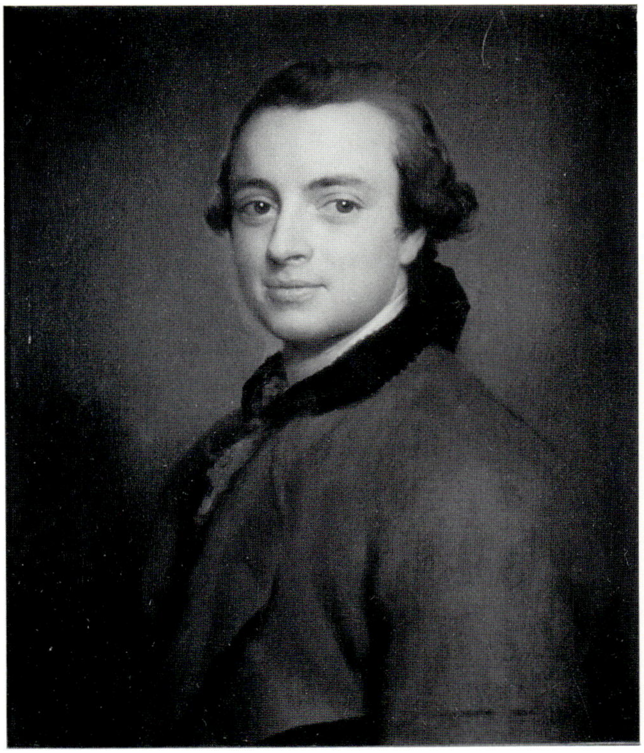

12. A. R. Mengs, *Portrait of Thomas Robinson, later 2nd Baronet of Grantham*, 1760, Newby Hall, Robert Compton Esq.

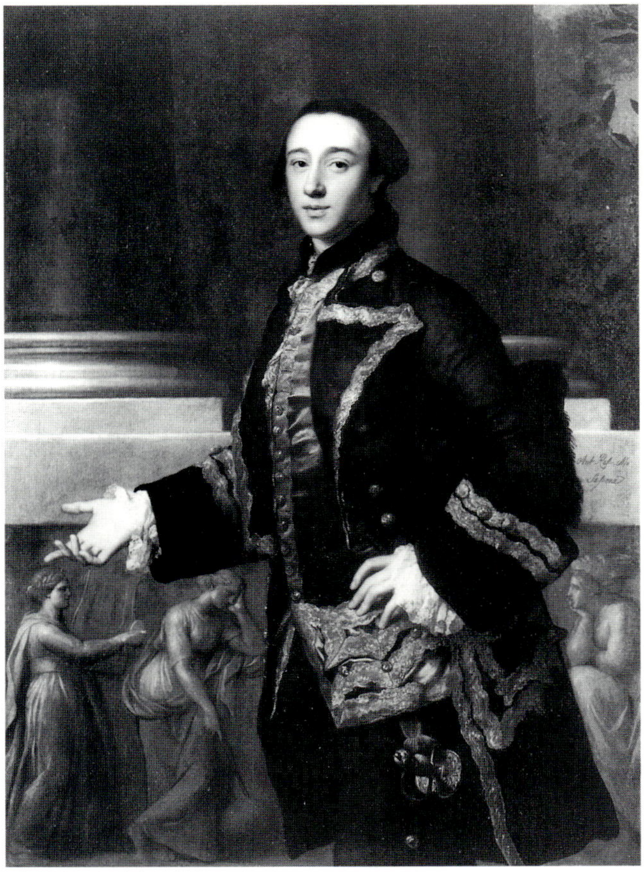

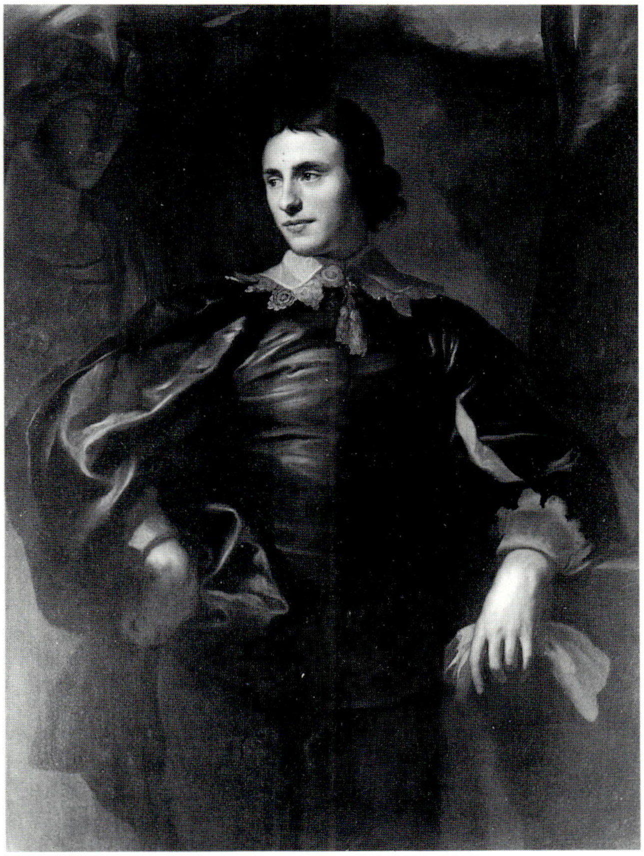

14. A. R. Mengs, *Portrait of Charles Lennox, later 3rd Duke of Richmond*, *c.*1755, Goodwood, The Earl of March

LEFT: 13. A. R. Mengs, *Portrait of Thomas Conolly of Castletown*, 1758, sold at Christie's, London, 29 Nov 1974, lot 13 (present whereabouts unknown)

Petersburg (fig.16) and another in Salzburg (fig.17) for reasons of cost.

A special case is the allegorical historical portrait which Mengs painted of the patron of the arts Lord Charlemont (cat.no.4). For a time, Charlemont had created something of a stir in Rome, and here Mengs made a striking attempt to combine portraiture and history into a new type of picture. The likeness to the sitter is suppressed in favour of an idealised generalisation. At the same time the programmatic statement of the picture is so specific that it characterises the sitter better than a pure physiognomic likeness could

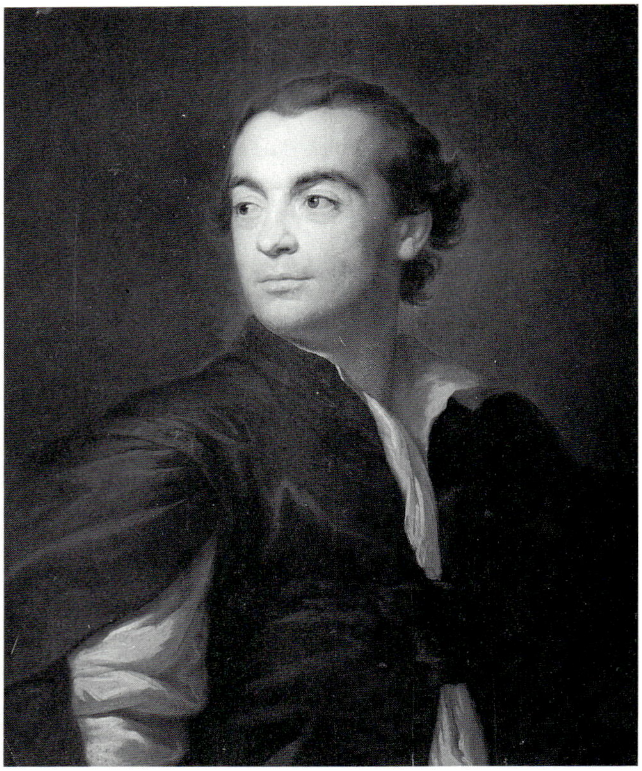

16 A. R. Mengs, *Portrait of an unknown English Sitter*, *c.*1758, St Petersburg, Hermitage

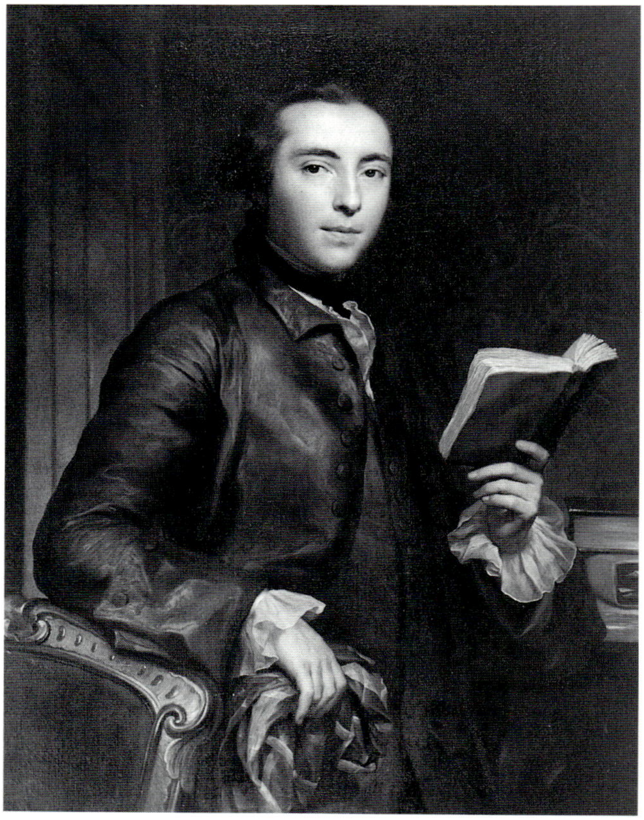

15 A. R. Mengs, *Portrait of an English Sitter*, here identified as Henry Willoughby, later 5th Baronet Middleton, *c.*1754, Providence, Rhode Island School of Design

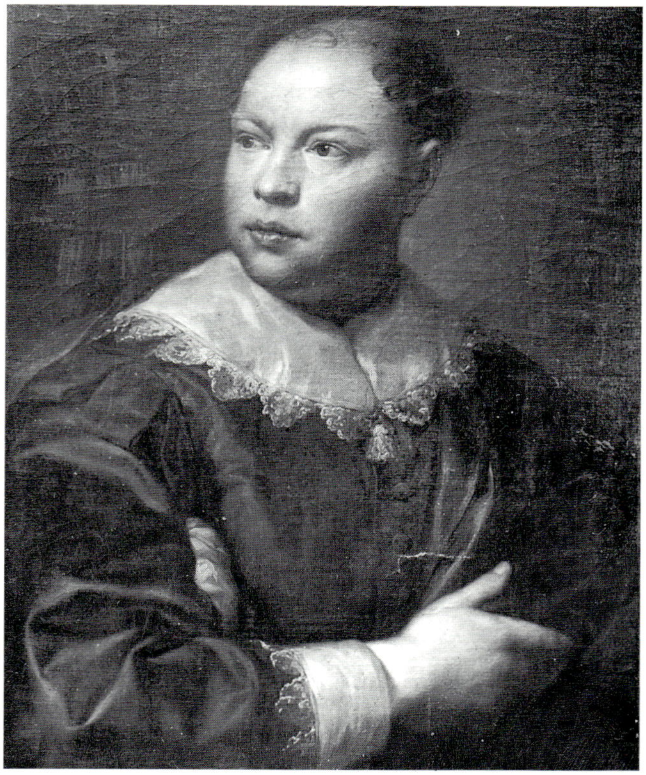

17 A. R. Mengs, *Portrait of an unknown English sitter*, *c.*1756-8, Salzburg, Museum Carolino Augusteum

do. One may recall Gavin Hamilton's painting of 1758 showing the *Discovery of Palmyra by Dawkins and Wood.*

Paintings for British Patrons and in British Collections
Mengs's first major commission from a British client after the Raphael copy was *The Judgement of Paris* for the Duke of Bridgewater, which he worked on in 1757. It has been suggested that Robert Adam, who was working in Rome as agent for the Duke in 1755, arranged the commission, which apparently was never completed.[78] The unfinished painting appears to have remained in the painter's studio and after his death it was sold to Catherine the Great of Russia. A drawing shows what was presumably the first planning phase of the composition, with life-sized figures (fig.18). The gentle swing of their movements and the

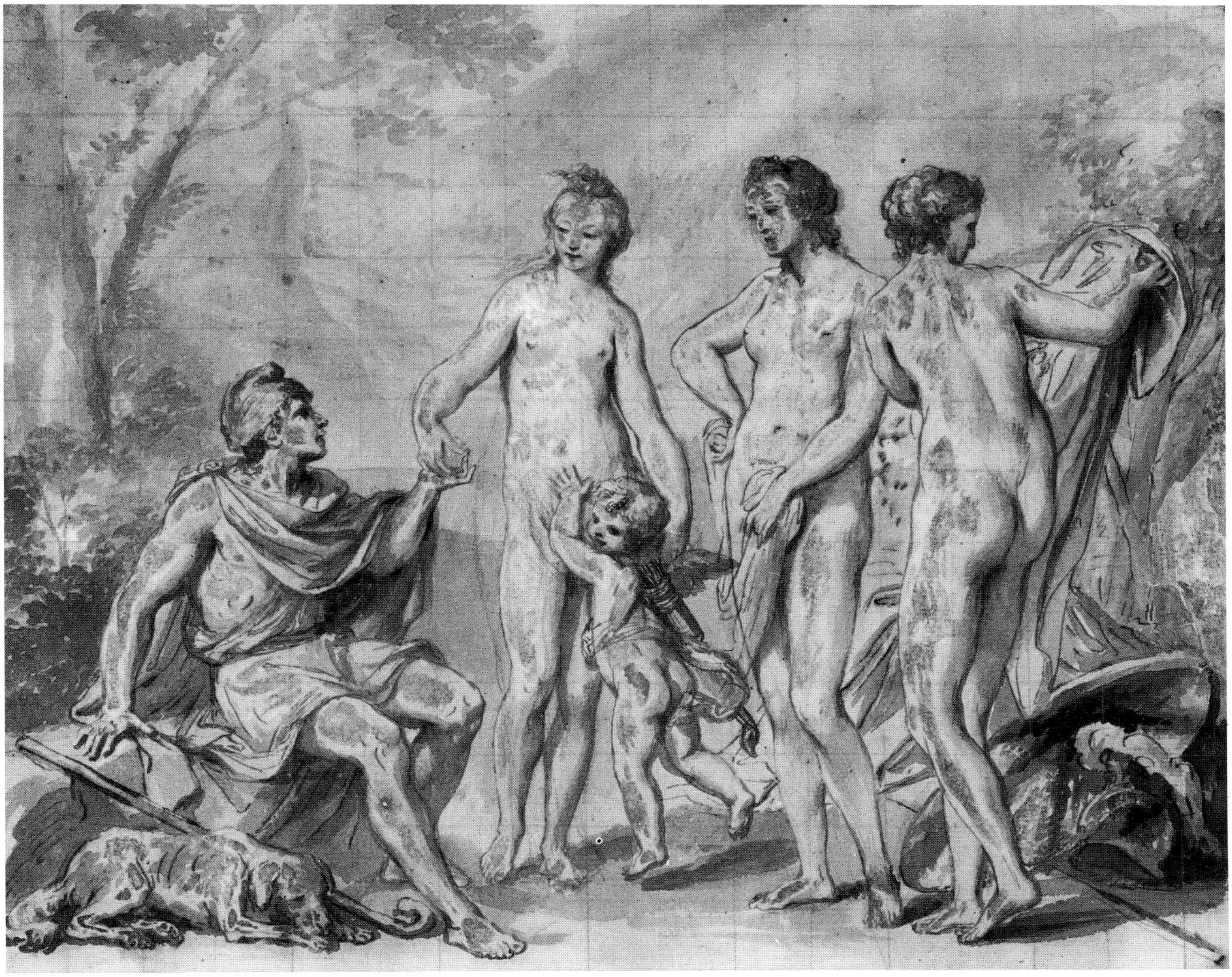

18. A. R. Mengs, *Sketch for a Judgement of Paris*, commissioned in 1756 by the Duke of Bridgewater, Private Collection

childlike expressions of the faces have a Rococo grace which gives way in the painting to a more sculptural and rather stiff severity.

Mengs's most important British commission in the late 1750s was the painting ordered by Henry Hoare around 1758–9 and which, according to the patron's instructions, shows the scene described by Plutarch of the meeting between *Augustus and Cleopatra* (cat.no.34). The painting was expressly intended to form a pair with the *Apotheosis of Marchese Pallavicini* by Carlo Maratti, which Hoare had purchased on the advice of Mann. The idea of giving the commission to Mengs may possibly have come from Mann, who had been in frequent contact with the artist about the copy for Lord Northumberland.

Evidently more important to Hoare than the thematic relationship to Maratti's work, which is barely noticeable, was the stylistic relation. The model which Hoare had in mind, both thematically and formally, was Guercino's depiction of the subject (Musei Capitolini, Rome), which he may have known from an engraving.[79] From one of the letters which document the execution of the painting and Hoare's reaction to it is clear that the engraver Robert Strange, who was in Rome at the time in question,[80] had shown Mengs an engraving of a *St Mary Magdalen* by Guido Reni, the expression of which Hoare regarded as appropriate for Cleopatra (cat.no.34). This episode shows the models that dictated taste, not only for Hoare but for most of the British collectors of his day as well. The *Grand Manner*, influenced by Italian seventeenth-century painting, was in demand. Hoare informed the painter of his criticisms of the painting, and the artist defended it in an equally detailed answer. It is a programmatic, and unambiguous statement of his approach to painting and a defence of his Cleopatra's expression in comparison with the work of Guido Reni and Guercino's composition, although the latter was the model for his composition.

In the *Augustus and Cleopatra* for Stourhead (fig.24), Mengs chose a moderate path stylistically, despite its formal severity and antique attributes. This is evident if one compares the painting with what was presumably the first version (fig.19). Originally Mengs had intended to set the scene in an Egyptian interior, and he kept strictly to antique models when arranging this very much more severe composition. With Piranesi's decor for the Café degli Inglesi, which was in the Egyptian style, the Egyptian interior of the earlier version is one of the earliest examples in Rome of the 'Egyptian Revival'. The café was at the bottom of the Spanish Steps, and it was one of the main meeting places for foreign visitors to Rome, and the scene of numerous contacts between artists and connoisseurs. The intellectual and artistic points of contact between Piranesi and Mengs that are illustrated by the portrait of Lord Charlemont (cat.no.4), are also confirmed by the study for the portrait of Pope Clement XIII (cat.no.5). The two artists were living only a few yards away from each other until 1758, in what is now the Via Sistina.

The decisive and pioneering innovation of the Stourhead *Augustus and Cleopatra* painting is the concentration on two main figures, who approach each other with measured steps and calm gestures, despite their intensely emotional state of mind and dramatic situation. Instead of Baroque emotion there is a disciplined and reasoned moderation of action and feeling. That Mengs had an evident preference for compositions in which two protagonists talk or turning to each other with restrained gestures can be seen from three other paintings for British clients: the allegorical portrait of Lord Charlemont (cat.no.4), *Noli me tangere* in Oxford (cat.no.30) and *Perseus and Andromeda*, painted in 1778 for Watkin Williams-Wynn and now in St Petersburg (fig.27). It may be coincidence that all three paintings were for British patrons; however, it cannot be denied that the British taste, influenced by portraits and conversation pieces, held a certain affinity for restrained parallel compositions. Mengs even commented on this in connection with *Noli me tangere*, maintaining that in this composition he had taken into account the taste of the nation for which he had painted it (see p.32).

Thomas Jenkins was at any rate very impressed by the painting for Hoare, and although the picture was never exposed to much publicity, the composition was greatly praised by Mengs's contemporaries and pupils. Chief among them was Benjamin West, who visited Stourhead in 1763 and closely followed Mengs's example in his own painting of *Pætus and Arrias* in 1766 (Yale Center for British Art).[81] Angelika Kauffmann also took up the theme of the Stourhead painting in a work of 1783.[82] When the Stourhead picture was finished, in the middle of 1760, Mengs was overwhelmed with commissions and at the highest point of his career since his early successes as court painter in Dresden. Several of the commissions on which he was working were for British clients. They included three half-figures, the subjects of which are not mentioned in the Azara–Fea catalogue of works. Very probably they were one of the two *Magdalens* (cat.nos.21 and 22), the *Sibyl* (cat.no.23) and a *St Cecilia*, now in a private collection.

The most important commission was probably the *Holy Family* for Lord Fordwich, later Earl of Cowper (fig.23). We know that Mengs already knew Cowper personally at this time from the portrait study he made then (cat.no.7). The *Holy Family* reappeared only a few years ago. Shortly after its completion it was copied by Benjamin West in Florence in 1762 for his American patron. After Cowper's death the painting entered the collection of Carlo Rinuccini in Florence. It stands chronologically between the *Holy Family* of 1749 (cat.no.19) and that painted in 1765 for King Charles III of Spain from the Wellington collection (cat.no.24).

While the *Magdalen* and the *Sibyl* are in a *neo-Seicento* style, clearly related to Bolognese seventeenth-century painting, the three compositionally related paintings of the *Holy Family* show how persistently Mengs worked to achieve a stylistic approximation to Raphael. The careful copy of the *School of Athens* had made him more familiar with Raphael's style, and the *Holy Family* for Cowper comes much closer to his aim of reviving Raphael's formal language than that of 1749. The *Holy Family* of 1765, formerly in the Palacio Real in Madrid, is one of the few works by

19. A. R. Mengs, *Augustus and Cleopatra*, *c.*1759, Augsburg, Städtische Kunstsammlungen

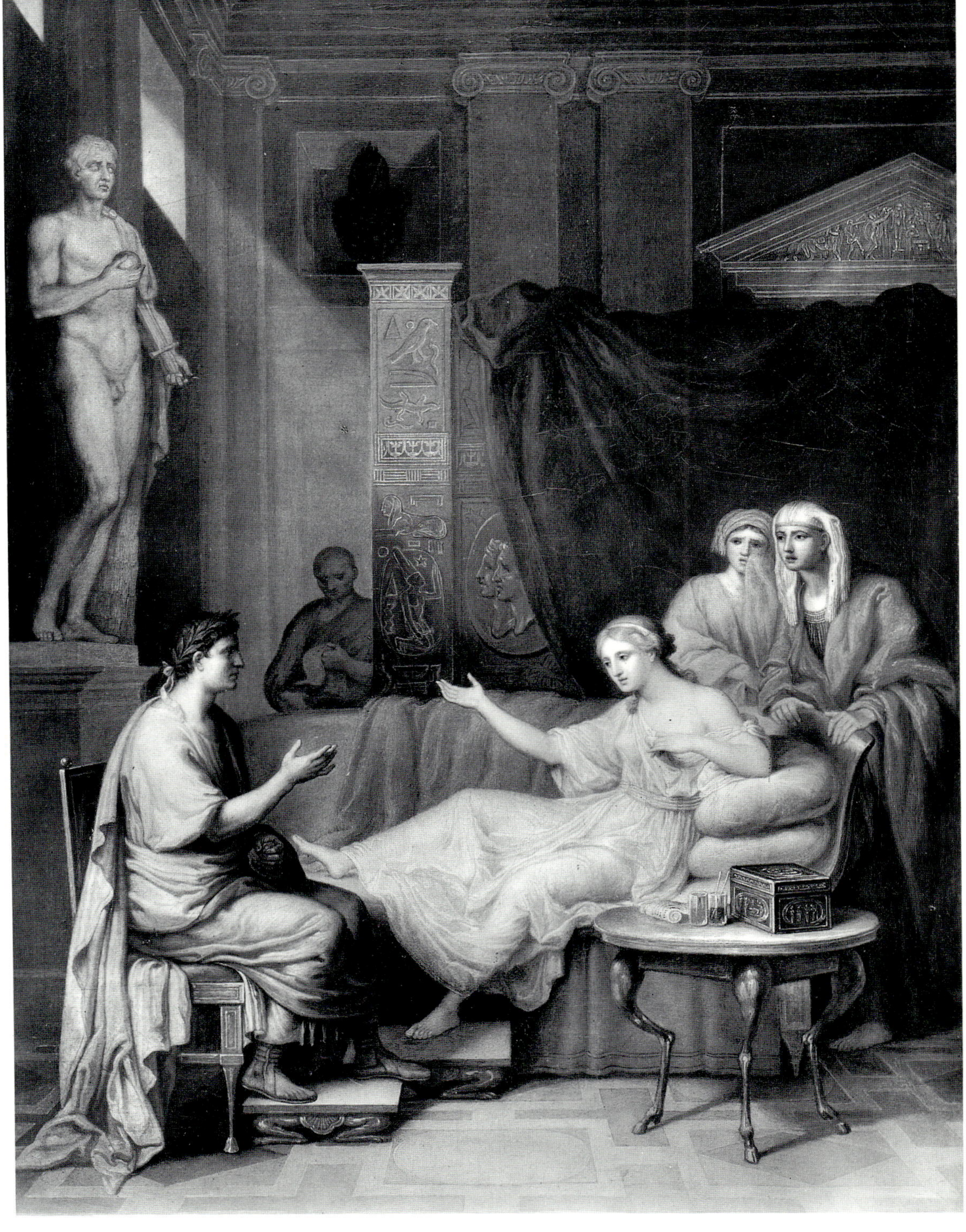

Mengs that are signed and dated, and it reveals an additional model to Raphael, from the Spanish tradition: Murillo. The setting is an interior which with its everyday utensils suggests a homely atmosphere recalling Murillo's *Holy Family* in the Prado, a painting that was then already in the royal collection.

Mengs's Contacts with Great Britain while in Spain

In Madrid Mengs was occupied chiefly with directing the work on the ceiling frescos of the Palacio Real. After Giaquinto left the court, in 1763 Mengs became the de facto supervisor and organiser of the decorative work on the palace. Tiepolo and his two sons were working on the interior of the throne room at the same time, but they were not under Mengs's supervision.[83] The coloured drawing in the Victoria and Albert Museum (cat.no.43) gives an insight into the painter's work as designer of ceiling paintings, which included sketches subsequently executed by other painters.

Because of his work as a fresco painter and portraitist, Mengs only found time to work again on more demanding easel paintings from 1765. The first example of these was the aforementioned *Holy Family* of 1765. At the same time he also started work on the *Lamentation* for King Charles III, which was not finished until 1769. This painting was initially intended to be a counterpart to the famous 'Spasimo di Sicilia' by Raphael, *Christ bearing the Cross*,[84] which was later placed in the King's bedchamber. Four scenes of the Passion by Mengs were added, creating a chronological depiction of the Christian story, which was usual in Spanish royal residences.

Another version of this painting, equal in quality to the original, reached England and since the early nineteenth century has been in the chapel of St John's College in Cambridge (cat.no.27), where it went long unnoticed. As with the two versions of *The Pentinent Magdalen* both by Mengs's hand and hardly distinguishable (cat.no.21 and 22), this case of a replica barely differing from the original also displays the degree of academic perfection which Mengs and his workshop had achieved. In handling and quality the second painting, the original destination of which is unknown, is in no way inferior to the first.

Faced with this Old Master-like technical care and workshop discipline, the rules by which art historians usually ascribe paintings prove inadequate. They generally judge by an often too schematic idea of the way tasks were divided between the master and his assistants. Replicas faithful to the original and by the master's own hand probably were due both to demand and the price the client was prepared to pay. For an artist like Mengs this would have been much more important than the question of originality, often overrated today, which derives from the idea that the artist had no choice but to embark on the search for a new solution, more 'developed' from a modern point of view, for each commission. How far this is from the reality of the eighteenth century can be observed in many artists and in many different genres of painting. Many collectors and patrons wanted an identical version of a successful painting from the artist himself. If they offered a good price he would naturally be prepared to provide a second and a third version of equal quality. However, that does not mean that he did so without any assistance. The different versions of the *Annunciation* which Mengs painted, and to which the model-like sketch here shown refers (cat.no.26), are good examples of this.

In the case of portraits replicas were normally only required of state commissions. In Mengs's output, however, we find a case where a faithful replica of one of his portraits of a client on the Grand Tour was made and given the same signature. This was the portrait of Tom Conolly of 1758 (fig.13), and the second version was probably made for the sitter's mother, for Horace Walpole mentioned it as being in her possession.[85] The signature did not necessarily mean that both versions were entirely by Mengs; it only means that the second portrait was also made in his studio, under his supervision and with his participation. As the official portrait of a prince often had to be reproduced, usually for dynastic or family reasons, the workshop of a court painter like Mengs was equipped for such cases (cat.no.13). The decisive factor in the overall appearance of the painting or portrait was that the master's hand should be recognisable in the quality of the finishing, while the preparatory work could be done by his assistants.

Most of the reports on court life in Madrid in the eighteenth century, and the most exact accounts, come from British visitors. One reason why they included distant Spain in their itineraries may be that it was less known, being further away, and so held out more promise of adventure than other European destinations. Certainly the number of British travellers to Spain greatly increased in the course of the eighteenth century.[86] Mengs met two old British acquaintances in Spain; one was Louis de Visme, whose profile he had already drawn in Rome in 1758 (fig.20), and whose portrait he now painted in Madrid in courtly style (cat.no.16).

The atmosphere at the court of Madrid and the harsh and

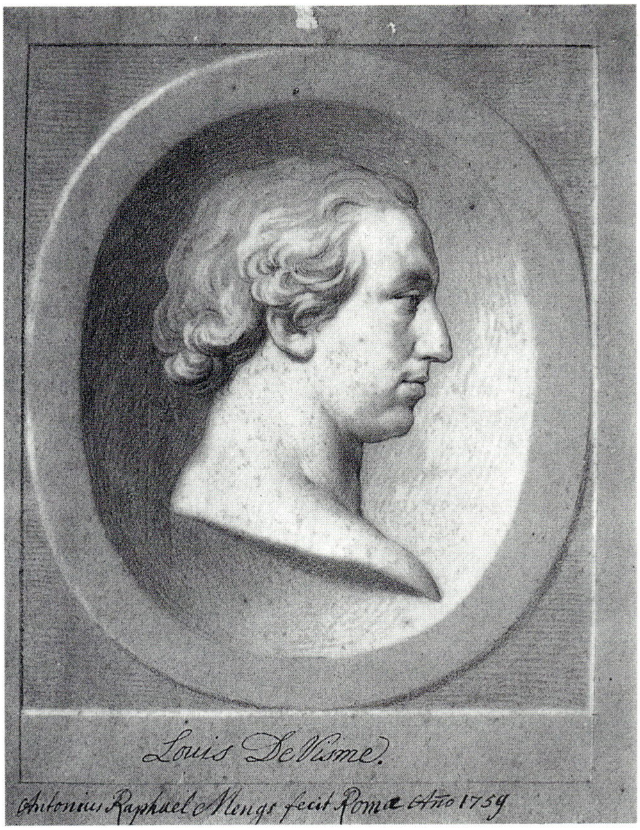

20. A. R. Mengs, *Portrait of Louis de Visme*, dated 1758, Otterlo, Museum Kröller Müller

depressing living conditions, compared with Rome, induced Mengs to seek a remedy after only two years. In the spring of 1763 he was offered the chance to go to Great Britain, as Winckelmann told the publisher Johann Kaspar Füssli in Zürich, adding in confidence that four of the richest noblemen had made the offer to the artist.[87] Later that year Mengs turned down the offer, according to Winckelmann, as the King had now given him such good terms that he was hoping soon to be able to return to Rome.[88] However, another four years were to pass before Mengs was able to go back to Italy for a few years, in 1769. There was no further talk of visiting Britain. No doubt influential British diplomats had suggested that Mengs should go to England as a freelance painter, but apart from Winckelmann's letter no other information on this has survived.

Occasionally British artists also came to Spain. One was the Scot Richard Cooper, son of the engraver of the same name who had been Robert Strange's teacher. Cooper seems to have worked in London between 1761 and 1764 for Strange, who had called on Mengs in Rome. As Cooper announced in a letter from Paris written on 4 January 1767, he intended to approach Mengs in Madrid with recommendations from British artists: 'Meng [sic], the famous Painter from Italy, is now there. I can be recommended to him in the warmest manner by Artists who were his Intimates in Rome, he is in a great esteem with his Prince [*i.e.* King Charles III] & a person that might not a little contribute [word illegible] both by his interest and good advice as a Painter'.[89]

That Cooper did indeed gain access to Mengs's studio is evident from his drawings, which show some of the works which were then there. Cooper's drawings are now in Edinburgh, and they are a valuable source of information on the contents of the Madrid workshop, as some of the works he copied are no longer extant.[90] They also provide valuable information for the dating of some paintings. Among the works he copied were two small paintings of *St John the Baptist* and, as counterpart, *The Penitent Magdalen.* Both were intended for the bedchamber of Charles III and they were among the artist's most highly praised works. For that reason they were taken from Madrid by Napoleon's brother Joseph Bonaparte and were then part of the war booty which came into the hands of the Duke of Wellington at the battle of Vitoria on 21 of June 1813. In 1819 they became part of his collection (cat.nos.28 and 29). Another of the works drawn by Cooper can be seen in our exhibition, the draft sketch for a cameo by Johann Pichler, which was in the possession of Lord Brudenell (cat.no.39). It can be seen as an irony of fate that precisely some of the works by Mengs that were spoken of with disdain by Richard Cumberland in his *Anecdotes of Eminent Painters in Spain* of 1782 (cat.no.57) were those that reached Great Britain.

Lord Cowper and the British Colony in Florence

Shortly after completing the two small paintings for Charles III Mengs, who was seriously ill, was given leave of absence in 1769 and set off for Italy. His journey took him via Monte Carlo, Genoa and Parma to Florence, which he reached in June 1770. He found three old acquaintances in the city. One was Count Orsini-Rosenberg, whose portrait he had painted in Rome in 1756 (cat.no.12) and who had been accredited Austrian Imperial ambassador to Madrid from 1757 to 1765. Orsini-Rosenberg went from there to Florence in 1766, where he took over the business of

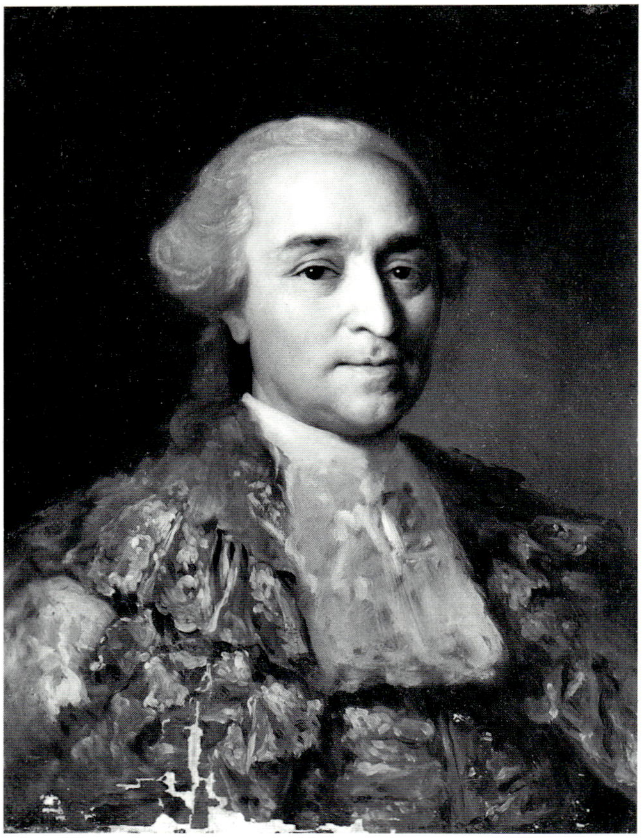

21. A. R. Mengs, *Portrait of a nobleman*, here identified as Franz-Xaver Orsini-Rosenberg, painted 1770 in Florence, sold at Sotheby's, London, 25 July 1973, lot 65

government for the young Grand Duke Pietro Leopoldo until 1771. Mengs painted another portrait of Orsini-Rosenberg (fig.21), but this also appears never to have been finished.

The second old acquaintance he saw in Florence was Lord Cowper. Cowper had commissioned the *Holy Family* (fig.24), mentioned above, from Mengs as early as 1760, and West had made a copy of it. Mengs had also painted Cowper's portrait (cat.no.7). The painter made a second portrait in Florence, and Lord Cowper gave this a few years later to his friend Carlo Rinuccini, who himself was a great admirer of Mengs.[91] Whether this second portrait, which was not finished until the summer of 1773, was a finished version of the study made in 1760, which was later in Mengs's studio, or a new portrait, must remain an open question, for the work was auctioned in London in 1945 and has never reappeared.[92] Of all the collectors in Florence Cowper owned the most works by Mengs, apart from the Grand Duke Pietro Leopoldo. They included the self-portrait by Mengs that is now in Liverpool (cat.no.1). It was painted during the artist's second stay in Florence in 1773/4 and will be discussed later.

Cowper was very vain and self-indulgent, and around 1780 he also had his portrait painted by the Florentine artist Giuseppe Maria Fabbrini (1740-*c.*1795).[93] Fabbrini was a pupil of Mengs and after his death copied his last, unfinished work, a *Lamentation* painted for Carlo Rinuccini, for Lord Cowper in 1782 (fig.26).[94] The cartoon of the painting was to bear an inscription in hexameters, composed by Cowper's chaplain William Sandys after ideas by Cowper.[95]

At this time the British artistic colony in Florence was experiencing what was perhaps its most intense interaction with the world of the Florentine Habsburg-Lorraine court. The main reason was the friendship which Cowper had formed with the young Grand Duke Pietro Leopoldo. Cowper had settled in Florence in 1760 and both his palace in the Via Ghibellina and his villa in Fiesole had become important centres of artistic life and elaborate social entertainments. Cowper was a major collector, but he also distinguished himself as a patron to British artists who came to Florence.[96] He employed the miniaturist Giuseppe Macpherson, a Scot born in Florence, commissioned works from the landscape painter John More[97] and sponsored Zoffany when he came to Florence in 1772 to paint the famous picture of the *Tribuna* for Queen Charlotte of England.[98] As Zoffany remained in Florence until 1777 he presumably met his teacher Mengs there on his second stay in the city, from autumn of 1773 to spring 1774.

The third old acquaintance whom Mengs re-encountered in Florence in 1770 was Horace Mann (1706-88). He was still head of the British embassy there, now with the rank of Envoy Extraordinary.[99] Mann had become famous in Florence, and his and Cowper's assistance after the catastrophic fire in Santa Maria del Carmine of 28-29 January 1771 was specifically mentioned in a Florentine newspaper.[100] Mengs also witnessed the fire, and shortly before he left Florence for Rome he endeavoured to ensure that Masolino's and Masaccio's frescos in the Brancacci chapel would be properly restored by his pupils.[101]

British Commissions and Contacts in Rome from 1771 to 1779

Mengs had hardly arrived in Rome when he was installed in his office as principal of the Accademia di San Luca. James Byres and Piranesi were present at the first meeting of the members of the Academy under his chairmanship.[102] Byres acted as agent for the commission for the altarpiece which Mengs was to paint for All Souls College in Oxford (fig.22). The entire correspondence and the invoices were handled through Byres.[103] Mengs received 600 Roman scudi as fee for the painting. The price, which was the equivalent of 315

22. A.R. Mengs, *Noli me tangere*, painted 1771 for All Souls College in Oxford. Oxford, All Souls College

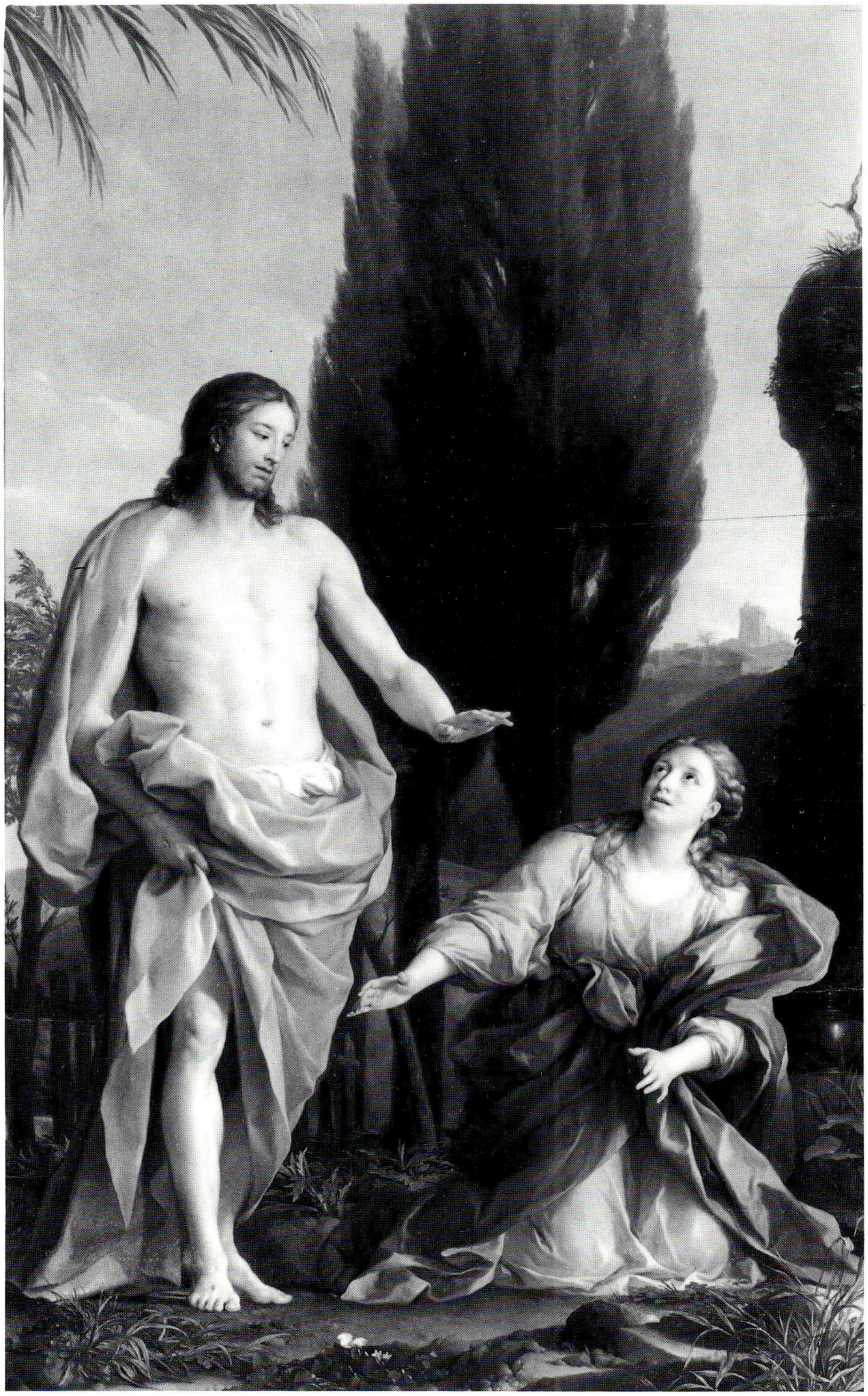

English pounds, was regarded as very high for one painting with two figures.[104]

The painter appears to have started work on the subject soon after he arrived in Rome, having already started on the sketches in Florence.[105] After its completion the wooden panel was displayed to the public in the Villa Medici in November 1771, having previously been shown to the Pope. Reaction was remarkable and, as was only to be expected, opinions were very divided. The sketch for the painting was acquired immediately by William Beckford at a high price. The painting was sent to England by sea and exhibited in London before reaching its destination. We know this from a letter from the Jesuit priest John Thorpe, who discusses the picture in detail in his correspondence with Lord Arundell. Thorpe compares the posture of Christ, which he found too similar to the Apollo Belvedere, with that of a dancing-master, and he also complains that the folds in St Mary Magdalen's dress are too heavy. However, Thorpe was Arundell's agent and a determined supporter of Batoni[106], so this critical attitude is hardly surprising. What is particularly remarkable is Mengs's reply, which Thorpe has recorded: 'When Mengs heard of some remarks made upon his performance he allowed the justice of them, but added he conformed himself to the taste of the nation, where his painting was to be placed. I dare not say how far this may be taken as a compliment to England. But I know that he was paid above twelve hundred Crowns for this picture, which he is said to have done in less than six weeks work'.[107]

James Barry complained in a letter to the Duke of Richmond on 14 October 1773: 'Mengs and other natives of foreign countries where art and human mind have been long since in a vitiated, sickly and dying state, are employed without scruples in pictures for the churches of our universities.'[108]

On the other hand the painting also earned much praise, as from the French painter Julien de Parme and the Flemish painter Corneille Lens, who was influenced by it in his *Noli me tangere* for the church of La Madeleine in Lille in 1778/9.[109] The spectacle of the public exhibition in Rome certainly put Mengs's name on everyone's lips, and his absence of ten years from the city had clearly advanced his reputation as a painter. During the next two years, which he spent partly in Rome and partly in Naples, he was mainly occupied with painting the Stanza dei Papiri in the Vatican library. Apart from that his important office as principal of the Accademia di San Luca brought him representative commissions and he was much engaged with academic teaching. He was also becoming more preoccupied with questions of art theory. As a result of his recent stay in Parma in May 1770, and a new edition of Vasari's *Lives of the Artists*, Mengs began to concern himself in detail with the life and work of one of his two favourite painters, Correggio. In Madrid the works by Correggio which were then in the possession of the Spanish monarch had evidently reawakened the interest in Correggio he had shown in his youth, when he was influenced by him in Dresden. Moreover, he shared a name with the Italian painter, whose real name was Antonio Allegri, as he did with Raphael.

Mengs had leaned towards Correggio's style in some of the works he had painted in Madrid, particularly the two small ones showing *St John the Baptist* and *The Penitent Magdalen* (cat.nos.28 and 29). With his renewed interest in Correggio he had also copied the small painting by Correggio showing *Christ praying on the Mount of Olives* in Madrid, which is now in the National Gallery in London. Mengs gave this drawing to the copper engraver Giovanni Volpato in Rome in 1772 to reproduce for the reference book *Schola italica* (cat.no.56), published by Gavin Hamilton.

On his return to Madrid Mengs again broke his journey in Florence, remaining there from October 1773 to spring 1774. During these months he painted a second version of *The Dream of St Joseph* for Lord Cowper, whose first version was in the possession of the Grand Duke Pietro Leopoldo in the Palazzo Pitti, a *Christ Bearing the Cross* and the self-portrait already mentioned (cat.no.1). The self-portrait confirms that at this time he was also working on a painting which Sir Watkin Williams-Wynn had commissioned as early as 1768 to match one commissioned at the same time from Batoni, showing *Bacchus and Ariadne*. While Batoni had completed his painting in 1773,[110] Mengs put off the work on his commission, and it was not until he was leaving Rome that he promised James Byres, who was again acting as his agent, that he would do the work in Florence.[111]

The self-portrait shows the painter at his easel; the painting of *Perseus and Andromeda*, now in St. Petersburg, is to be seen in the right half of the picture. As the self-portrait was painted for Cowper, it was assumed for a long time that Cowper had also commissioned *Perseus and Andromeda*, until Brinsley Ford produced documentary evidence to show how the painting had been commissioned.[112] Cowper did however have one of the many sketches for the painting, which is now in Venice (Pinacoteca del Seminario Patriarcale). It differs considerably from the composition in the Liverpool self-portrait.

The work on the painting took a long time, and when

23. A. R. Mengs, *Holy Family*, painted 1760 for Lord Cowper. Private Collection

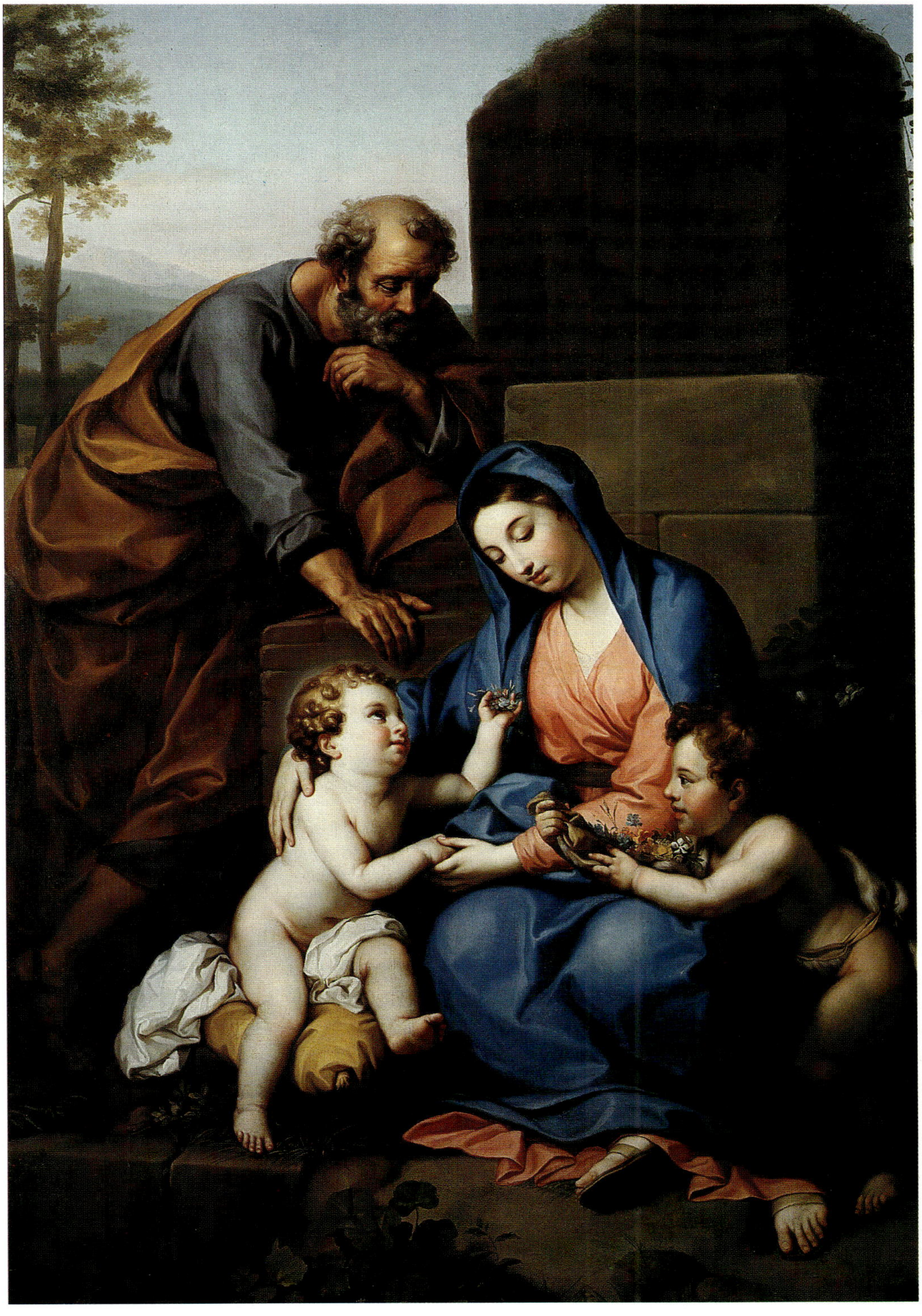

Mengs returned to Madrid in the spring of 1774, the completion of the ceiling frescos in the Palacio Real was awaiting him. In Madrid he re-encountered Thomas Robinson, since 1770 the Second Lord Grantham, who had been among Mengs's admirers in Rome in 1760 and was now British Ambassador to Madrid. Possibly it was his old familiarity with Mengs which enabled Thomas Pelham to view the paintings in the royal collection escorted by Mengs. Pelham recounted this event in 1776 in letters to his parents.[113] Mengs also gave the young Briton important advice for the itinerary of his proposed visit to Italy.[114] Lord Grantham's predecessor in Madrid was Mr Harris, who had supplied Mengs with the commission for the All Souls College chapel altarpiece in Oxford in 1769. With his position as 'primer pintor de camára' and a European reputation, Mengs had become a leading personality in Madrid, a man whom any visitor interested in culture could not ignore. He was also responsible for the supervision of the royal collctions, and in 1776 he worked out a plan for the re-hanging of the museums, although this was not carried out as his ill-health caused him to return permanently to Rome at the beginning of 1777.

Shortly after Mengs arrived in Rome the remains of an ancient house were uncovered on the site of the former Villa Montalto, now the Villa Negroni; they included rooms decorated with frescos of unusually high quality. Thomas Jenkins was selling the collection of antiquities from the villa to British collectors at this time. The excavation, which was undertaken by Mengs's friend Azara, aroused Mengs's interest due to the quality and good condition of the paintings, and he decided to make careful tracings of the frescos and copy them in miniature. The paintings and their copies aroused considerable interest in the Roman press and among the art public.[115] Thomas Jones made an oil sketch of the site and recorded his visit to the villa on 5 July 1777, commenting that 'the painted ornaments [are] much in the Chinese taste'.[116] Mengs was probably drawing there about this time. Thomas Jones was travelling in the company of Henry Tresham, who purchased the paintings when they were taken down shortly afterwards and sold them again in December to Frederick Hervey, who had only just arrived in Rome, where he was known as 'Lord Bristol'. He intended to decorate his villa in Downhill in Ireland (his 'Tusculum') with the frescos but apparently never did so. The frescos acquired by Hervey included those which Mengs had drawn. The three engravings from his drawings which appeared in 1778 (cat.nos.49 and 50) were dedicated to Lord Bristol, as were the majority of the later engravings.

The completion of *Perseus and Andromeda* for Sir Watkin Williams-Wynn in 1778 brought Mengs his last great public triumph (fig.27). Like the *Noli me tangere* in Oxford, this painting was exhibited in his studio, in February of that year. Among the many records left by people who saw the painting and commented on the event, those by Thomas Jones and James Northcote stand out. Neither of them thought very highly of the work. For Jones its principle merit consisted 'in its laborious high finishing – the Result of German flegmatic industry'.[117] James Northcote expressed a similar view: 'He is a German and this is a true German picture. I did not much like it'.[118] Both painters have left very informative descriptions of the exhibition in Mengs's studio and of his expensive lifestyle, of which they also disapproved. Jones, who had been a pupil of Richard Wilson, nevertheless had direct contact with Mengs, and has also left us a vivid description of their last meeting, on 16 June 1779 near the Arco della Regina at SS. Trinità dei Monti.[119] Other artists, including the director of the French academy Joseph-Marie Vien and the Swiss sculptor Alexander Trippel, praised *Perseus and Andromeda* highly. Jacques-Louis David, who was then in Rome, does not seem to have been unimpressed by the work, which in its rigorous antique style and technical perfection is on the threshold of mature Neo-Classicism, the style of the last two decades of the eighteenth century.

The client, who according to Jones paid 500 zecchini, that is, about 1000 scudi for the work, never had it in his possession. The British warship 'Westmoreland' that was taking it to England was captured by a French vessel; the painting was commandeered as booty and presented to the French Minister of the Navy. He auctioned it in Marseilles, where more than 9000 Roman scudi were offered for it. It was finally purchased by Catherine the Great of Russia through her Paris agent Melchior Grimm, and formed the brilliant centrepiece of the considerable collection of works which she purchased at the end of June 1779 from Mengs's estate after his death. Even had Sir Watkin Williams-Wynn been prepared to ask the painter for a second copy, all hope of restitution had gone.

The sudden death in June 1779, at the peak of his fame, of an artist blessed with such great success caused great grief not only in Rome. His friend José Nicolas de Azara endeavoured to make arrangements for the support of Mengs's seven children, whom the painter had left ill-provided for, despite his high earnings. The well-handled sale of his estate and the generosity of the Spanish King nevertheless resulted in a sum that put his family in a comfortable position.

24. A. R. Mengs, *Augustus and Cleopatra*, 1760-1. Stourhead, National Trust

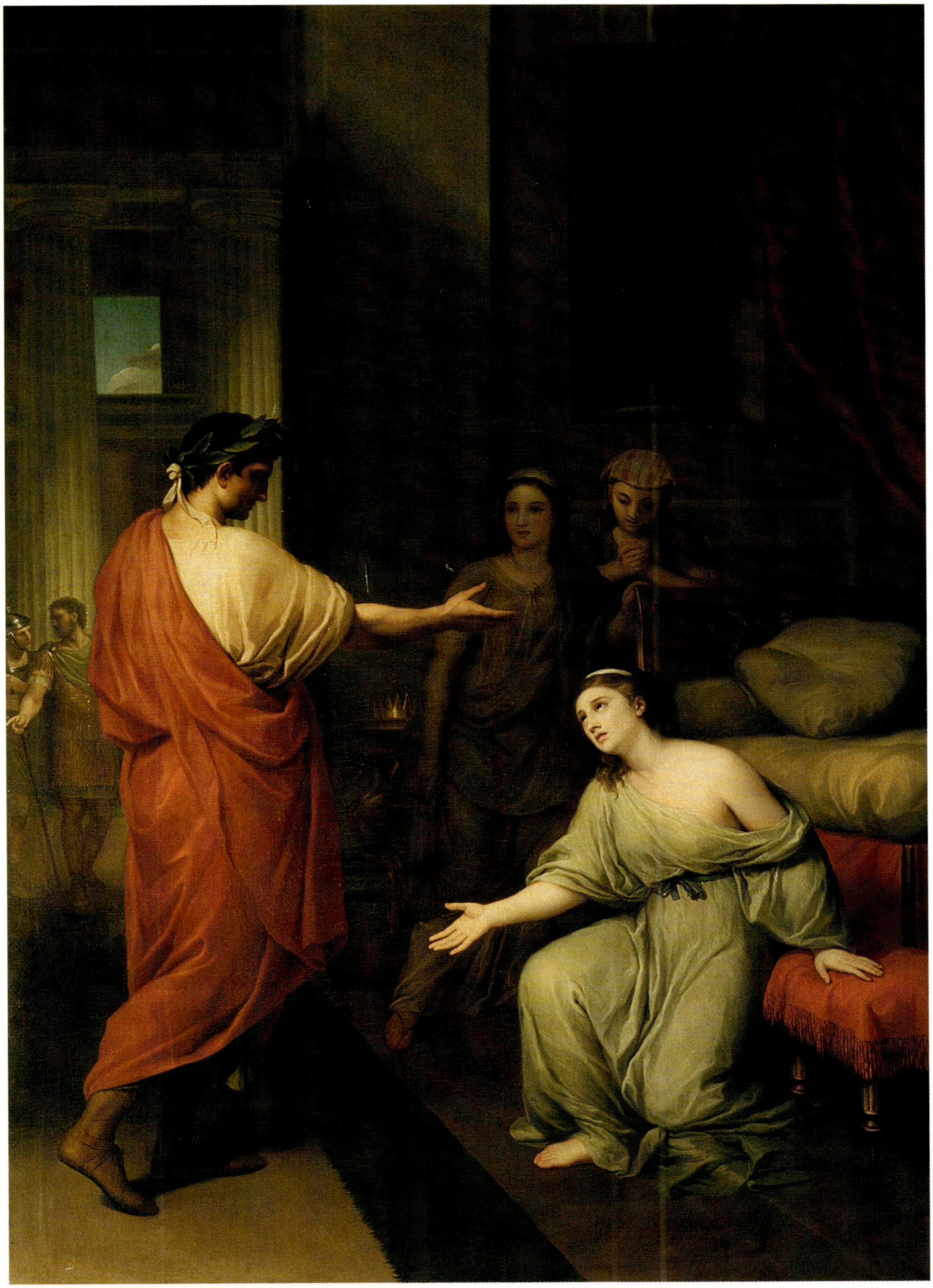

Azara also funded a memorial to the painter in the Pantheon, consisting of a bronze bust with an inscription.[120] The bust was by the Irish sculptor Christopher Hewetson, who since 1765 had been living in Rome where he had good relations with Thomas Jenkins and Gavin Hamilton.[121] Azara recorded a visit by the sculptor to the painter's studio in March 1779.[122] The bronze bust was replaced in 1782 by a marble version (fig.25) which Hewetson made from the bronze. The memorial was removed in the nineteenth century and the bust was placed in the Protomoteca Capitolina in Rome, while the bronze bust may be that which is now in the Institut de France in Paris.

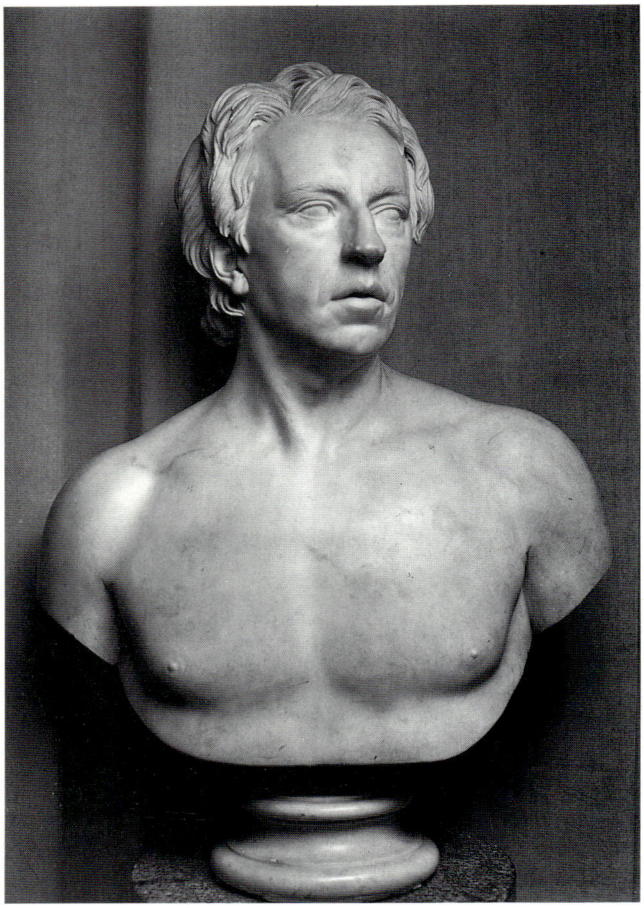

25. Christopher Hewetson, *Bust of A. R. Mengs* (marble), collocated 1782 in the Pantheon in Rome. Rome, Protomoteca Capitolina

The Decline in Mengs's Reputation

In his bust Hewetson created a strongly idealised portrait of Mengs, whom many of his contemporaries thought unsurpassed as a painter, and it reflects the high honour in which his supporters held him. However, Reynolds was to be proved right in his prophecy that Mengs and Batoni, like all the Roman school of their time, would soon be forgotten. Many factors contributed to the decline in Mengs's reputation, particularly rapid and thorough among British critics, which even so ardent an admirer as the influential Benjamin West could not prevent.[123]

The main reason for this decline was the far-reaching change in taste which affected British art earlier and much more deeply than continental art. While aristocratic and court society still revered Italian taste and antiquity, artists, writers and critics began to see art and its history from a new angle, as they did man and the real world. For the younger generation of painters like John and Alexander Runciman, John Hamilton Mortimer, James Barry, George Romney and Johann Heinrich Fuseli, born around 1740, art had aquired a quite different dimension. It was no longer recourse to recognised models but experimentation with the possibilities of their own pictorial imaginations and an ironic questioning of reality and tradition which determined the new approach. Fuseli had utterly condemned Mengs, whom he had formerly admired, shortly after his arrival in Rome in 1770, reacting with bitter disappointment to his works, and probably particularly the ceiling frescos in the Villa Albani and the church of Sant'Eusebio. He could not understand how Winckelmann, whom he admired so much, could regard a painter whom he thought mediocre as so outstanding. Like Reynolds, Fuseli used the fiction of the objectivity of the later generation to give weight to his views: 'Posterity, which will judge impartially, will wonder how he could have written with such dignity of this art, setting a mediocre artist beside Phidias and Apelles'.[124] But in 1802, when Fuseli went in the company of West, John Opie and Joseph Farington to Paris, where they saw and discussed *The Rape of the Sabine Women* by David, he did concede that this painting was not as good as Mengs's work.[125]

What Fuseli, Reynolds and soon other artists failed to see in the work of the painter who had been so admired during his lifetime was expressed perhaps over-forcibly by Richard Cumberland: 'Mengs was an artist who had seen much, and invented little; ...he dispenses neither life nor death to his figures, excites no terror, rouses no passions, and risques no flights; ... by studying to avoid particular

26. Giuseppe Antonio Fabbrini after A. R. Mengs, *Lamentation*, painted 1782 for Lord Cowper, sold at Sotheby's, London, 8 July 1987, lot 320

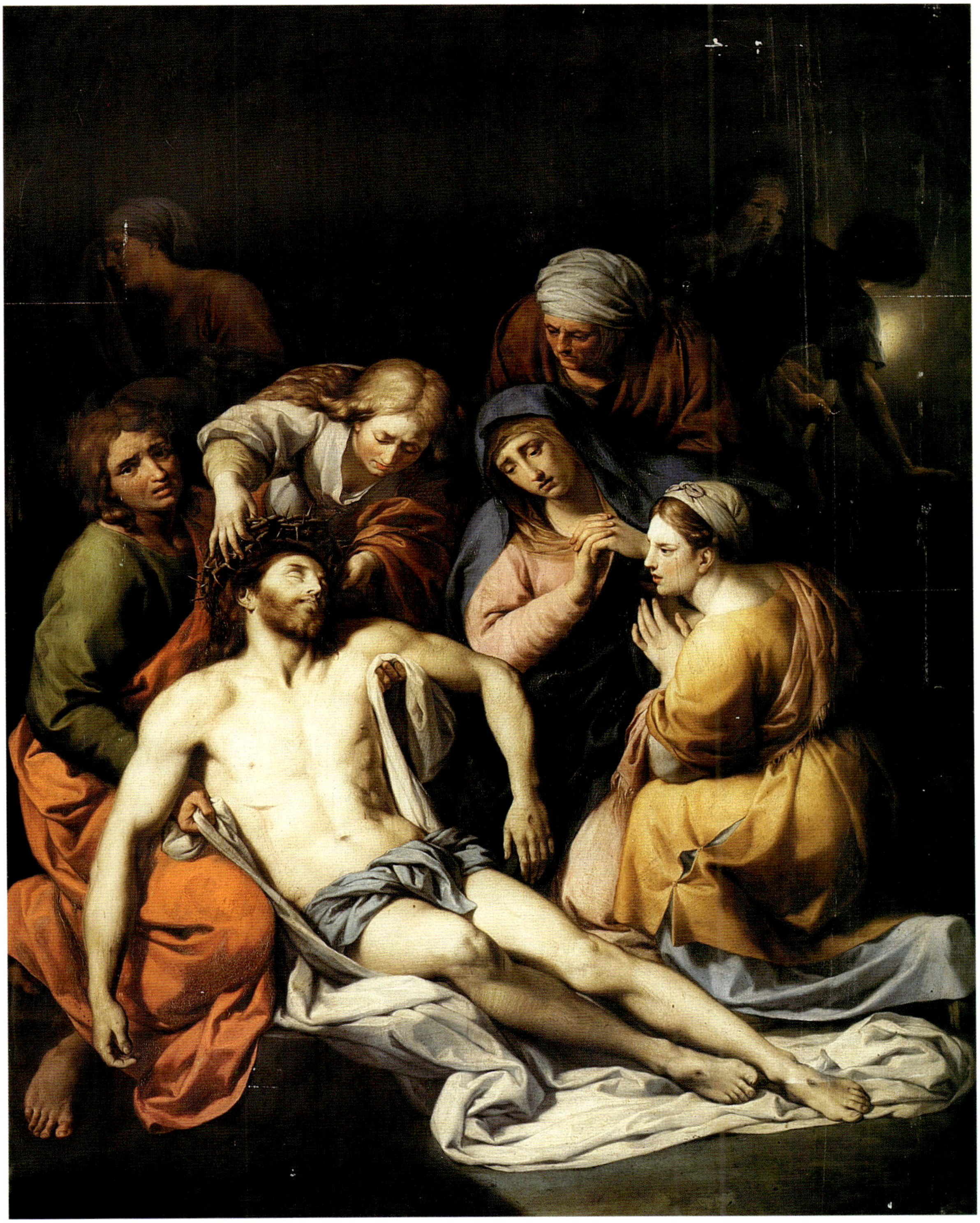

defects, he incurs general ones, and paints with tameness and servility; ... in all or most of his compositions, in which a finished delicacy of pencil exhibits the Hand of the Artist, but gives no emanations of the Soul of the Master; if it is beauty, it does not warm, if it is sorrow, it excites no pity ...'.[126]

This criticism has characterised attributes to the painter right into our century. The 'Sturm und Drang' artists, and the later Romantics, kept an aggressive distance from the artistic taste of Winckelmann's age, and they had hardly a good word to say for an artist like Mengs. Collectors however, particularly in Great Britain, do not seem to have bothered greatly about such prejudices. During the nineteenth century also a number of his works reached British collections or were offered for sale.[127] On the other hand, many portraits and works remained untouched in older collections, and this is one reason why they survived relatively unscathed the long period when Mengs was almost totally forgotten. The German Karl Gustav Waagen in his *Treasures of Art in Great Britain* of 1854 only mentions a single work supposedly by Mengs, and in fact it is not by him.[128]

It is to be hoped that this study will help to bring further works to light that have survived away from the light of publicity, and that this may help to improve and complete the picture sketched out here. More research in British archives and diaries of the age of the Grand Tour may yet yield many a surprise.

Notes

1. Jeremy Black, *The British and the Grand Tour* (London, Dover, 1985), p.165.
2. Francis Haskell, 'Some aspects of taste, fashion and collecting in England and France', *Rediscoveries in Art* (Phaidon Press, 1976), pp.19-20.
3. Black, (n.1), pp.189, 201-2.
4. Black, (n.1), pp.220-1.
5. See the articles by Christopher White and Michael Kitson in the exhibition catalogue *Zwei Jahrhunderte englischer Malerei. Britische Kunst und Europa 1680 bis 1880* (Munich, Haus der Kunst, 1980), passim.
6. *Pompeo Batoni and his British Patrons* (London, Iveagh Bequest, Kenwood, 1982).
7. A full and informative account of his British contacts is to be found in Ulrich Finke, 'Mengs und England', *'Sind Briten hier?' Relations between British and Continental Art 1680-1880* (Munich, 1981) pp.57-82.
8. I refer to this in my monograph with a full catalogue raisonné: *Anton Raphael Mengs 1728-1779. Ein deutscher Maler in Europa*, to be published by Hirmer Verlag, Munich in 1994.
9. *Elogio storico del Cavaliere Anton Raffaele Mengs scritto dal Consiglier Bianconi con un catalogo in fine delle opere da esso fatte* (Milan 1780), pp.29-30. According to this the painter was to receive an annual salary of 25,000 thalers for five years and a further 25,000 thalers in the form of subsistence and accommodation allowance. In return he was to paint pictures and portraits for his patron. The sums are so high that the offer hardly seems credible; however, it is known that British portrait painters earned far more than their colleagues on the continent, see Peter Helfrich Sturz, *Briefe im Jahre 1768 auf einer Reise im Gefolge des Königs von Dänemark geschrieben* (London, 1768).
10. Black (n.1), p.167. William, Fourth Earl of Essex, was in Munich in 1751.
11. Doray de Longrais, *Oeuvres de M. Mengs, traduites par J. P. Doray de Longrais, avec un éloge historique de Mengs, rédigé par L. T. Hérissant, sur des notes qui avaient été envoyées de Stuttgard au traducteur par Guibal, élève de Mengs* (Regensburg, 1782), pp.36-7.
12. William Hogarth dedicated one of his engravings of the election campaign that appeared in 1755 to Williams, see Frederick Antal, *Hogarth and his Place in European Art* (first edition, 1962, German edition Dresden, 1966), p.106.
13. *Horace Walpole's Correspondence with Sir Horace Mann* (New Haven, vol.4, 1960), p.330.
14. Walpole *Correspondence* (n.13), vol.4, pp.330-1.
15. Leslie Lewis, *Connoisseurs and Secret Agents* (London, 1962), passim. F. Noack, 'Des Kardinal Albani Beziehungen zu Künstlern', *Cicerone*, XVI (1924), pp.402-413, 451-459.
16. *Aedes Walpoliana or a Description of the Collection of Pictures at Houghton Hall in Norfolk, the Seat of the R. Hon. Sir Robert Walpole* (London, 1747), p.xxxv: 'In short, in my Opinion all the qualities of a Perfect Painter never met but in Raphael, Guido and Annibal Carracci'.
17. T. Pignatti, F. Pedrocco, E. Martinelli, *Palazzo Labia à Venezia* (Turin, 1982), pp.178, 208.
18. Letter from Walpole to Mann, 3.5.1757, see Walpole, *Correspondence*, vol.5, p.88.
19. *The Works of James Barry* (London, 1809), p.69.
20. Reported by Thomas Jones, who was a pupil of Wilson, see Farington's Diary, 21.6.1823, Windsor, Royal Library.
21. Edwards, *Anecdotes of Painters* (London, 1808), pp.78-9.
22. Inger Hjorth Nielsen, 'Richard Wilson and Danish Artists in Rome', *Burlington Magazine*, CXXI (1979), pp.439-443.
23. Thomas Ashby, 'Thomas Jenkins in Rome', in: *Papers of the British School at*

27. A.R. Mengs, *Perseus and Andromeda*, painted 1778 for Sir Watkin Williams-Wynn, St Petersburg, Hermitage

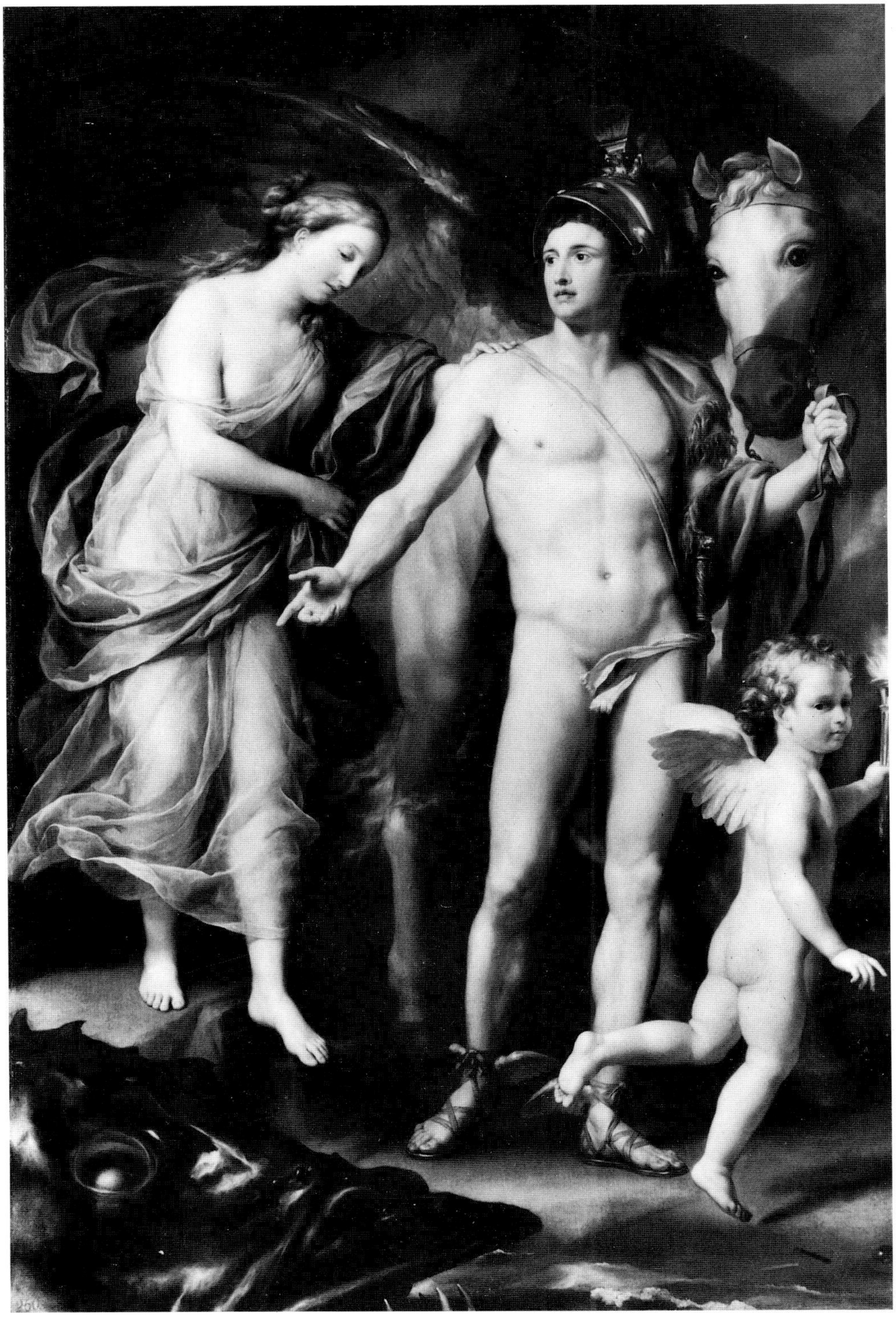

Rome, VI (1913), No.8, pp.487ff.

24. 'The Original was painted by Cavalier Mengs being a Portrait of his wife in the Character of diligence, now in the Possession of Thomas Jenkins for whom it was painted' (London, British Museum, *Mosmann Drawings*, VI, T.5-2, inv.no.206; 416 × 336 mm).
25. London, British Museum, Mosmann Drawings, VII, p.9, T.3-83 and T.3-84, inv.nos.239 and 240. Lord Exeter gave the set of Mosmann drawings to the British Museum in 1789. See Ashby (n.23), p.487, and Jakob Hess, 'Amaduzzi and Jenkins in Villa Giulia', in Jakob Hess, *Kunstgeschichtliche Studien* (Rome, 1967), vol.1, pp.309-326.
26. J. T. Smith, *Nollekens and his Times*, ed. Whitton (1820), I, p.233.
27. Antal, (n.12), pp.303ff.
28. Ford (1974), p.418.
29. On John Plimmer see Ashby (n.23), p.480 and K. Woodbridge, Henry 'Hoare's Paradise', *Art Bulletin*, XLVII, I, p.103-4.
30. Steffi Roettgen, 'Das Papyruskabinett von Mengs in der Biblioteca Vaticana. Ein Beitrag zur Geschichte und Idee des Museo Pio Clementino', in: *Münchner Jahrbuch der Bildenden Kunst*, 3rd series, vol.31 (Munich, 1980), pp.189-246.
31. Ford (1974), p.219: report by J. C. Hippisley, January 1780, who doubted that the drawings were by Mengs: 'Be they [by Mengs] so they are worth 5 sequins but the half I am sure are not so, and mere academic figures. He [*i.e.* Jenkins] however told us he had refused 100 sequins for them'.
32. Oliver Millar, *Zoffany and his Tribuna* (London & New York, 1966), p.37.
33. Finke, (n.7), p.64.
34. Louis Réau, 'Correspondance artistique de Grimm avec Catherine II', in *Archives de l'Art français* (1932), letter of 24.5.1781.
35. Noack I, p.324; Ford (1974), p.429 (copies for Lord Bristol). According to Thieme-Becker he died there in 1791, see *Journal of the Walpole Society* (1956-8), Letters of Jonathan Skelton p.37 (note). According to Olivier Michel (information given orally), Nevay was later friendly with the French painter Gabriel Bouquier, who was in Rome in 1776-7.
36. On Winckelmann's contacts with Morison see his letters of 26.9.1758 to the publisher Walther (Winckelmann, *Briefe*, I, p.416), of 30.9.1758 to Francke (*Briefe*, I, p.422) and of 16.11.1758 to Hagedorn (*Briefe*, I, p.435). He intended travelling to Sicily with Morison. Winckelmann reported on Morison's progress and said of him that he could draw very well. On Morison see also Fleming (1959), p.24, and Ford (1974), p.451.
37. In 1763 Jenkins brought Winckelmann an offer from Thomas Brand Hollis to share in financing the copperplates for Winckelmann's *Geschichte der Kunst des Alterthums* (letter from Winckelmann to Muzell Stosch of 7.12.1763, *Briefe*, II, p.361). Winckelmann maintained that Jenkins owed all his good fortune to Thomas Brand. On him and his relation to Jenkins see Fleming (1959), p.26.
38. Philadelphia, American Philosophical Society, see Ford (1974), p.461, n.27.
39. On Byres's influence and his career as antiquarian and art dealer see the essential account by Brinsley Ford, 'James Byres, Principal Antiquarian for the English Visitors to Rome', in Ford (1974), pp.446-461.
40. Ford (1974), p.447.
41. On 6.3.1774 he sent his best wishes to Byres from Florence through Maron, see Herbert von Einem, 'Anton Raphael Mengs, Briefe an Raimondo Ghelli and Anton Maron', in *Abhandlungen der Akademie der Wissenschaften in Göttingen*, Göttingen (1973), p.69.
42. According to Fleming (1962), p.144, on 24.2.1755.
43. Fleming (1962), pp.169ff.
44. On 8.5.1757, Rome, Archivio Acc. Naz. S. Luca, *Libro de' Decreti*, vol.51, f.96 v. On 28.7.1762 Winckelmann informed Mengs, who was in Madrid, of the sale of Cardinal Albani's drawings and said of James Adam 'è il fratello minore di quello che avete consciuto voi' (Letters II, p.255).
45. Fleming (1956), pp.79-84, Fleming (1962), p.174
46. 'The Naples Yellow has a salt in it which it is thought necessary to wash out. Mr. Meenx says that it ought to be ground as they grind the fine white at Rome'. The document is quoted by Alastair Smart, *Allan Ramsay: Painter, Essayist and Man of Enlightenment* (New Haven & London, 1992), p.292.
47. Letter of thanks from George Field to Sir Thomas Lawrence of 19.6.1820, see John Gage, *George Field and his Circle* (Cambridge, Fitzwilliam Museum, 1989), p.67. On the influence of Mengs's colour theory on Turner see John Gage, *Colour in Turner, Poetry and Truth* (London, 1969) passim.
48. M. James Craig, *The Volunteer Earl, being the Life and Time of James Caulfield, First Earl of Charlemont* (London, 1948), pp.83ff. and Fleming (1959), p.27.
49. Letter to Muzell Stosch of 28.10.1758, *Briefe*, I, p.311. At this time Charlemont was in Florence.
50. In April 1752 Reynolds was in Naples, in May he went from Rome to Florence, Bologna, Parma and Venice and on to Paris, and from thence to England. A meeting might have taken place in Florence, where the two appear to have been at about the same time.
51. Sir Joshua Reynolds, *The Discourses on Art* (London, Collier Macmillan, 1969), p.218.
52. The comment is recorded by Azara, who in turn quotes it from Cumberland (1782). It presumably refers, not to the first English editions of the 'Discourses', which appeared annually from 1769,but the Italian edition of 1778. This is suggested by the formulation, which Azara has translated from Cumberland, 'Mengs disse che il libro dell' inglese Reynolds può condurre i giovani nell'errore, poichè si lascia ai principi superficiali che sono i soli noti a quell'autore' (Azara-Fea (1787), p.XXXIX).
53. Northcote wrote to his brother Samuel on 11.8.1778: 'Unfortunately for him they have hung Sir Joshua's close to it, which makes it look like a devil, for they ought not to come together, for Mengs' is finished so that you can almost tell the hairs of his beard and Sir Joshua's appears as if it was painted with his fingers.' Quoted from Whitley, *Artists and their Friends in England 1700-1799* (London & Boston, 1928), II, p.311. The comment by Siries is in a letter to Angelika Kauffmann, see

Whitley, I, p.314. See also Finke (n.7), pp.75-6.

54. Heinrich Meyer, in *J. W. von Goethe, Winckelmann und sein Jahrhundert* (I, 1805), (Leipzig, 1969), p.164.
55. Ellis K. Waterhouse, 'The British Contribution to the Neo-Classical Style in Painting', *Proceedings of the British Academy*, vol.XL (1954), pp.60ff.
56. Letter of 27.11.1762 to Usteri, see *Briefe*, II, p.273. The same view was expressed by Giovanni Casanova, Etienne Falconet and Azara, see Finke (n.7), p.70 and n.38 (with literature).
57. Johannes Dobai, *Die Kunstliteratur des Klassizismus und der Romantik in England* (Berne, 1975), III/2, p.726.
58. Letter to R. Rutherford of 17.3.1763, in Algarotti, *Opere* (1779), vol.VIII, p.345/6.
59. Letter from West to Joseph Shippen of 1.9.1763, see Erffa/Staley, p.445–6.
60. Erffa/Staley, p.548 (n.689), from Galt (1816), pp.101-123.
61. Erffa/Staley, p.548.
62. *Des Ritters Anton Raphael Mengs ersten Mahlers Karl III, König in Spanien hinterlassne Werke*... ed. M.C.F. Prange (1786), I, p.114; *Ceres and Flora*.
63. See report by Francis Cotes on the pastels in Whitley (n.53), I, p.268, and Finke (n.7), p.58.
64. Exhibition catalogue *Painting in Italy in the Eighteenth Century: Rococo to Romanticism* (Chicago, 1970), p.192 (A. M. Clark).
65. Bianconi (1780), p.31.
66. Ford (1974), p.418.
67. Francis Haskell, 'Pompeo Batoni e gli inglesi', in exhibition catalogue *Pompeo Batoni* (Lucca, 1987), p.77.
68. Andrea M. Kluxen, *Das Ende des Standesporträts, Die Bedeutung der englischen Malerei für das deutsche Porträt* (Munich, 1989), p.75. According to André Bouquet, *L'état des arts en Angleterre* (1755), the British were only interested in portraits. John Moore, *Views of Society and Manners in Italy* (London, 1781), also complained that the Italians did not fully appreciate portraiture.
69. Jonathan Richardson, *An Essay on the Theory of Painting* (London 1715), pp.7ff.
70. Francis Haskell (n.67), p.75.
71. Aileen Ribeiro, 'Batoni's use of Costume', in exhibition catalogue *Pompeo Batoni and his British Patrons* (London, Kenwood House, 1982), p.21.
72. A. M. Clark, 'La carriera professionale e lo stile del Batoni', in exhibition catalogue *Pompeo Batoni* (Lucca, 1967), p.48.
73. Frederick Antal, *Hogarth and his Place in European Art* (first edition 1962, German edition, Dresden, 1966), p.74.
74. On a comparison with Reynolds, for instance the portrait of Lord Fortescue of 1756, see Renate Prochno, *Joshua Reynolds* (Weinheim, 1990), p.63. Also Benjamin West's portrait of Edward Hase of 1768, see Erffa/Staley, no.636. Antal has pointed out that Hogarth followed van Dyck for aristocratic portraits and Rembrandt for bourgeois sitters (*Hogarth*, German edition, p.297).
75. J. J. Winckelmann, *Geschichte der Kunst des Alterthums* (first edition 1766, Darmstadt, 1972), p.231.
76. *E.g.* Carlo Giuseppe Ratti, *Epilogo della vita del fù Cavalier Mengs* (Genoa, 1779), p.111.
77. Anthony M. Clark, *Pompeo Batoni, A Complete Catalogue of his Works with an Introductory Text, edited and prepared for publication by Edgar Peters Bowron* (Phaidon, 1985), cat. no.179.
78. John Fleming, 'Lord Brudenell and his Bear-Leader', *English Miscellany* (1958), p.136.
79. An 18th-century engraving has not survived, see Luigi Salerno, *I Dipinti del Guercino* (Rome, 1988), p.268. Possibly Hoare's attention had been drawn to Guercino's painting by Jenkins or another art expert in Rome. Pope Benedict XIV had purchased it in 1748 together with the Sacchetti Collection for the Capitoline Museums.
80. On 11.8.1760 Strange had given Mengs a letter from the copper engraver Wille in Paris, whom he had visited. J. G. Wille, *Journal* (Paris, 1857), I, p.142.
81. Erffa/Staley, illus.pp.39 and 182. A drawing with a similar composition by West shows the same theme as that depicted by Mengs (Erfaa/Staley, p.38). West visited Stourhead in 1763 (Galt (1820), p.5).
82. Kansas University Museum, see Peter S. Walch, 'Cleopatra before Augustus', in *The Register of the Museum of Art, Kansas City*, III (1968), pp.25-6.
83. Catherine Whistler, 'G. B. Tiepolo at the Court of Charles III', *Burlington Magazine*, CXXXVIII (1986), pp.199-203.
84. S. Roettgen, 'Mengs e Raffaello, Rendiconto di un rapporto programmato', in *Raffaelo e l'Europa, Atti del IV Corso Internazionale di Alta Cultura*, ed. Marcello Fagiolo and Maria Luisa Madonna (Rome, 1990), p.638.
85. Horace Walpole, *Anecdotes of Painting in England*, ed. F. W. Hilles and P. B. Daghian, V (1937), p.52.
86. Black (n.1), p.24.
87. Letter of 9.4.1763, see *Briefe*, II, pp.307-8.
88. Winckelmann, letter to Johann Heinrich Wille in Paris of 28.1. 1764, see *Briefe*, III, p.12.
89. Letter to David Lord Cardross, later 11th Earl of Buchanan, Edinburgh University Library, Laing MSS; La IV. 26. Quoted from Duncan Hull and Enriqueta Harris, 'The Companion of Velasquez' Rokeby Venus and a Source for Goya's Naked Maya', *Burlington Magazine*, CXXXVIII (1986), p.647.
90. I am grateful to Mr Mungo Campbell, Assistant Keeper of the National Gallery of Scotland, for valuable help in preparing the photographs.
91. Cat. Sig. Rinuccini Verst. (Florenz 1852), p.90 HANC COWPERI IMAGINEM/ INTER MAGNAE BRITANNIAE PROCERES/ QUAM DIVINUS RAPHAEL MENGS/ FLORENTIAE ANNO MDCLXIX PINXIT COWPERUS IDEM NUNC S.R.I. CAROLO RINUCCINO BASELECAE TOPAR CHAE/AMICO SUAVISSIMO DONABAT.
92. Last known at an auction at Sotheby's, London, on 25.4.1945, Lot 58 (information kindly provided by Mr Hugh Belsey).
93. Cortona, Accademia Etrusca, illus. in exhibition catalogue *Firenze e l'Inghilterra* (Florence, 1971), p.39.
94. *Gazzetta Toscana* (1782), p.106.
95. Letter from W. Sandys to Cowper of 13.1.1780, Hertford County Record Office, Cowper Papers, D/EP F 310/106. I am grateful to Mr Hugh Belsey for drawing my attention to this letter.
96. Exhibition catalogue *Firenze e l'Inghilterra* (Florence, 1971), pp.39-40, with further literature.
97. Exhibition catalogue *Firenze e l'Inghil-*

terra, pp.59-60.

98. Oliver Millar, *Zoffany and his Tribuna* (New York, 1966), p.10.
99. Millar (1966), p.21. His portrait is in the Zoffany *Tribuna*. In 1770 he was portrayed by Mengs's pupil Maron. Later a portrait of Mann that can no longer be traced was attributed to Mengs.
100. Ugo Procacci, 'Il Vasari e la conservazione degli affreschi della Cappella Brancacci al Carmine e della Trinità in S. Maria Novella', in *Scritti di storia dell'arte in onore di Lionello Venturi* (1953), p.205. Report by Luigi Scotti on the generous donations from the British then living in Florence for the restoration of the chapel, among them Lord Cowper, Horace Mann and Mylord Tilly.
101. Umberto Baldini and Ornella Casazza, *La Cappella Brancacci* (Milan, Electa, 1990), pp.310-11.
102. On 3.3.1771, see *Libro de'Decreti*, Rome, Archivio Acc. Naz. di S. Luca, vol.52, f.77 r .
103. Sparrow (1960), passim, from archive material in the Bodleian Library in Oxford, MS. DD All Souls College.
104. One scudo was roughly the equivalent of DM 50 in 1968, so that the fee was about DM 30,000.
105. *Dr Burney's Musical Tours in Europe*, ed. Percy Scholes (Oxford, 1959) I, p.190 (ref. from Sparrow (1960), p.4).
106. Clark/Bowron (n.77), p.341.
107. Letter of 25.11.1771 to Henry, Eighth Lord Arundell of Wardor, Donhead St Andrew, Mr John Arundell of Hook Manor, ref. from Sparrow (1965), p.631.
108. *The Works of James Barry*, ed. Fryer (London, 1809), I, p.244. This reference is from Michael Levey ('Letters to the Editor', *Burlington Magazine*, Jan. 1960, p.36).
109. See P. Rosenberg, 'Une correspondence de Julien de Parme', *Archives de l'art français*, XXXV (1984), pp.212-213; A. Jacobs and A.C. Lens, exhibition catalogue (Antwerp, 1989), p.171.
110. Rome, private collection. See exhibition catalogue *Guido Reni und Europa*, Frankfurt am Main, Schirn Kunsthalle (1988-9), p.623.
111. Letter to Anton Maron from Florence of 23.11.1773: 'Onde sono a pregarla di farsi dare dal Signor Byres sudetto la misura del sudetto quadro... ma siccome già diverse volte il signor Byres mi ha dato la misura, ed io non ho fatto il quadro – non vorrei comparire questa volta per non parer ridicolo', quoted from von Einem (1973), p.67.
112. The circumstances under which the commission for the painting was given were clarified by Brinsley Ford, 'Sir Watkin Williams-Wynn, A Welsh Maecenas', in Ford (1974), pp.436-7.
113. Black (n.1), p.230; 26.2, 29.2 and 18.7.1776. The letters are in the British Library in London, add. 33126-7.
114. Black (n.1), p.221. Pelham also visited Genoa and Parma, possibly on Mengs's advice.
115. Betty Joyce, 'The Ancient Frescoes from the Villa Negroni and Their Influence in the Eighteenth and Nineteenth Centuries', *Art Bulletin* (Sept. 1983), p.423-30.
116. A. P. Oppé 'Memoirs of Thomas Jones', *Walpole Society*, XXXII, 1946-8 (London, 1951), p.62.
117. Oppé (n.116), p.68-9.
118. Letter to Samuel Northcote of 4.2.1778, quoted from Whitley (n.53), II, p.309.
119. 'Pars & myself on his arrival waited to receive his at the gate with all ye Defference due to so respected a Character, and assisted in Coverging him up stairs – for the last time – as he dyed on the 29th', Oppé, n.116, p.89.
120. The wording of the inscription is in José Nicolas de Azara, *Opere di Antonio Raffaello Mengs. Primo Pittore della Maestà di Carlo III re di Spagna* (Parma, 1780), p.XLVIII.
121. T. Hodgkinson, 'Christopher Hewetson, An Irish Sculptor in Rome', *Walpole Society*, XXXIV (1952-4), pp.42-54.
122. Azara (n.120), p.XXXVIII.
123. Franziska Forster Hahn, 'The Sources of True Taste. Benjamin West's Instructions to a Young Painter for his Study in Italy', *Journal of the Warburg and Courtauld Institutes*, XXX (1967), p.367-382.
124. Letter to Lavater of 30.7.1770, see Gert Schiff, *Johann Heinrich Füssli*, (Munich & Zurich, 1973), I, p.74.
125. Farington's Diary for 4.9.1802, quotes from Schiff, p.270.
126. Richard Cumberland, *Anecdotes of Eminent Painters in Spain with Cursory Remarks upon the Present State of Arts in that Kingdom* (London, 1782), II, p.209-210.
127. See the lists of auctions in Burton Fredericksen, *The Index of Paintings Sold in the British Isles during the Nineteenth Century*, I (1988), II (1990), ad vocem.
128. This was a copy of Batoni's altarpiece from San Gregorio al Celio in the Miles Collection in Leigh Court, see Clark Bowron (n.77), p.210.

Chronology of Mengs's life

12.3.1728 Mengs born in Aussig, Elbe, son of the Dresden Court Painter Ismael Mengs and Charlotte Bormann
1728-40 Childhood in Dresden, trained as a painter by his father
Autumn 1744 In the late autumn in Rome with his father and two sisters, Therese and Julie. Studies after Michelangelo and Raphael in the Vatican. Lives in the Palazzo dei Penitenzieri in the Borgo Santo Spirito
Christmas 1744 Returns to Dresden
6.4.1746 Appointed Court Painter in the Service of the Elector of Saxony, with a salary of 600 thalers a year
June 1746 A second visit to Rome with his father and two sisters
16.7.1749 Converted to the Catholic faith
16.8.1749 Marries Margherita Guazzi, daughter of a dustman in Borgo San Pietro
Christmas 1749 Returns to Dresden
2.9.1750 Birth of his first son (the first of about twelve children, of whom seven survived)
23.3.1751 Appointed Principal Court Painter at Dresden with a salary of 1000 thalers a year
September 1751 Leaves Dresden for Italy with his wife and two children and his two sisters
Winter 1751–Spring 1752 In Venice
25.4.1752 Visits the British Ambassador to Florence, Horace Mann
May 1752 Arrives in Rome and takes lodging in the Via Sistina, opposite the Palazzo Zuccari
20.8.1752 Becomes a member of the Accademia di San Luca in Rome
1755 Completes his copy of Raphael's *School of Athens* for Northumberland House, Charing Cross, London
December 1755 First acquaintance with Winckelmann, which soon develops into a close friendship
End of 1755 The Court at Dresden ceases to pay his salary
1757 Negotiates with the Court of Naples for commissions
1758 Moves to the Via Vittoria below the Spanish Steps
1757-59 Paints the ceiling fresco in the church of Sant' Eusebio in Rome
End of September 1759 Leaves Rome for Naples
May(?) 1760 Returns
Summer 1760 Completes *Augustus and Cleopatra* for Henry Hoare
July 1760 In the Villa Albani with his family, where he is working on the gallery
August 1760 Acquaintance with Thomas Robinson and Benjamin West
December 1760 Giacomo Casanova visits Mengs in the Villa Albani
Spring 1761 Completes the fresco in the gallery of the Villa Albani
23.7.1761 Enters the service of the Spanish monarch as 'Pintor de Camára', with a salary of 7000 scudi a year
8.8.1761 Leaves Rome for Naples with his wife and some of his children
15.8.1761 Embarks for Spain
22.9.1761 Arrives in Madrid
End of April 1762 Corrado Giaquinto leaves Madrid
June 1762 Publishes *Thoughts on Beauty and Taste in Painting (Gedanken über die Schönheit und den Geschmack in der Mahlerey)* in Zurich
4.6.1762 Tiepolo arrives in Madrid
Winter 1762 Takes over the supervision of the painting on the Palacio Real in Madrid
December 1762 Receives an offer to settle in England
February 1764 Asks to be relieved of his duties in the Academia de San Fernando in Madrid after a dispute over the defects in the teaching
October 1766 Winckelmann breaks off his correspondence with Mengs
1767-8 Second encounter between Giacomo Casanova and Mengs in Madrid
8.6.1768 Winckelmann murdered in Trieste
30.12.1768 Leaves the Academia de San Fernando
8.7.1769 Commission from All Souls College, Oxford for *Noli me tangere*
13.11.1769 Leaves Madrid owing to ill-health
Spring 1770 In Monaco and Monte Carlo to recuperate
17.3.1770 Tiepolo dies in Madrid
April, May, June 1770 Travels via Genoa and Parma to Florence
16.12.1770 Elected Principal of the Accademia di San Luca in Rome
February 1771 Leaves Florence for Rome
October 1771 Completes *Noli me tangere* for Oxford
November 1772–Spring 1773 In Naples
August 1773–April 1774 In Florence
End of April 1774 Leaves Florence, and travels via Bologna, Parma, Turin and Milan to Spain
9.7.1774 Arrives in Madrid
December 1774 Obtains position in the Madrid tapestry workshop for Goya

1776 Publication of his letter to Antonio Ponz on the most important paintings in the Royal collections in Ponz's work *Viaje de Espana*
June 1776 Praise for Goya's work at the workshop
July 1776 Requests leave of absence and permission to return to Rome
2.1.1777 Memorandum on setting up a picture gallery in Madrid
February 1777 Leaves Madrid
11.3.1777 Arrives in Rome
3.12.1777 Rents the Palazzo delle Convertende near the Piazza Scossa Cavalli, Raphael's former dwelling, near St Peter's
19.12.1777 Purchases the Villa de' Cavalieri Sannesi on Monte Santo Spirito near St Peter's (entailed)
February 1778 Completes *Perseus and Andromeda* for Sir Watkin Williams-Wynn
3.4.1778 Death of Margherita Mengs at the age of 48
29.6.1779 Death of Mengs in the former home of the painter Salvator Rosa near SS Trinità ai Monti at the age of 51, believed to be from chronic lead poisoning. He is buried in the church of San Michele in Sassia

Catalogue of Works

1

Self-Portrait

Oil on panel, 73.5 × 56.2 cm
Inscribed on reverse: RITRATTO D'ANTONIO RAFFAELLO MENGS / FATTO DA LUI MEDESIMO / PER LORD NASSAU CONTE DI COWPER / IN FIRENZE L'ANNO 1774
Liverpool, Board of Trustees of the National Museums and Galleries on Merseyside. Walker Art Gallery, inv.no.1227

PROVENANCE: George Nassau, Third Earl of Cowper, Florence (Cowper inv.1779, no.28, see Sutton); after 1826 Panshanger, Cowper inheritance; handed down to Lady Desborough, Panshanger; auctioned at Christie's, Manson & Wood, 16.10.1953, lot 92; Agnew's, London 1953.

LITERATURE: *Gazzetta Toscana* IX, no.17 (23.4.1774), p.66; (Giuseppe Ginori) *Serie degli uomini i più illustri in Pittura, Scultura e Architettura con i loro ritratti incisi in rame* (1769); *Supplemento (...) o sia Abecedario pittorico dall'origine delle belle arti a tutto l'anno 1775* (Florence, 1776), I, p.107; Jansen I, 1786, p.30; M. L. Boyle, *Biographical Catalogue of the Pictures at Panshanger* (1885), pp.442-448; *Burlington Magazine*, XCV (Dec, 1953), Suppl. T.XVI; exhibition catalogue, *European Masters of the Eighteenth Century* (London, Royal Academy, 1954-5), no.304; exhibition catalogue *Italian Art in Britain* (London, Royal Academy, 1960), no.177; exhibition catalogue, *Goya and his Times* (London, Royal Academy, 1963-4), no.12; Michael Compton, *Catalogue of Foreign Schools* (Liverpool, Walker Art Gallery, 1963), no.1227 (other editions 1966, 1977); Honisch (1965), no.62.

This portrait was commissioned and first owned by the Earl of Cowper, a close friend of Mengs, whom he met twice in Florence (in 1770 and 1773-4). Lord Cowper also owned other works by mengs. The picture is listed in the inventory of the works of art in Lord Cowper's villas (the villa Palmieri and the Villa Cipresso) near Florence in 1779 (see Sutton). However, it must have been sent to England before Cowper's death in 1790, as it is not included in the inventory of his Italian estate (information kindly provided by Benedetta Rousseau). Presumably Cowper took the work to England on his brief trip to London in 1786; certainly he offered it to King George III, but his gift was declined (information kindly provided by Mr Hugh Belsey). On the same occasion Lord Cowper gave the King the 223 miniature copies of self-portraits of artists in the Uffizi, which Giuseppe Macpherson had made by 1779.

The painting can be dated to 1774 from the inscription on the reverse and from a dated drawn copy by Friedrich Hackert in Braunschweig. It was therefore painted during Mengs's stay in Florence from autumn 1773 to May 1774, only a few months after the self-portraits for the Uffizi and the collection of Count Firmian (now in the Neue Pinakothek in Munich). It is closest to the latter in type and posture. The difference in the approach is thus all the more striking. The face appears older and more flaccid, the eyes are tired and disinterested. This is a disillusioned, critical self-examination, and the portrait has that undercurrent of resignation and pessimism that was to be characteristic of Mengs's self-portraits from that point on. The simple, unassuming presentation is all the more conspicuous as Mengs has depicted himself with one of his own works, *Perseus and Andromeda*, which he only completed in 1777. The work was commissioned by Sir Watkin Williams-Wynn and is now in the Hermitage in St Petersburg. Mengs first began to make concrete plans for the work in November 1773, and this coincidence in time is probably the reason why he included the sketch of this composition in his self-portrait. The composition on the easel is shown in its first state, that is, after the drawing has been transferred to the canvas, and the gesture of the pointing hand not only shows that this is the painter's own work, but also indicates that he is still working on the picture.

The painter showing himself with one of his own works was a familiar device in Baroque artists' self-portraits. Mengs also used it for his portrait of Richard Wilson in 1752, while his many other self-portraits are based on a different typology. Like all his self-portraits, the Liverpool work has been copied many times. One copy was in the J. Singer Collection in London in 1941 (photo Courtauld Institute), and others are in Prague, Salzburg and the Palace of Jemniste in Bohemia.

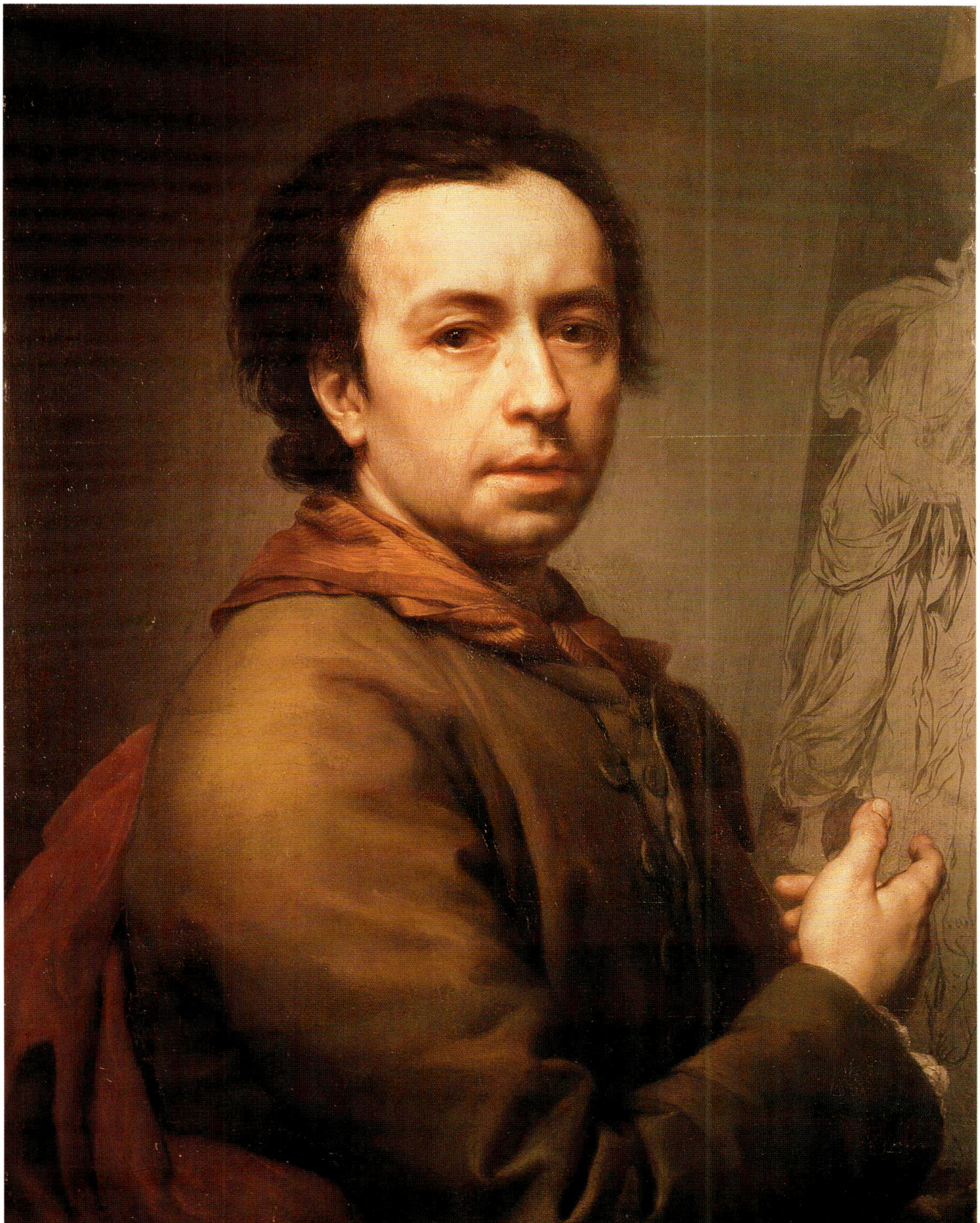

2

Portrait of John Brudenell-Montagu, later Marquess of Monthermer (1735-70)

Oil on canvas, 244 × 171.5 cm
The Duke of Buccleuch Kt.

LITERATURE: Exhibition catalogue *European Masters of the 18th Century*, (London, Royal Academy, 1954-5), no.301; Hermann Voss, review of the exhibition in *Kunstchronik* 8 (1955), p.40; Fleming (1958), pp.127-141; exhibition catalogue *Il Settecento a Roma* (Rome, 1959), p.153; exhibition catalogue *German Art 1400-1800* (Manchester, 1961), no.184; Russell (1979), p.16; Clark Bowron (1985), p.270.

John Lord Brudenell, who bore the title of Marquess of Monthermer from 1766, was the only son of George Brudenell, Fourth Earl of Cardigan and from 1766 Duke of Montagu, who was one of the founders of the British Museum. At the age of 17 he was sent on the Grand Tour, in the company of his tutor Henry Lyte. Lord Brudenell's and Henry Lyte's visit to Rome was the last stage of their Tour, which began in 1751 and took them through Paris, Turin and Genoa to Rome, which they reached for the first time in 1756. However, they only remained a month in the city, and then went on through Naples on a tour of southern Italy which lasted almost two years. According to the letters from Lyte to the Earl of Cardigan, which Fleming consulted for his reconstruction of the Grand Tour, Brudenell was particularly interested in Greek antiquities in southern Italy, visiting among other places Paestum and Agrigento. In 1758 he made contact with Winckelmann in Rome, who presumably gave him more exact information on the monuments he had seen in Magna Graecia. Brudenell's marked interest in Greek art is an interesting phenomenon, as Fleming points out, and it makes a striking difference between his Grand Tour and that of other contemporary Britons. While he was in Italy, Brudenell collected mainly ancient works, and Fleming believes that his entire collection of antiquities was acquired from Thomas Jenkins. Mengs made a copy of an Athena cameo owned by Brudenell for Jenkins. A cameo by Giovanni Pichler showing *Priam before Achilles* (see cat.no.39) and made from a design by Mengs was also in Brudenell's possession. After his return to England he became a member of the Society of Dilettanti. Fleming believes that Henry Lyte, whose portrait was also painted by Mengs (cat.no.10), was the initiator of the commissions for both Mengs and Batoni. However, both painters were so well known among the British colony in Rome as portraitists that it was not difficult to commission a portrait from them.

The two portraits differ considerably, both in type and in the perception and characterisation of the sitter. Mengs shows Brudenell seated at a table, with the figure in full-length. A pile of books is on the table before him, beside a bust of Cicero. A dog lies at his feet, looking up at him. In the background, through the half-open curtain, trees can be seen, suggesting a park in the English style. The mood of the room and the presentation of the sitter create an atmosphere representative of the sitter's social milieu, with the dog and the park as status symbols.

The documents published by John Fleming give us detailed information on how the commission was given to Mengs and the time the portrait was painted. Brudenell's tutor Henry Lyte wrote on 1 March 1758 to Brudenell's father, the Earl of Cardigan: 'Mengs and Batoni have both begun my Lord Brudenell's portrait, the former a full-length and the other a half-length. They have promised to finish them out of hand and they will both be fine pictures the more so as there is great emulation between those two celebrated painters'. Lyte wrote to Lord Cardigan on 21 June of the same year that the two portraits were ready to be shipped to England on the next freighter.

It is striking that here, where Batoni and Mengs were painting the same subject at the same time, and, as Lyte says, were rivals, Batoni should choose the type of half-length, close-up view with a neutral background usually preferred by Mengs, and that Mengs should use the type Batoni generally preferred. This reversal of their usual practice is particularly obvious when the two portraits are seen side by side, but the reasons for it have not as yet been explored. The possibility cannot be excluded that each painter deliberately chose the type of portrait usually favoured by his rival in order to show that he could equal the other's achievements. So far Mengs's portrait of Brudenell has not been judged favourably by scholars (Clark, Voss, Fleming), but this is hard to understand. Batoni's version has been seen as a peak in his 1750s portrait work, and Mengs's work deserves no less a place in his œuvre.

Each artist shows a different side of Brudenell's personality. Batoni depicts him with violin and music book; his expression is dreamy and he is looking slightly away from the viewer, with his gaze fixed on an indeterminate point. He seems to be thinking of a musical score he has just finished reading, and the almost child-like naïveté of his facial expression makes him seem much younger than his 23 years. Mengs, on the other hand, shows Brudenell as a scholar. He looks his true age and appears serious, collected and highly intellectual. Mengs seems to have perceived Brudenell – perhaps influenced by Winckelmann – more as

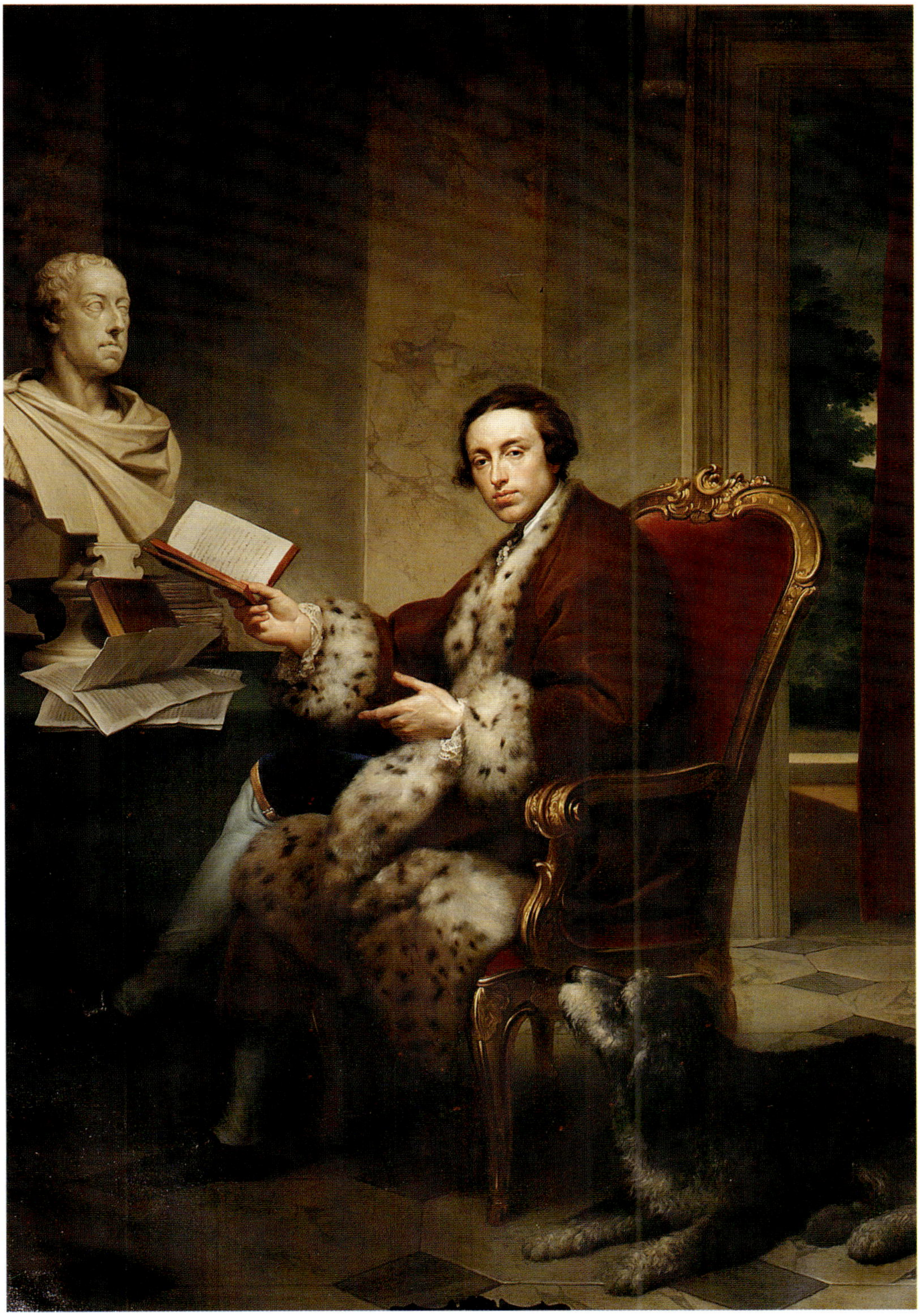

an experienced scholar and explorer of southern Italy, while Batoni saw in him rather the bored and romantic young man, used to luxury and perhaps a little unsteady, his activities hardly extending beyond those of cultivated leisure.

A relatively finished compositional study for the portrait was in the collection of José Madrazo in Madrid in 1856. It has been identified from the description in the catalogue of the collection (p.131). The collection of the Duke of Buccleuch in Bowhill contains a bust of high quality, made from the face of the portrait (76.2 × 50 cm).

For another portrait of Brudenell, see cat.no.3.

3

Follower of Anton Raphael Mengs (? Thomas Jenkins): Portrait of John Brudenell-Montagu, later Marquess of Monthermer (1735-70)

Oil on canvas, 95 × 71.2 cm
Lord Montagu of Beaulieu

LITERATURE: Russell (1979), pp.12, 16; exhibition catalogue *Treasure Houses of Great Britain*, no.174, (Washington DC, 1985-6)

This portrait was originally ascribed to Batoni, but it was attributed to Mengs by Sir Ellis Waterhouse and A. M. Clark. However, a second portrait of Brudenell by Mengs is not mentioned in the sources or the correspondence between Henry Lyte and the sitter's father (see cat.no.10). The nature of the modelling and the handling of the folds are clearly influenced by Mengs; the same applies to the choice of apparel, which, as in many of Mengs's portraits, is in the van Dyck style. There can be no question that this portrait was painted at the same time as the two by Mengs and Batoni in Rome. The main similarities to Batoni's portrait are the general approach and the facial expression, which in many respects almost seems to be a mirror image of that painting.

The position taken in this work between the portraits by the two most celebrated practitioners in Rome at the time seems almost calculated, as if the painter deliberately wanted to demonstrate aspects of the style of each. A painter like the Frenchman Gabriel Blanchet, who was a rival of Mengs and Batoni in Rome and from whom many British visitors commissioned portraits, cannot be compared in the same way. It is however, quite possible that the evident contrast of stylistic preferences in the portraits of Lord Brudenell by Batoni and Mengs could have something to do with the combination of the best aspects of both in the third. This could have been intended as an example of what a synthesis could look like. Certainly, to permit himself such paraphrase and combination of elements from both, which would be evident to anyone who saw the work, the painter must have been on very friendly terms with both Mengs and Batoni.

These facts apply to no-one so well as Thomas Jenkins, and I also believe that a number of stylistic arguments support the attribution to him, not least a comparison of this picture with his portrait of Thomas Brand of 1758 (see Introduction, fig.5). We know that Jenkins worked as a painter between 1753 and 1761, otherwise he would hardly have been accepted as such in the Accademia di San Luca in 1761. Jenkins had studied portraiture in England under Hudson, and it could have been he who first drew Mengs's attention to the advantages of the van Dyck style for contemporary portraiture, and the fondness for that type of costume in certain British circles.

Should this attribution prove correct, it would greatly help to further our knowledge of Jenkins's role as artistic intermediary between Great Britain and the painters in Rome. So far we have had too negative a picture of him, seeing him as a cunning and unscrupulous dealer, and this image could be somewhat softened by a knowledge of his undoubted abilities as a painter.

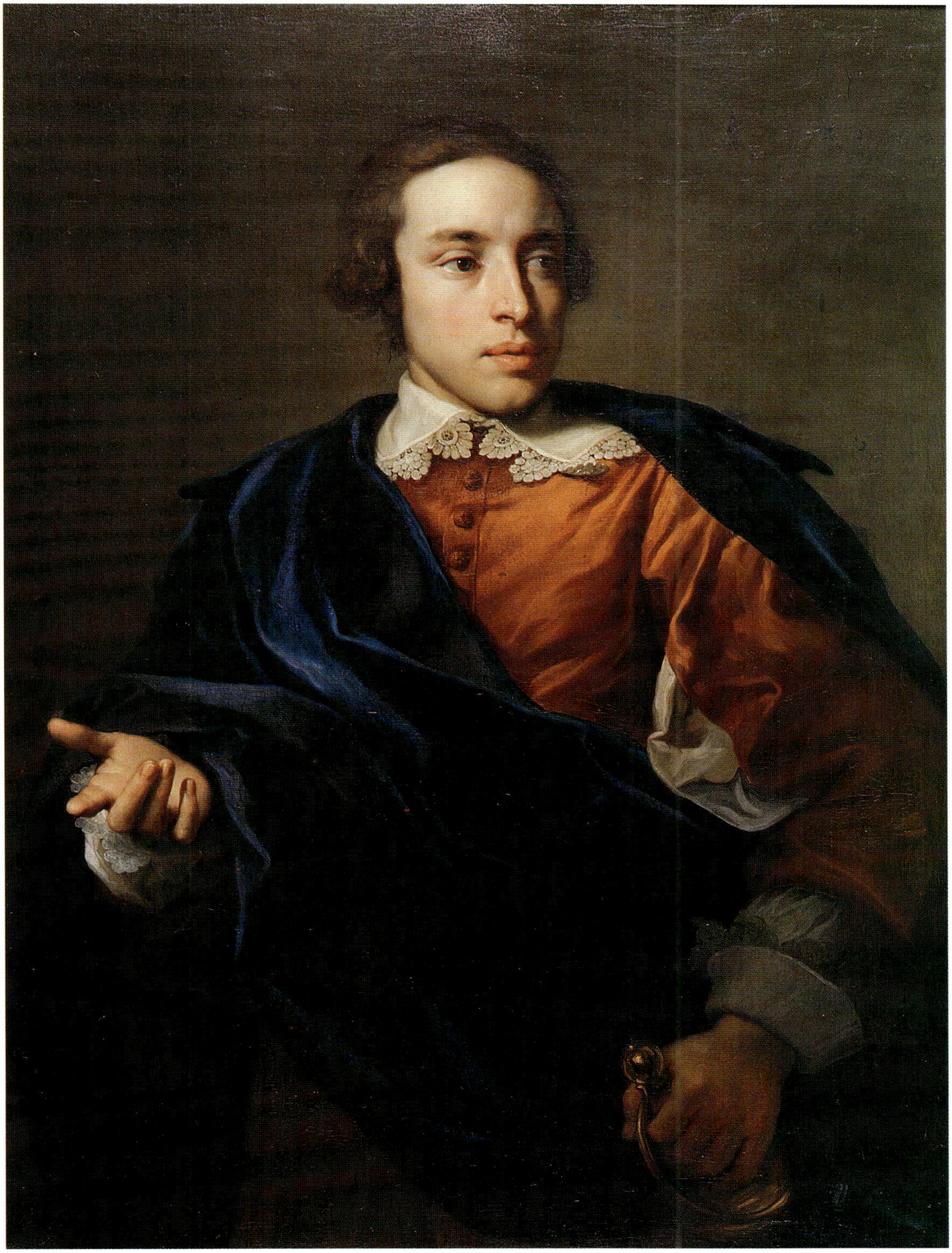

4

Allegorical Portrait of James Caulfield, Lord Charlemont (1728-99)

Oil on canvas, 137 × 101 cm
Inscribed at lower right: Ant: Raph: Mengs pinxit.
Beneath the bust of Palladio: Andreas Palladius Architect(us) Vincent(inus)
On the memorial stone: D(icatum) M(emoriae) / M(arcii) VITRVVI POL (lio) NI/ ARCHITEC (ti) / POLLION M(onumentum B(ene) M(erenti) P(osuit)
On reverse: Export stamp in German, no date
Prague, National Gallery, inv.no.DO 4561

PROVENANCE: Kilmorey (until 1924); Schicht Collection, Aussig/ Elbe (until 1945)

LITERATURE: Carlo Giuseppe Ratti, *Epilogo della vita del fù Cavalier Mengs* (Genoa, 1779), p.iii; catalogue of the Kilmorey auction sale, Sotheby's, London, 3 December 1924, lot 45; Steffi Roettgen, review of the exhibition The Age of Neoclassicism, London, Royal Academy 1972: Dipinti e Disegni, *Arte Illustrata*, 52 (Feb 1973), p.63; Russell (1979), p.19; Steffi Roettgen, 'Un ritratto allegorico di Lord Charlemont dipinto da Mengs e alcune annotazioni sul rapporto tra Piranesi e l'ambiente neoclassico romano', in *Piranesi e la cultura antiquaria*, ed. Maurizio Calvesi (Rome, 1984), pp.149-70; Legrand (1990/1), p.138.

This painting must be regarded as one of the most astonishing and also one of the most important of Mengs's Roman works, with its combination of the genre of portraiture with history painting. The composition was influenced by Batoni's early works (*Prometheus and Minerva*, 1740-3, Lucca, Conte Minutoli Tegrimi) and Andrea Sacchi's allegorical portrait of the singer Pasqualini (New York, Metropolitan Museum). The early date, 1755-6, makes it one of the seminal works of Roman Neo-Classicism. The stylistic features relate directly to the content and reflect the significance of one of the outstanding personalities of the Grand Tour.

The picture is described by Carlo Giuseppe Ratti, who first came to Rome in 1756, as among the pictures in Mengs's studio at that time: 'Molti (ritratti) che mi ricordo di aver veduti in quel tempo da lui dipinti erano vestiti alla Vandikesca, e fra questi uno di non so quale Signore, pure Ingelese, che poteva dirsi piuttosto un quadro storico, stantechè sendo quegli dedito a studi architettonici lo ritrasse in atto di apprendere precetti dall'Architettura medisima, additantegli il simulacro di Vitruvio.' Ratti does not describe the subject of the portrait as an architect, although the attributes in the picture would certainly make this seem appropriate, but as 'signore inglese'. Nor is he correct in his identification of the bust and clothing. However, one must remember that he was writing from memory in 1779.

There are two studies for the picture in Besançon, showing the composition in reverse with a putto. Despite the antique clothing the features of the sitter are certainly portrait-like, and they are very similar to those of Lord Charlemont, well-known from other portraits. He was in Italy from 1748 to 1754, living mainly in Rome, although he went on frequent tours. Charlemont was caricatured by Pier Leone Ghezzi and by Sir Joshua Reynolds, and painted in three-quarter length by Batoni (New Haven, Yale Center for British Art); there is also a portrait by William Hogarth (Smith College Museum of Art, Northampton, Mass., fig.7).

Although it is difficult to compare the caricatures with the portraits, they do all have striking features in common: the fleshy lips and receding forehead, and the shape of the face – full but long, with the top of the nose strongly indented. While these features are strongly exaggerated by both Ghezzi (Philadelphia Museum of Art) and Reynolds in his caricature of the *School of Athens* (Dublin, National Gallery of Ireland) the face is strongly idealised by Mengs. The view from below does much to soften the solidity of the mass, yet nevertheless the similarity is still evident. For comparison I have included the portrait by Hogarth, where the likeness is most clear (fig.7).

Anthony M. Clark concurred with this identification (in conversation), although it should be mentioned that it is not accepted by Brinsley Ford (oral statement). Francis Russell has suggested that the sitter is Daniel Webb; Mengs did portray Webb, but the ideas expressed in this historical portrait are not appropriate for Webb.

I believe that the identification proposed by Clark and accepted by Margot Wittkower is substantiated, not only by a comparison with the known portraits of Charlemont but also by the references to architectural theory in this picture. I have explained in detail in my article of 1983 the consistent theoretical programme displayed in Mengs's portrait work, and the ideas expressed in this painting are a warrant which will go far to identify the subject. Shown in the pose of Raphael's Isaiah, the young man is leaning on an antique memorial stone with an inscription referring to Vitruvius. A ruler and several books are leant against the stone. The man has just interrupted his work on a drawing, which shows the groundplan of a simple, rectangular house. Behind him is a bust of Palladio, but he is taking no notice of it. He is looking at the personification of Architecture, who has just approached him, and who is drawing his attention to the bust of Palladio and the colonnade of Tuscan pilasters in the background. I interpret this to mean that Architecture is making clear to the draughtsman that dilettante studies of architecture based on Vitruvius are useless

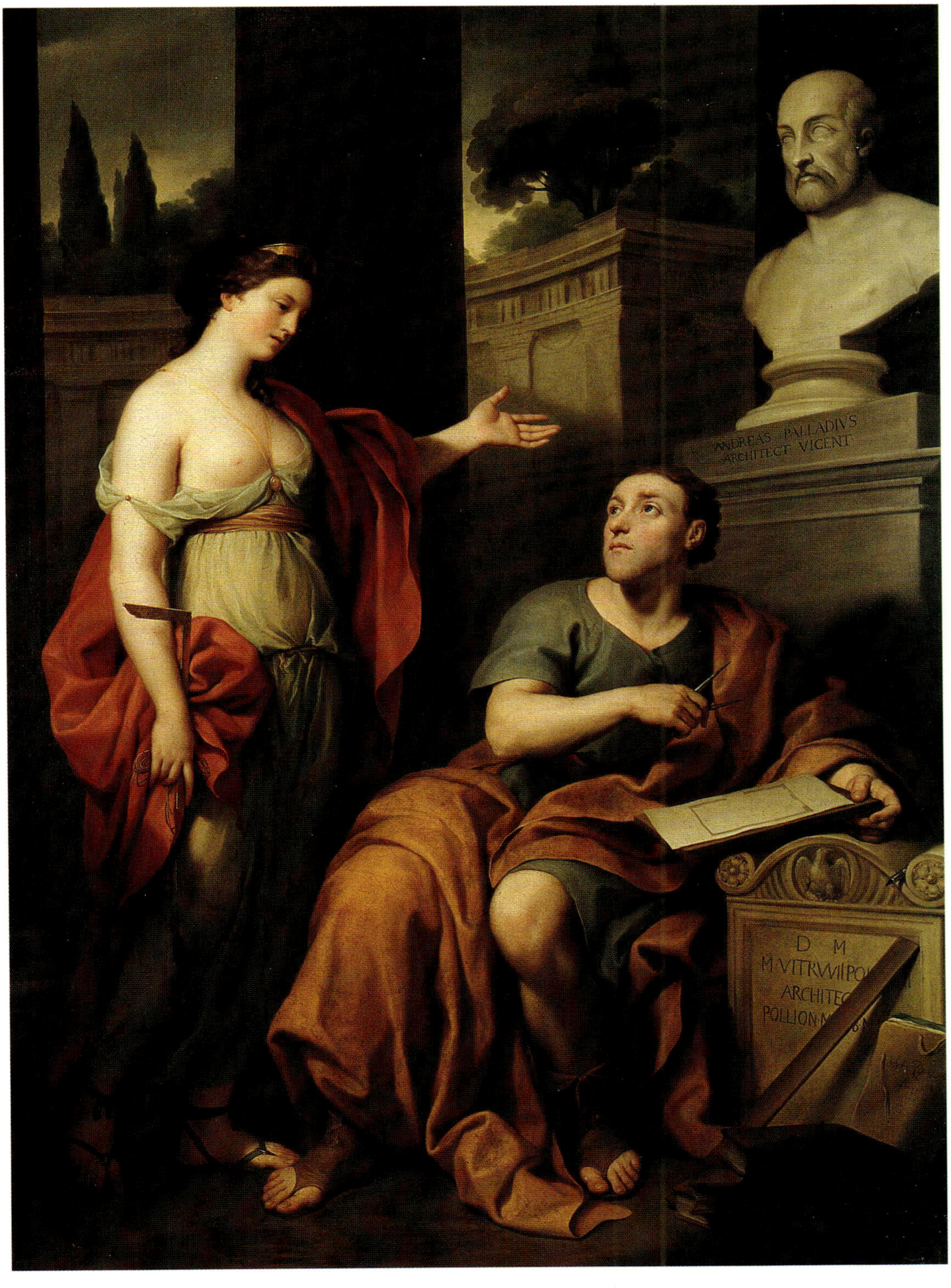
ANDREAS PALLADIVS
ARCHITECT VICENT
D M

and that he should concentrate instead on the practice of architecture as represented by Palladio.

The picture is like a painted commentary on the events that characterised the last and turbulent years of Charlemont's stay in Rome. Born the second son of James Caulfield, Third Viscount Charlemont, in Dublin, Charlemont stayed in Italy from 1746 to 1754, kept there by his extraordinarily strong interest in classical antiquity. During this period he also travelled in Sicily, Greece, Asia Minor and Egypt. In 1748-49 he commissioned drawings of Roman *vedute* from Thomas Patch, and together with John Parker, who was his artistic adviser and agent in Rome, he founded an Academy of English Professors of the Liberal Arts in Rome. He also funded the expedition to Greece by Stuart and Revett and in 1753 promised Piranesi financial support for the publication of his *Antichità Romane*, although this was not in fact given. He also made contact with William Chambers in Rome, who had come from Paris to look for future clients. The first commission which Chambers received after his return did in fact come from Charlemont; it was to design the Casino of the villa which Charlemont built from 1758 in Marino near Clontarf.

Charlemont's interests accordingly shifted, while he was still in Rome, and particularly after his return to Ireland, from the study of classical monuments, mainly architecture, to the active promotion of building. This was presumably also the reason why he lost interest in financing Piranesi's publication on Roman *vedute* and instead turned to the practice of building in the Neo-Classical style. Apparently, the first designs for the Casino in Marino came from Charlemont himself (see Roettgen (1983), further literature there). Piranesi was angry at the withdrawal of the promised support and reacted loudly and vehemently. He took his revenge in his *Lettere di Giustificazione scritte a Milord Charlemont*, published in 1757, which he distributed among his Roman and British friends (see J. Scott, *Piranesi*, London 1975). Mengs also received a copy of this polemic, but his portrait of Charlemont was presumably already finished by then and he had left Rome. Charlemont was in Italy again in 1758, but apparently not in Rome. The fact that Winckelmann sent best wishes to him through his patron Muzell Stosch in Florence shows that Charlemont had met Winckelmann, who only arrived in Rome in November 1755. So presumably he travelled more frequently between Ireland and Italy than one would imagine today.

John Parker remained in Rome as Charlemont's trusted correspondent, particularly to look after the transport of the paintings which Charlemont had purchased in Rome. In the correspondence with Parker (Clark Bowron (1985), p.265) a full-length portrait is mentioned, as well as the portrait painted by Batoni in Florence in 1754 which he was still working on after Charlemont left. It was not finished until the end of 1755 and is now lost (see Clark Bowron (1985), p.264). Whether the portrait by Mengs is mentioned in the Charlemont papers has not as yet been ascertained.

The events leading up to the commission are also unclear. The provenance from the Kilmorey collection can only be followed back to the date of the auction from what is known at present. Certainly the portrait cannot be a member of the Kilmorey family. Lord and Lady Kilmorey were in Rome in 1755, but they were both very much older than the young man in this picture.

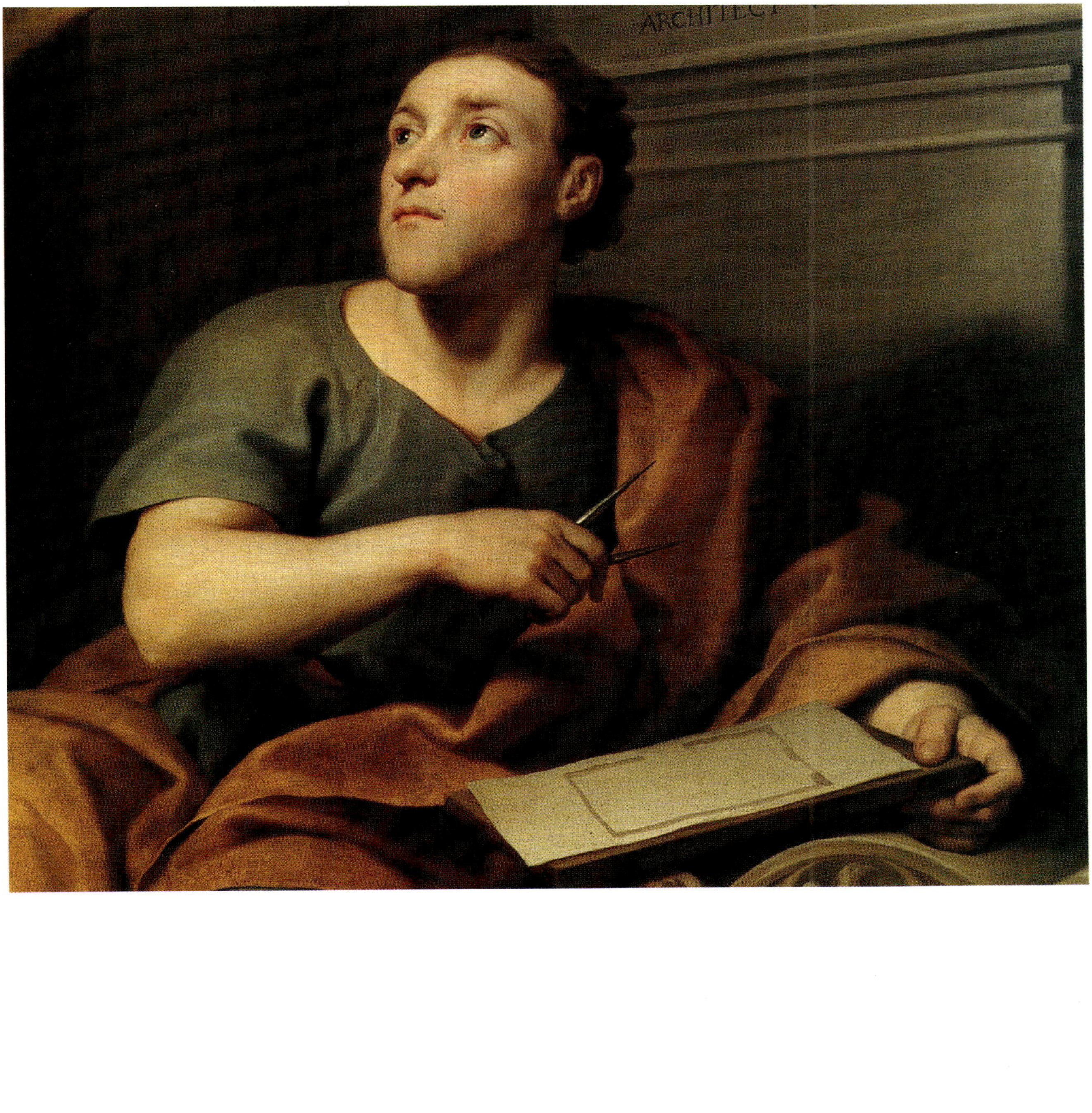

5

Portrait of Pope Clement XIII Rezzonico (1693-1769)

Oil on canvas, 58.4 × 47 cm
Stratfield Saye, the Duke of Wellington

PROVENANCE: Acquired in 1956 by the 7th Duke of Wellington at an auction
as the portrait of an old woman. Previous owner Edith Lady Wolverton.

LITERATURE: Azara-Fea (1787), p.XLV; B. Ford, 'The Pictures at Stratfield Saye', *Apollo* (July 1975), p.29.

This portrait study appears to have been made at the same time as the two three-quarter length portraits of Pope Clement (Bologna, Pincacoteca Nazionale and Milan, Pinacoteca Ambrosiana), that is, between his enthronement on 16 July 1758 and 1760. Despite some deviations, the similarities of approach are so strong that this must be a study from life for the portrait in Bologna. It has the characteristic features of a study from life. We know that it remained in the painter's studio, and it is probably the 'testa di papa Rezzonico' mentioned in the inventory of his estate in 1779.

The study of the head served as the model for the portrait engraving of the Pope by Piranesi in 1761. Winckelmann says in a letter to Usteri on 28 July 1761 (*Briefe*, II, p.171) that the engraving work was finished, apart from the portrait of the Pope, meaning the engraving itself and not the model it was derived from. Piranesi's engraving was a three-quarter length portrait and it generally follows the portrait of Clement XIII by Mengs of 1758 (Bologna, Pinacoteca Nazionale). However, according to Azara-Fea he used as a model a portrait of which only the head was finished and which differed from the other two. A comparison with the engraving which served as the frontispiece to Piranesi's 'De Romanorum magnificentia et architettura', published in 1761 in Rome, shows that this was the study of the head which he used. Mengs having produced so masterly a study from life, the engraving, a joint production by Piranesi and Cunego, provided a representative depiction of the Venetian Pope, and the medium ensured that it became much more widely known than the painted portraits. It is not easy to see why the caption under the engraving does not give any indication that Piranesi used a study by Mengs. There can be no doubt that it was used with Mengs's permission, as it was in his workshop.

Mengs's portrait of the Pope appears to have aroused considerable interest among the art-loving public in Rome, largely due to the fact that the Pope had his portrait painted also by Batoni in 1760 (Rome, Galleria Nazionale d'Arte Antica, see Clark-Bowron (1985), no.227). Prange (I, 1786, p.177-8) records an episode in connection with the painting of what is presumably this portrait.

Mengs apparently refused to paint the Pope's portrait, that is, the study from life, with him kneeling, as Subleyras had portrayed Pope Benedict XIV. When his demands had been met, he started to sing and whistle in the Pope's presence, and the Monsignore in attendance requested him several times to cease, but in vain. Mengs replied that it was his custom to whistle while he was working. It was probably his unconcern even in the presence of the supreme representative of the Church that gave his study such life and so unpretentious a character. Certainly, the episode throws a characteristic light on Mengs's unconventional behaviour, which was so different from Batoni's. Thomas Robinson says in a letter of 1760 (cat.no.51) of Batoni's public demeanour: 'He is besides of a very devout Exterior & Appearance in this Prelatical world not a useless Recommendation'. While a Venetian observer preferred Batoni's portrait of Clement XIII to Mengs's, but thought both inferior to a work by Tiepolo, Thomas Robinson, who mentions both portraits in his letter, appears to have esteemed Mengs's work more highly.

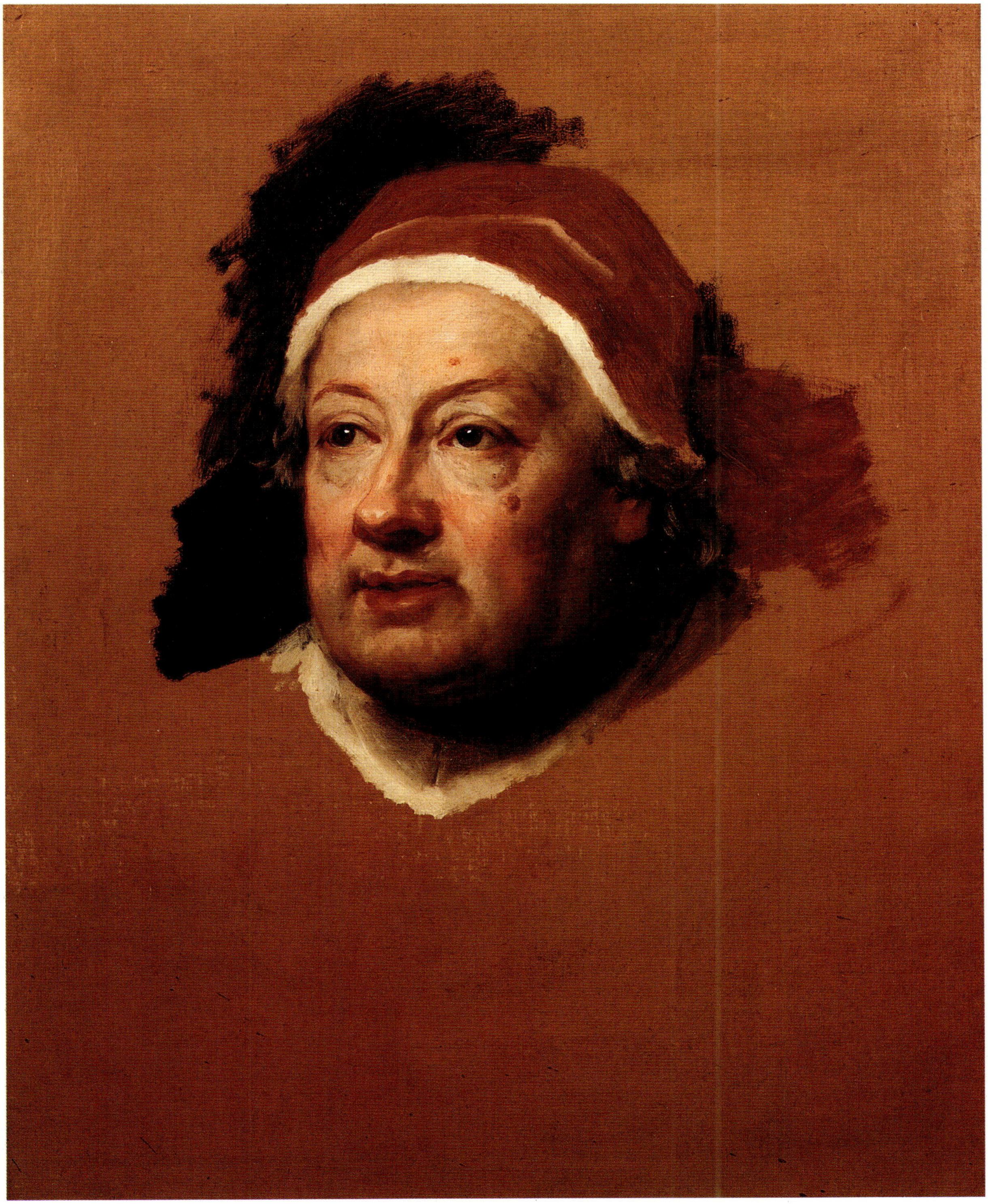

6
Portrait of William Burton Conyngham (1733?-96)

Pastel on parchment (or paper), 65 × 48.7 cm
Private collection

LITERATURE: Russell 1979, pp.13-14, 16.

As Francis Russell has pointed out, this portrait was presumably made to match a pastel of Lord Boyne by Rosalba Carriera. This is suggested not only by the matching frames on the two works, both of which date from the eighteenth century, but also by the pastel technique, unusual for a Grand Tour portrait.

Mengs had made his name as a pastellist in Dresden, and the quality of his portraits in this medium in the Royal pastel collection was greatly admired by British travellers to the city (see Introduction). In Rome his use of pastel was rare after 1752, the technique being very popular amongst amateur artists and no longer adequate for his ambitions as a history painter. However, he continued to use it for studies from life, no doubt because the medium was easier to use. This portrait of William Burton, which is finely executed in every detail, therefore was an exception, the result of a special request to match the technique of another artist.

Mengs was familiar with the portraits by Rosalba Carriera in Dresden, as his work there in 1745 had to stand comparison with the masterpieces by the Venetian woman artist which were already in the Royal collection. Hence he was perfectly aware of his technical advantage over the Venetian painter whom he so greatly revered, and he made appropriate use of it. His superiority lay mainly in an unusual degree of saturation of pastel colour; he could achieve such strong and powerful colours that the effect is like oil painting, and this was seen by his contemporaries as proof of his technical mastery. Mengs achieved this effect by using and blending strong and pure pastels, as he described later in the essay 'Riflessi sopra differenti tinti di carne' written before 1760 (Azara-Fea, (1787), pp.257ff).

In the portrait of William Burton this technique is particularly evident in the highly plastic modelling of the face; it is also apparent in that the lights on the nose, lips and hair have the same effect as in an oil painting. The rendering of the velvet cloak also has a material quality that is hardly less than one would expect from the use of oils.

Mengs deviates here from the type of portrait which he used for most of his other pictures of British sitters, choosing the Baroque type of head and shoulders. The luxurious folds of the cloak are cut off at the picture edge and so give an impression of volume and richness. The slightly dramatic turn of the head over the shoulder adds to the effect, while also giving an impression of spontaneity and naturalness. The open and eager expression of the face and the hand reaching into the cloak support that impression. As Russell has stressed, the work is of a quality, not least in its harmony of colour, that makes it 'rank as one of Mengs' most satisfying portraits'. Because the type of portrait is unusual, it does not offer stylistic clues to its exact date. The posture is similar to that in the *Portrait of an Englishman* in Salzburg (fig.17); it was made between 1752 and 1760 but cannot be more exactly dated either. The brilliant modelling of the cloak recalls the *Portrait of Sir Charles Hanbury Williams* (cat.no.17) of 1751, and so it is likely that this work dates from the first years of Mengs's stay in Rome, that is, before 1755.

According to Russell, William Burton Conyngham, who later played an important role in Ireland in commissioning architecture, was also portrayed by Nathaniel Dance who was in Rome from 1754 to 1765. It is to be hoped that documentary evidence of Burton's stay in Rome may come to light, allowing a more accurate dating of the portrait, and a clearer idea of his contacts and acquaintances. This would also throw more light on his relations with Mengs and his circle. The sources mentioned by Clark Bowron on Robert Clements (1732-1804) and his stay in Rome might provide the appropriate information. Clements was later First Earl of Leitrim and the builder of Killadoon. So far it has not been possible to ascertain what the relationship was between William Burton and Francis Burton Conyngham of County Clare, a nephew of Baron Conyngham of Slane and one of the companions of Lord Charlemont (cat.no.4) on the journey to Constantinople which he undertook in April 1749 (see M. Charles Craig, *The Volunteer Earl, being the Life and Times of James Caulfield, First Earl of Charlemont* (London (1948), pp.44-5).

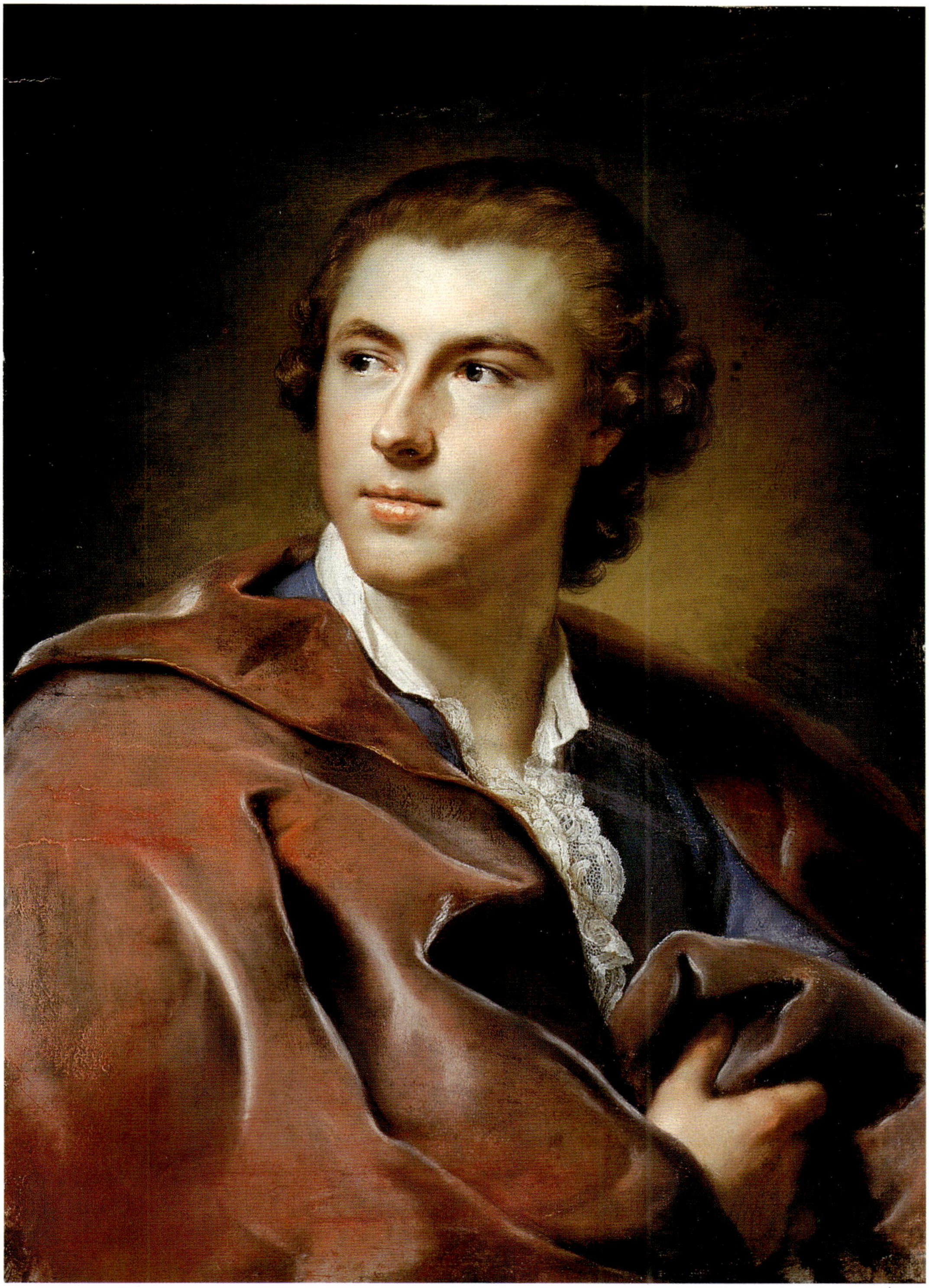

7

Portrait of George Clavering Nassau (1738-90 Florence), Lord Fordwich, later Third Earl of Cowper

Oil on canvas, 50.2 × 40.7 cm
Yale Center for British Art, Paul Mellon Collection

LITERATURE: Exhibition catalogue *Old Master Paintings* (London & Rome, Chaucer Fine Arts & Galleria Gasparrini, 1987), no.34.

The Earl of Cowper was well-known for his vanity and his appearance was mockingly likened to that of a Doge of Genoa by Horace Walpole in 1786 (*Letters of Horace Walpole*, ed. Cunningham, IX (Edinburgh, 1906), p.51); in its rich iconography the portrait of him by Mengs, which reappeared only in 1976, is certainly one of the most important.

This work is presumably the study from life which Mengs made, probably in 1760, intending to use it for a representative and larger portrait. In the same year he was also working on a commission from Cowper for a *Holy Family*, which was finished before he left for Spain (see Introduction, fig.23).

The study from life remained in Mengs's studio and it is mentioned in the inventory of the artist's estate after his death in 1779 as follows: 'Ritratto di Milord Cowper da giovane scudi 70'. The value put on the work confirms the suggestion that it was this picture, now at the Yale Center. It was the usual practice for the study from life to remain in the artist's possession, and here this appears to be confirmed by a letter dated 1765 in the Cowper archive, which states that Mengs was keeping the study for the portrait in order to paint other versions (information given by Hugh Belsey in the Chaucer catalogue).

The second portrait which Mengs painted of Cowper, in 1769 according to the inscription on the reverse, is known from descriptions but not from photographs. It was painted on wood and bore the inscription on the reverse: 'HANC COWPERI IMAGINEM/ INTER M;AGNAE BRITANNIAE PROCERES/ QUAM DIVINUS RAPHAEL MENGS/ FLORENTIAE ANNO MDCCLXIX PINXIT COWPERUS IDEM NUNC S.R.I. PRINCEPS/ CAROLO RINUCCINIO BASELECAE TOPARCHAE / AMICO SUAVISSIMO DONABIT'.

The portrait was later given by Cowper to his friend Carlo Rinuccini, who was also an admirer of Mengs and collector of his work. After 1852 the portrait passed from Rinuccini's possession to the Corsini Collection, where it was recorded for the last time in 1911. In 1945 it was auctioned with the collection of Sir Buckston Brown at Sotheby's in London (25.4.1945, lot 58; information kindly provided by Mr Hugh Belsey). It is clearly identifiable in the catalogue from the inscription on the reverse, but it cannot now be traced.

It is therefore not possible to say how the study from life relates to the finished portrait which was only completed in summer 1773. At any rate, the artist was concerned with the gilding of the frame and the packaging of the work at that time (letter to Anton Maron of 28.8.1773, see von Einem (1973), p.66). It cannot be ruled out that the incorrect dating on the reverse might simply have been a lapse of memory, for the inscription was certainly written as a dedication to Rinuccini when the gift was made and so some years after the portrait was painted.

The fact that the inventory of the artist's estate calls this study a portrait of Lord Cowper in his youth suggests that it is not the study on which Mengs based the later portrait. That is also suggested by the difference in the clothing. In the lost portrait Cowper wore a carmine red waistcoat and a cloak of the same colour, with an embroidered jabot and lace ruffles, while here he wears a relatively simple light blue coat over a greenish-blue waistcoat. Admittedly, the clothes the sitter wore for the first study from life were not necessarily those which would be used for the final portrait, as is evident from a number of works (cat.nos.10 and 11). Moreover, the letter mentioned above is further evidence, as it says the study in the artist's possession can be used several times for portraits. But in the lost portrait Cowper also wore a powdered wig and was shown with his right arm outstretched.

Compared with the portraits by Macpherson, Fabbrini and Zoffany (in the famous picture of the *Tribuna in the Uffizi*, London, Her Majesty the Queen) Cowper does look rather younger here. Nevertheless, it is hard to imagine that this is the portrait of a man of only twenty-three.

A head and shoulders portrait which came onto the London art market a few years ago (Chaucer Fine Arts, London 1987, cat.no.34) can be seen as a copy, with variations, of the portrait by Mengs. However, it is odd that the features and clothing are painted as if they were taken from a fully executed portrait. This cannot be the portrait with the inscription on the reverse which was formerly in the Corsini Collection in Florence, as the colours and handling of the clothing are the same as those on our study. Hence the possibility cannot be excluded that a finished version of the oil study existed.

Cowper was obviously a devoted admirer of Mengs, and in Florence he owned the most works by the artist (see Introduction).

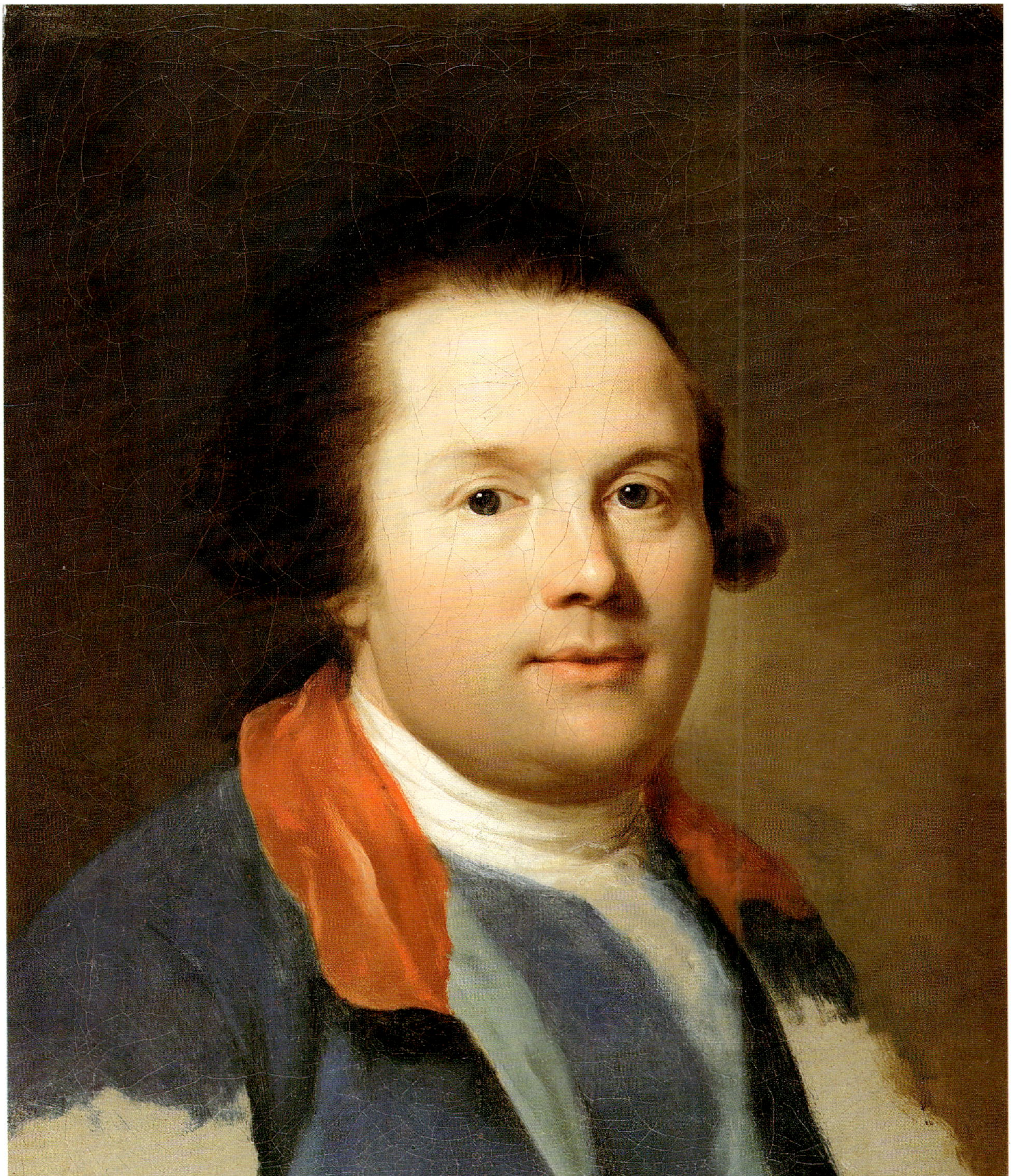

8

Portrait of William Fermor of Tusmore, Oxfordshire (1737-1806)

Oil on canvas, 61.5 × 47 cm
Inscribed on the stretcher 'Wm. Fermor in a Masque dress, price 10 guineas
Anton Rafael Mengs Pinxit May 1757'
Oxford, The Visitors of the Ashmolean Museum

PROVENANCE: Auctioned by King and Chasemore, Pulborough, 7.2.1978; Colnaghi's London.

LITERATURE: H. Walpole, *Anecdotes of Painting in England* (ed. 1937), vol.5, p.52; The Times, London, 8 February 1978 (G. Norman, Sale Room Correspondent); cat. *Paintings by Old Masters*, Colnaghi & Co (London, 1978), no.43, p.41; *Apollo* (July 1978), p.71; Russell (1979), pp.10, 16-17; *Annual Report of the Visitors of the Ashmolean Museum 1977-8* (Oxford, 1979), pp.33-4; Clark-Bowron, (1985), p.271.

The sitter was the eldest son of Henry Fermor of Tusmore in Oxfordshire (died 1746). As is evident from the inscription on the back of the painting, he was on the Grand Tour in 1757, and appears to have returned just after the middle of 1758 (letter from J. Skelton of 28.6.1758). Fermor had his portrait painted also by Batoni (Kress Collection, Houston, see Clark-Bowron (1985), no.205). Batoni's portrait dates from rather later and it is more elaborate and elegant than Mengs's. However, the difference is a matter of presentation rather than perception and the two works are very similar in the depiction of the heads.

It is not easy to interpret the inscription on the stretcher, which must be regarded as authentic as it does give the correct date. Above all, it is hard to see why this was noted as a masquerade costume. The coat is slightly more elaborate than the garb usually worn by travellers on the Grand Tour, with its gold embroidery on the collar, expensive buttons and lace jabot, but it is certainly not so unusual that one could call it festive attire. Moreover, none of the other attributes associated with a masquerade portrait, like the mask, are to be seen (cat.no.15).

The inscription states that the portrait fee was 10 guineas. According to contemporary sources this was the equivalent of 20 Zecchini or 40 Scudi, and so it was 10 Scudi above the price Batoni was asking at the same time.

In type the portrait is extremely simple. Although it is almost a half-length, the sitter's hands are not shown, and this lowered the price. The depiction itself is also simple, and there is no suggestion of a theatrical pose. Distinguished reserve, mixed with an impersonal friendliness, are the dominant features. Apart from the portrait of Louis des Visme (cat.no.16) none of Mengs's other portraits of British sitters has such conscious modesty imbued with courtly flair.

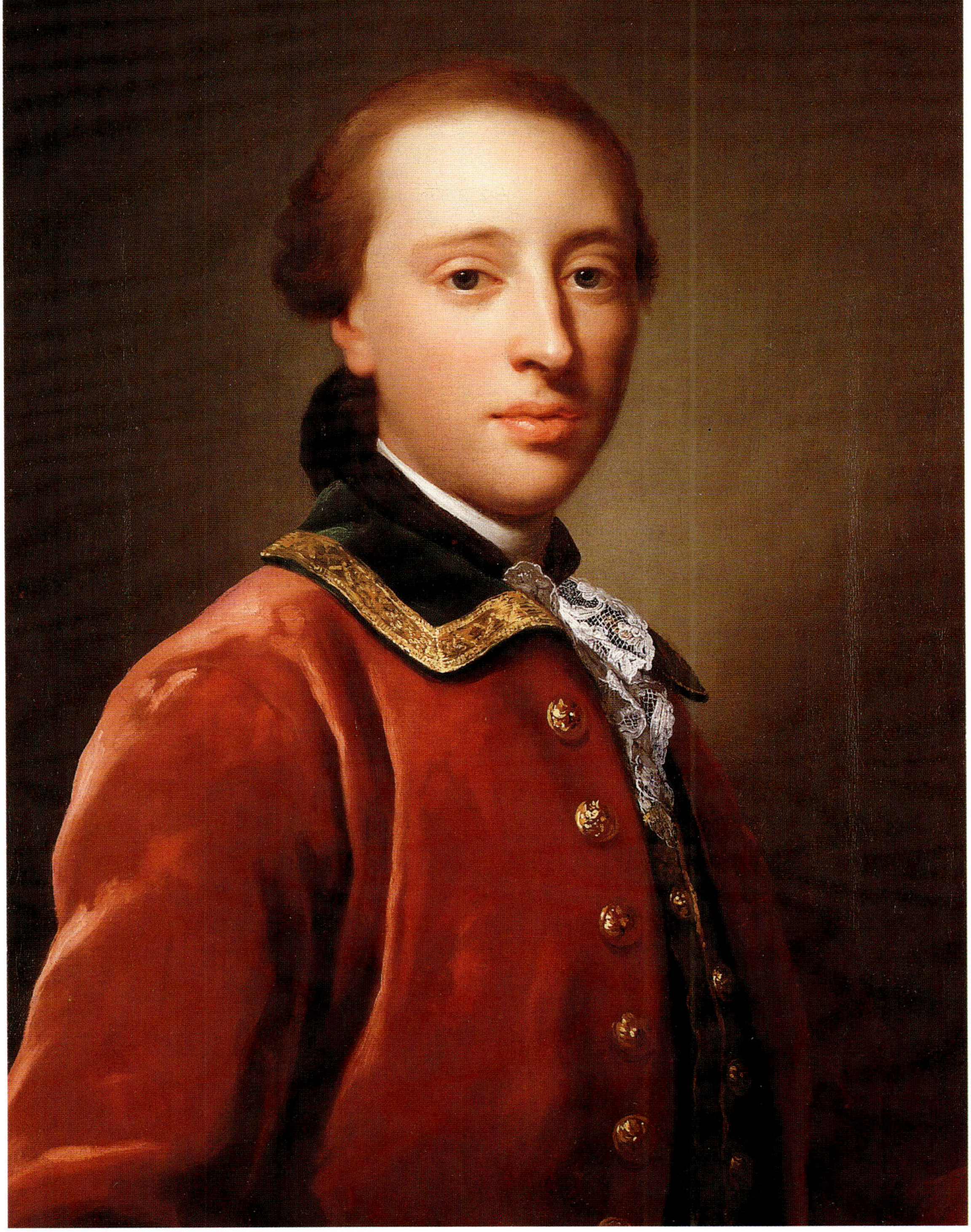

10

Portrait of Henry Lyte (1727-91)

Oil on canvas, 73.7 × 47.8 cm
Inscribed lower right by another hand later:
'Henry Lyte Esq./Sub Preceptor and Master of the Rolls/and Privy Purse to H.R.H. the / Prince of Wales, afterwards George the 4th/ and Auditor of the Duchy of Cornwall./Died 1791/ By Raphael Mengs.'
London, Sir Brinsley Ford, C.B.E., Hon F.R.A., F.S.A.

PROVENANCE: Auctioned at Sotheby's, 4.11.1953, lot 73.

LITERATURE: Fleming (1958), pp.127-141; exhibition catalogue *Il Settecento a Roma* Rome (1959), no.380; exhibition catalogue *The Eighteenth Century, Italy and the Grand Tour* (Norwich, 1958), no.38; exhibition catalogue *Italian Art and Britain* (London, Royal Academy, 1960), no.301; J. J. Winckelmann, *Kleine Schriften*, ed. Walter Rehm (Berlin, 1968), p.447; Russell (1979), p.17.

Lyte came from Somerset and may, according to Fleming, have been a descendant of the celebrated seventeenth-century botanist and antiquarian of the same name. He was educated at Peterhouse and Cambridge, where he was a fellow at Queen's College from 1749 to 1763. In 1751 he acted as tutor to the seventeen-year old John Brudenell on the Grand Tour of France and Italy. He directed the young lord's academic studies in Paris and wrote regular reports back to his father, the Fourth Earl of Cardigan, and later Third Duke of Montagu. This correspondence has survived and it is now in the possession of the Duke of Buccleuch at Dalkeith Palace in Scotland, where it was consulted by John Fleming for his reconstruction of Lord Brudenell's and Lyte's Grand Tour.

In December 1754 the two were in Genoa, having spent some time at the court of Turin. Robert Adam, who saw them in Genoa in the picture gallery of the Palazzo Balbi, called Lyte a 'clever-like fellow', while his opinion of Lord Brudenell was less favourable. In April 1756 Brudenell and Lyte arrived in Rome, but they only spent a month there, continuing through Naples for a tour of southern Italy which lasted almost two years.

The first meeting of Lord Brudenell, Lyte and Mengs may have happened through Winckelmann, whom Brudenell contacted regarding his tour of southern Italy and his archaeological findings. Like the portrait of Lord Brudenell which Mengs painted during his second visit to Rome, which lasted until about August 1758, this portrait of Henry Lyte must have been executed at that time, as their first visit to Rome was too short. Whereas Henry Lyte mentions the portrait of Lord Brudenell in his reports to his pupil's father, so that it can be dated fairly exactly, he never mentions the portrait Mengs painted of himself. Fleming thinks that Lyte kept silent on the matter because Mengs painted his portrait as a favour in return for the commission to paint Brudenell.

Unlike in Brudenell's portrait, Mengs chose his favourite portrait type for Lyte, a half-length. As he was painting both the young lord and his tutor, it was essential to make a clear distinction between them. The difference in their rank had to be clear, but this is done very discreetly. Lyte, like Lord Brudenell, is shown as a scholar, with books on the table and one in his hand; his clothing is elegant. His posture, gesture and facial expression seem hardly less self-assured than those of the lord, although his corpulence and pose make them seem rather more deliberate. His outer appearance is detached from reality by the slightly fantastic garb. The emotional expression achieved by the view from below and the turn of the head monumentalises and distances the picture, making it something of an idealised image of authority.

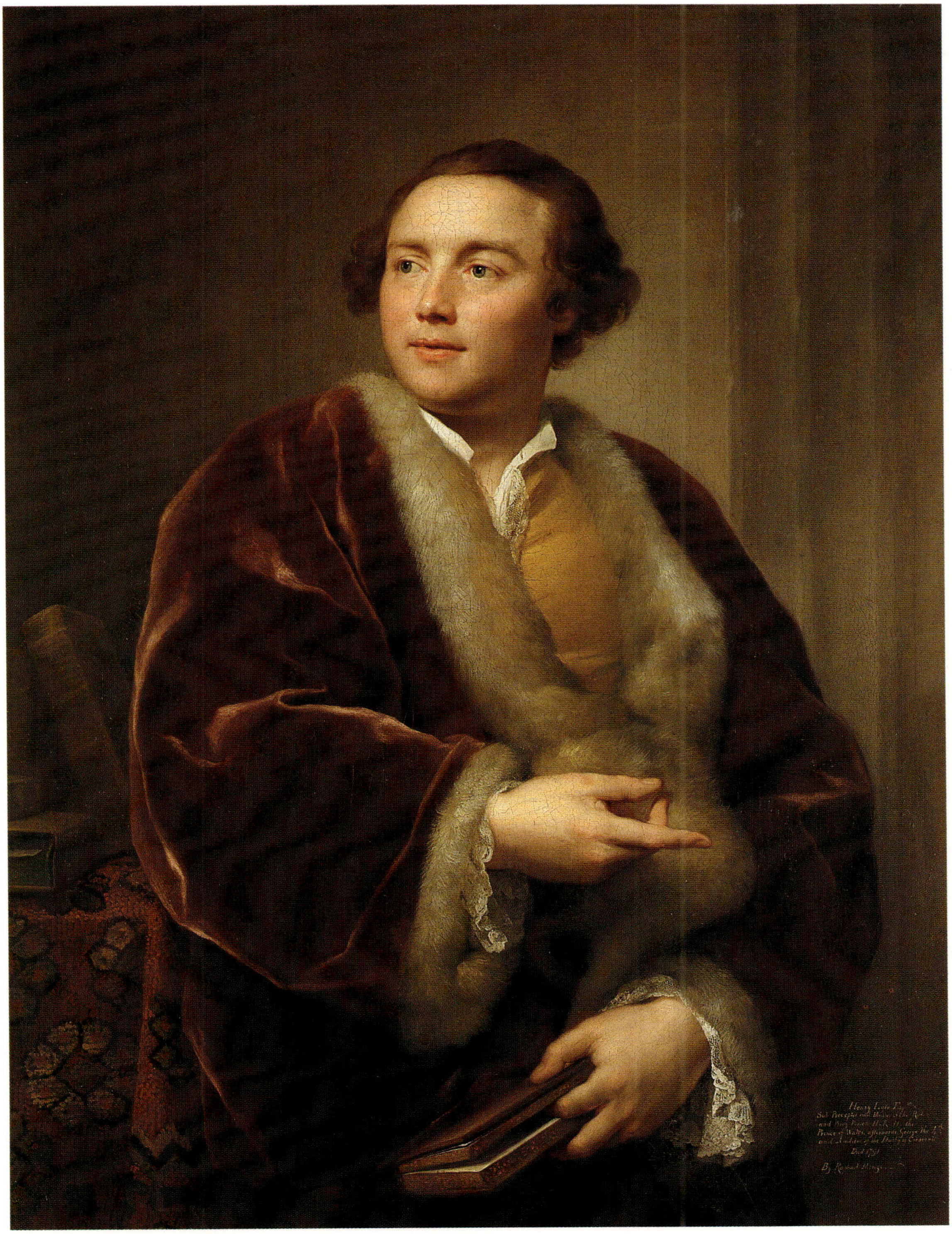

11
Portrait of Henry Lyte

Oil on canvas, 47.5 × 37 cm
Germany, Private collection
This work has been assigned to Mengs by Michael Levey.

My thesis, which is not accepted by Brinsley Ford, that this is a study from life for the portrait of Henry Lyte, is based on the undeniable similarity in the physiognomy of the two images. The position of the head and the shape of the face are so alike that the evident variations must be explained by the difference between a study and a finished portrait. No importance should be attached to the fact that the clothing and hairstyles differ, for these are details that would naturally only be decided when the portrait was executed. The rather more slender face in the study, which makes the sitter look slightly older than in the finished portrait, can also be explained by the type of portrait rather than a difference in the identity of the sitter.

The painter's interest in the sketch, which is loose and broadly laid out, is focussed on a realistic depiction of the physiognomy and the facial expression. The dark coat, buttoned up high, and the unpretentious and lively expression give the work a simple, almost 'bourgeois' character.

The executed portrait, on the other hand, seems more aloof. The sitter is made to appear very much younger and more attractive, both in his features and in his well-groomed and carefully chosen clothes. The difference between the study from life and the executed portrait illustrates the range in Mengs's work between the naturalistic and direct portrayal of the study and the more demanding and representative portrait.

The turn of the head shows, on the other hand, that the gesture which is such a decisive feature of the executed portrait was calculated right from the start, as was the slightly theatrical element of the view from below and the sitter's gaze, which is directed diagonally upwards out of the picture.

There are many other examples in Mengs's portraiture where considerable differences can be found between the study from life and the portrait as finally executed.

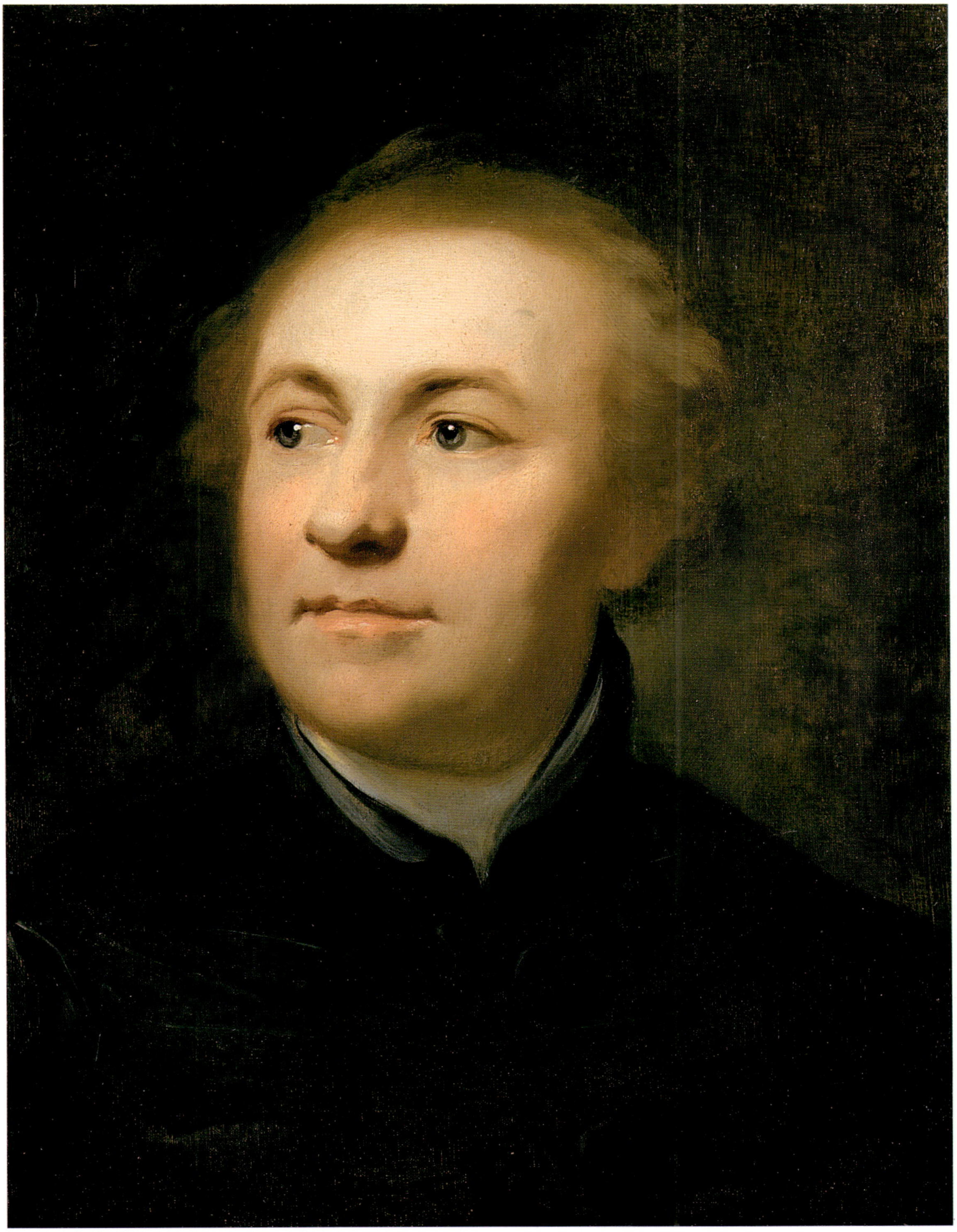

12

A Portrait Sketch of Count Franz Xaver Orsini-Rosenberg

Oil on canvas, 61 × 47.5 cm
Inscribed below likeness: *Portrait de Mr De Rosenberg Gentilhomme Suedois, Peint par A. R. Mengs. En Deux Heures de Temps. A Rome l'année 1756*
London, Private collection

PROVENANCE: The Collection of Prince Belosselsky-Bolozersky, St Petersburg; his sale. Lair-Dubreuil. Paris. 17 June 1921, for FF 3,800 (E. Benezit, *Dictionnaire... des peintres, sculpteurs, dessinateurs et graveurs*, Paris 1953, VI, p.61).

LITERATURE: Honisch 1965, No.462, p.155; sale catalogue. W. Doyle Galleries, 25.10.1989, lot 70, p.13; exhibition catalogue, *A Collectors Miscellany. European Paintings 1600-1800.* London, Colnaghi's 1990/1. p.36/7.

Born in Carinthia in 1723, Rosenberg moved to Vienna at the age of fourteen. He finished his studies there and then entered the diplomatic service. He took up posts in England, Milan and Copenhagen. Next he went to Madrid as Ambassador, serving there from 1757 until 1765. He represented Peter Leopold, the second son of Emperor Franz Stephen, in his nuptial ceremony held in Madrid in 1764 and then accompanied the bride, the Infanta Maria Luisa, to Innsbruck, where he received the Order of the Golden Fleece from the hands of Franz Stephen, shortly before the latter's death, in recognition of his services in forwarding the Spanish match.

In 1766 Rosenberg was sent to Florence by Maria Theresa, and immediately won the affection of the Grand Duke's subjects without losing the trust of Maria Theresa and Joseph II. An Italian courtier noted at the time that Rosenberg 'was a man of esprit and heart and merits the trust of the Grand Duke Leopold'. In 1771 Rosenberg returned to Vienna and in 1773 began building a new castle and park *alla italiana* in his native Carinthia. In 1774 he was recalled to Vienna by Maria Theresa who made him Chief Chamberlain. In 1776 he also became Director of the Court Theatres. Rosenberg was a regular member of Joseph II's intimate coterie. In 1790, on the occasion of his coronation as Emperor, Peter Leopold, now Leopold II, raised his old friend to the dignity of imperial princehood. Rosenberg died in 1796.

The original lining canvas of this sketch bore an identical inscription to that under the image of the sitter identifying him as a *Mr De Rosenberg Gentilhomme Suedois.* It was signed by Giovanni Casanova, half-brother of the infamous Giacomo and pupil and friend of Mengs in Rome from 1752 to 1761. In 1764 Casanova went to Dresden where he remained until his death in 1795. In 1771 he returned to Rome for a brief visit with Prince Belosselsky, then on his Grand Tour. It must be supposed that this *Portrait Sketch* was bought at that time by the Russian nobleman and that it was authenticated by Casanova, who continued to make use of the fact that he had been Mengs's favourite pupil. The mistake about Rosenberg's nationality arose at this time because Casanova confused Rosenberg's position as Imperial Ambassador to Copenhagen with his being Swedish. Casanova was, after all, a painter and not a geographer!

This *Portrait Sketch of Count Orsini-Rosenberg*, executed in two hours, was intended to serve as an aid to memory during the preparation of a formal portrait of the sitter, as was Mengs's usual studio practice, although no finished portrait of Rosenberg by Mengs is known. The Saxon artist did, however, paint a further study of Rosenberg (Sotheby's, London, 25 July 1973, lot. 65), during the former's Florentine sojourn of 1770).

It would have been only natural for Mengs and Rosenberg to renew their acquaintanceship at that time, especially as they probably met each other, after the brief Roman encounter, at the Court of Charles III in Madrid in the early 1760s.

It is obvious that both sketches show the same man notwithstanding the difference in age. So similar are pose and conception that it is likely that the Sotheby canvas was conceived to replace the present sketch for the preparation of a grand, formal portrait, given that the latter no longer closely resembled Rosenberg. The identification of the sitter with Rosenberg is further confirmed by comparison of both sketches with C. Vinazer's 1783 engraving showing the Count in profile and a three-quarter length portrait of 1790, still in possession of the Rosenberg family.

This *Sketch* of the young Rosenberg is similar in style and composition to the portraits of the Saxon royal family executed by Mengs while he was Court Painter at Dresden between 1746 and 1751, especially that of the Prince Elector Friedrich Christian of 1751 (cat.no.13). The manner in which the likeness is taken from below, emphasizing the sculptural quality of the features, is characteristic of these canvases. As well as imparting vivacity to the expression it confers that sense of importance and distanced dignity which are the requisites of official portraiture. These iconographic elements are, at the same time, tempered by Mengs's conception of portraiture which aimed at the realistic rendering of the sitter's face. The personal and, as it were, visual contact between Mengs and his client finds its natural expression in Rosenberg's quickened, vivid glance. By using van Dyck as his model, he found a way of getting around the antiquated conventions of his day, thus tending towards a new naturalism.

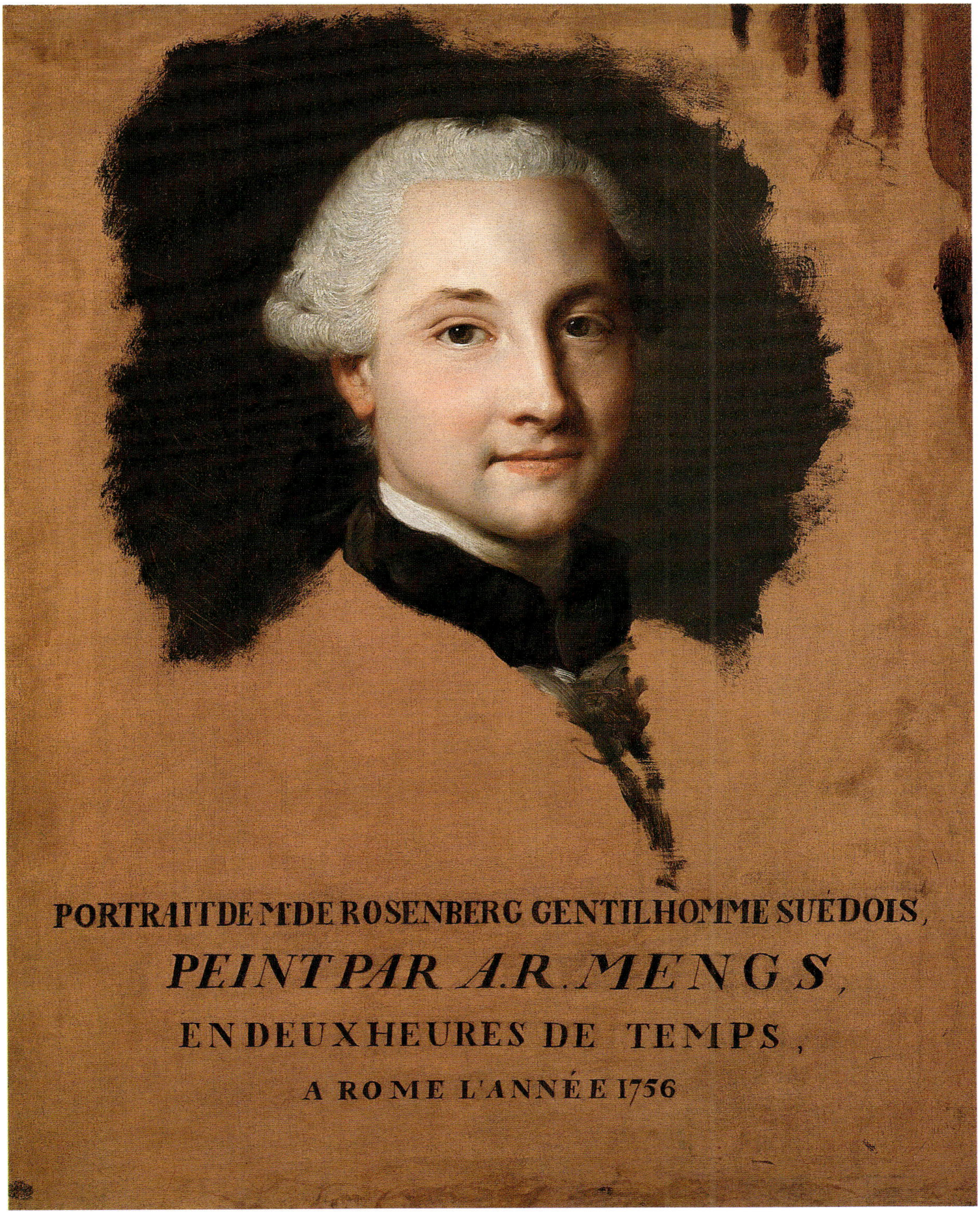
PORTRAIT DE Mr DE ROSENBERG GENTILHOMME SUÉDOIS,
PEINT PAR A.R. MENGS,
EN DEUX HEURES DE TEMPS,
A ROME L'ANNÉE 1756

13

Portrait of the Elector Friedrich Christian of Saxony (1722-63)

Oil on canvas, 152 × 116 cm
Inscribed at top right '775'
London, Count A. S. Ciechanowiecki

PROVENANCE: Rome 1779 (A. R. Mengs estate)

LITERATURE: Exhibition Catalogue: *Zbiory Fundacyi Ciechanowiecki* (*The Ciechanowiecki Foundation Collection*) (Warsaw, Royal Castle, 1989), cat.no.29.

The inscription in white paint on the front identifies the portrait as one of the Electoral Prince of Saxony which was in Mengs's possession when he died. With its companion piece, a portrait of the Prince's spouse Maria Antonia, a Princess of Bavaria, it was valued in the inventory after Mengs's death at 12 Scudi. The picture shows clear signs of deliberate (war?) damage and retouching, particularly to the head, and this reduces its impact. Nevertheless, with the version in the Palazzo Reale in Naples (*Il Palazzo Reale di Napoli*, ed. Marina Picone Causa (Naples, 1986), pp.64-5) it must be regarded as qualitatively the best of the replicas of the original that have survived, and it can be taken as certain that Mengs himself was responsible at least for part of the work. The original was painted in 1751 and is now in the possession of the heirs of the Saxon dynasty. The companion portrait came into the Old Masters Gallery in Dresden in the nineteenth century.

The portrait of the young heir to the throne of Saxony and its companion were the first state portraits Mengs painted in his new office as Principal Court Painter in Dresden. The fact that several replicas of the portrait exist, including some of only head and shoulders, shows that right at the beginning of his career Mengs had assistants in his workshop. This would be essential given the great demand for replicas of official portraits of the ruler and his family. The basis for this portrait was presumably the pastel which has survived in very bad condition and is now in the gallery in Dresden.

The type of portrait chosen here derives from French models: the portrait of the Prince's father, Elector Prince Friedrich Augustus II as Crown Prince by Nicolas de Largillière (1715, Museum in Melbourne, Australia) and that of the young Friedrich Christian painted by the French artist Pierre Subleyras in Rome (1739, Dresden, Old Masters Gallery). From this portrait Mengs has adopted particularly the view of a peaceful park-like landscape visible beyond the interior, which terminates in a low balustrade.

This is a decisive change from the Baroque iconography of the royal portrait, in which a battle or a hall with columns is usually shown. Only the fine balustrade and the staff in the sitter's lowered right hand remain of the earlier genre. Otherwise, the Electoral Prince has all the heraldic attributes of his rank and dignity. He wears on his right hip the blue ribbon of the Polish Order of the White Eagle, the star of which is fastened to the left breast of his coat.

His face is shown very much from below and thus appears strong and radiant with health and strength. Mengs shows himself a master at portraiture that flatters while still achieving a strong likeness, although in this case he comes close to idealisation. In reality the Prince was rather sickly. This kind of embellishment for dynastic considerations was one of the most important tasks of the Baroque court painter, and Mengs owed part of his great success to this ability. Later he was to use it in the service of other dignitaries and rulers, as with Pope Clement XIII (cat.no.5). The portrait also shows Mengs's remarkable skill in rendering the various textures of the clothing and the heraldic insignia.

A comparison of this portrait with that of Sir Charles Hanbury Williams painted only a short time later (cat. no.17) reveals a number of features in common, particularly the total command of technique and the idealised, yet lifelike portrayal. It also shows the huge gap which separated the full-blown state portrait from one which, while following courtly conventions, could still retain the character of a private work. The great diversity in portraiture which Mengs had already mastered – he was only just 22 – suggests already that he would not in future be content to tread the usual path of the court painter.

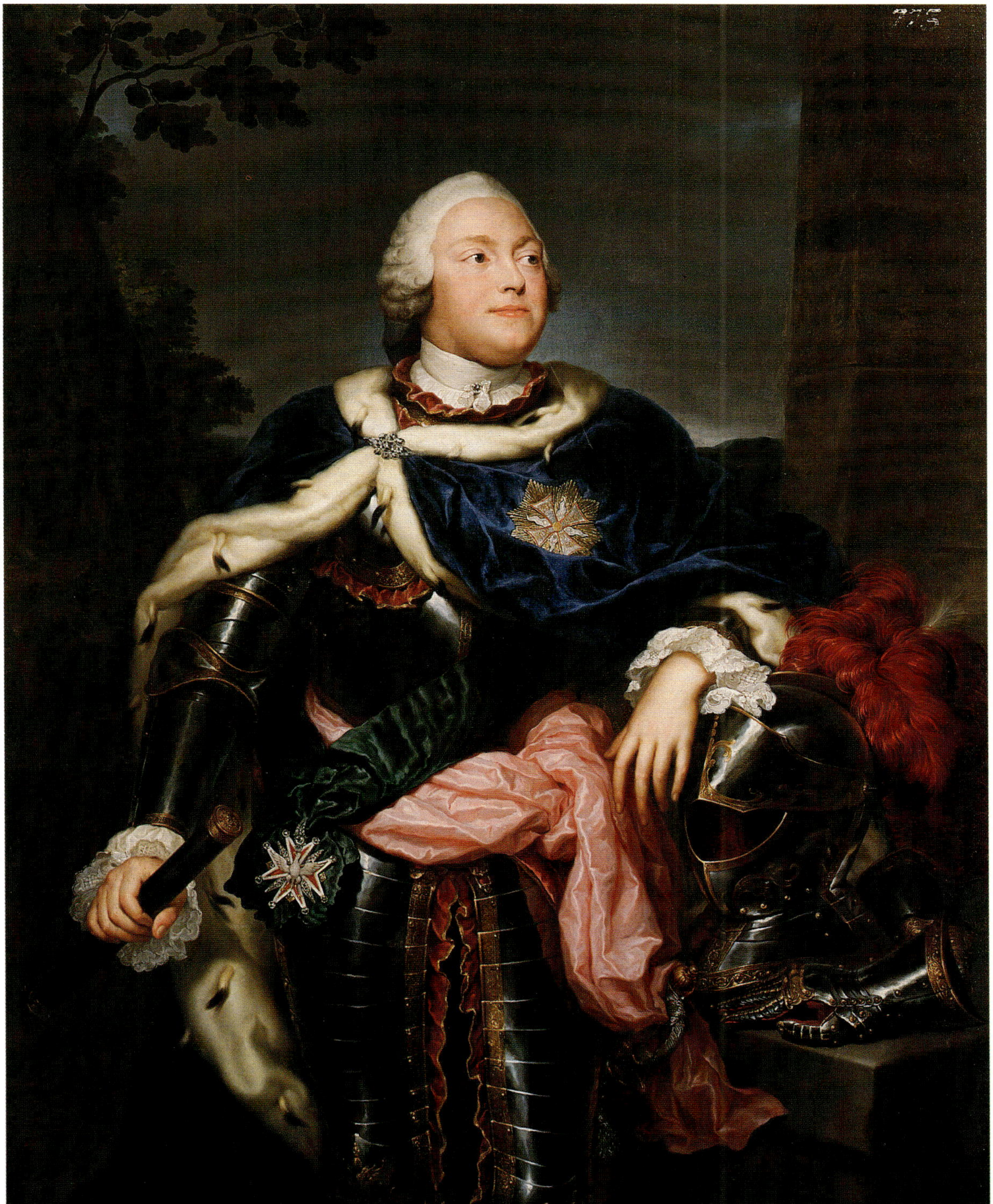

14
Portrait of Robert Stewart, First Marquess of Londonderry (1739-1821)

Oil on canvas, 100 × 72.5 cm
Inscribed centre left: Antonio Raphaele Mengs Año 17[58?]
Mount Stewart, The Londonderry Collection (The National Trust)

LITERATURE: Russell (1979), pp.8, 18; Clark Bowron (1985), p.326.

The sitter was the eldest son of Alexander Stewart (1700-81), of Mount Stewart, and Mary, daughter of Alderman John Cowan of Londonderry. So far no information has come to light on the date or duration of his Grand Tour.

The attributes, posture and gesture in this portrait are very subdued. However, the elegant restraint of the clothing and the voluptuous folds of the luxurious velvet raise the image to a level which must be seen as representative of nobility. This is also suggested by the stump of the great Doric column in the left background, which can hardly be interpreted as a reference to the sitter's stay in Rome. Columns are a frequent motif in portraits of rulers. Here it may possibly be a reference to the fact that Robert Stewart was the eldest son and so the future heir to the title. It cannot be denied that this discreet touch of aristocratic flair is extremely effective. It gives the posture a hint of grandeur, further strengthened by the slightly open left hand which is pointing discreetly to the column.

The sitter's younger brother Alexander (1746-1831) was painted in 1773 by Pompeo Batoni (Clark Bowron (1985), p.325). His portrait (Mount Stewart, National Trust) is of about the same dimensions and it was probably designed to match this one at the request of the client, as Francis Russell has rightly pointed out. The intentional matching of the two portraits can be seen in that both are slightly more than half-length, and that Batoni has chosen a costume in the style of van Dyck, a mode that was out of fashion again by 1770. Apart from this work, Batoni very rarely used van Dyck-style costume in earlier portraits. Again apparently with Mengs's portrait in mind, Batoni has chosen the simple and non-decorative format, which was also unusual in his œuvre. Significantly, a comparable motif to the column is not included, and again this is unusual for Batoni. It substantiates the interpretation of the column motif suggested here.

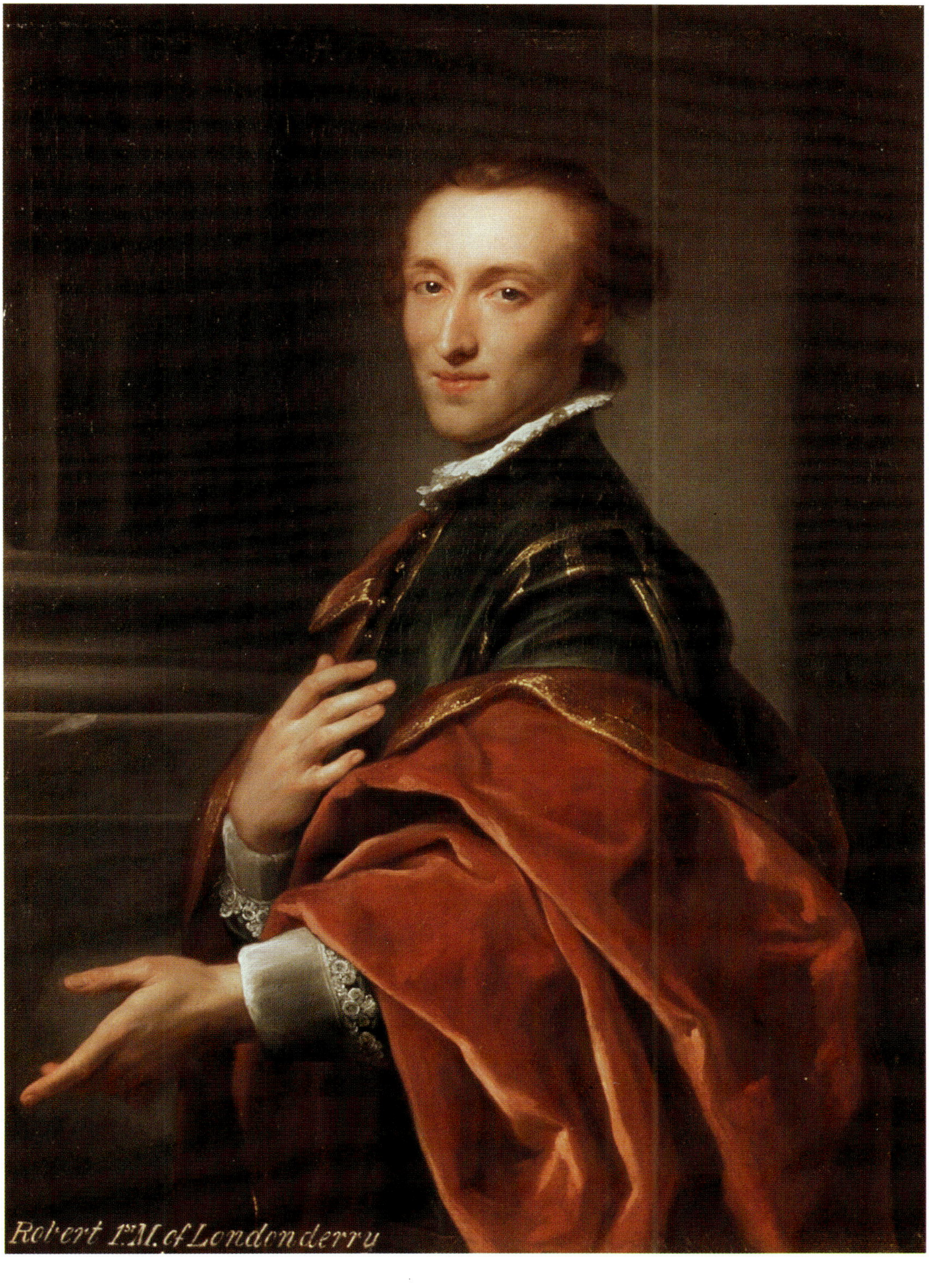
Robert Iˢᵗ M. of Londonderry

15

Portrait of Arabella Swimmer, later Lady Vincent (died 1795)

Oil on canvas, 153 × 111 cm
Dalmeny House, Scotland, the Earl of Rosebery

LITERATURE: Doray de Longrais (1782), pp.33-35; Prange I (1786), p.116; Azara-Fea (1787), p.XLII; Honisch (1965), p.124, no.247; Russell (1979), p.18.

The sitter was a daughter of Sir John Astley, Baronet of Patschul. Anthony Langley Swimmer, a rich merchant from Jamaica, was her first husband. It is clear from the documents which Brinsley Ford has published that Swimmer left London in September 1752 to travel to Rome (see Russell). He left Rome again on 21 April 1753.

Through the sitter's second marriage to Francis Vincent of Stoke d'Abernon, Surrey, the portrait later came into the possession of the Rosebery family, as the only daughter of that marriage, Mary, married the third Earl of Rosebery around 1780. Arabella's third husband was James O'Donnell, a baronet (J. R. Burke, *Extinct and Dormant Baronetcies of England, Ireland and Scotland,* (second edition, London (1844), pp.23-4).

The dimensions of this and the portrait of Mr Swimmer given by Doray de Longrais and Prange are about the same as those of the portrait of Mrs Swimmer in Dalmeny House ($6\frac{1}{2} \times 3\frac{1}{2}$ Paris feet). The description leaves no doubt that this is the portrait in question. The portrait of Mr Swimmer, shown seated at a table and with account books as mercantile attributes, is lost. The two portraits may have been separated when Mrs Swimmer married a second time after the death of Mr Swimmer in 1760. Doray de Longrais has left an account of the execution of the portraits from information given by Nicolas Guibal, who was in Rome at the time. Mengs also did a pastel of *Flora and Ceres* for Swimmer. There was a disagreement between the painter and his sitter over the fee for the portraits, which Doray de Longrais describes as follows: 'Lorsque M. Mengs eut fini ces tableaux, on lui demanda combien il vouloit en avoir. Comme c'était un des primières qu'il faisait pour le public, & qu'il ne savait pas comment se règler dans cette affaire, pour que le prix n'effrayat pas les gens, & que pourtant il y trouvat son compte sans compromettre sa considération, il consulta M. Guibal, qui ignorait ce que Rigaud & Largillière les faisaient payer, lui dit qu'il ne connaissait que M. Nattier, peintre renommé à Paris, qui faisait payer de cette espèce de 1500 liv.; c'est à dire 300 écus romains. Suimars comme un homme de commerce qui connaissait plus les prix des espèces que de la peinture, & d'ailleurs mal conseillé par un nommé Bl qui était jaloux de n'avoir pas fait ces deux portraits, parla d'abord de crever les tableaux & de les bruler. Eh, qu'il fasse tout ce qu'il voudra, dit M. Mengs, pourvu qu'ils les paye – Il se serait relaché du prix, si M. Guibal ne lui eut fait voir les conséquences, tant pour son intéret que pour sa considération. Suimars enfin paya et s'en retourna content'.

According to Prange, the painter who made Swimmer suspicious of the price Mengs asked could have been Blanchet. He is probably right, for Blanchet was a portrait painter in Rome frequently commissioned by British visitors.

The subject is shown standing on a terrace before a low balustrade, beyond which extends a landscape. The ruined wall on the right, crowned by a vase, contains a fragment of a relief that has not as yet been identified. On the left in the background the ruins of the Imperial palace on the Palatine hill are to be seen, as is a small building, which according to Doray de Longrais is the Temple of Romulus. In using a landscape background Mengs is adopting a convention particularly favoured by Batoni in his portraits of British subjects after 1750. However, the pose, with Arabella Swimmer in a magnificent ball gown in the courtly style and with a mask in her hand, is in striking contrast to the idyllic Roman park landscape. Characteristically, Batoni clothed his female sitters in antique robes when painting them against a landscape background.

This work shows how greatly Mengs's portrait style was still influenced by court portraiture at the beginning of his third visit to Rome. Guibal, who criticised the inappropriate juxtaposition of a landscape background with a ball gown (see Doray de Longrais), praised the picture solely for the masterly handling of the paint. The depiction of the fabrics, lace and embroideries is indeed brilliant.

The dress is intended to be seen as festive attire for the carnival season, as the mask in Arabella Swimmer's hand makes clear. The Swimmers were in Rome during the carnival season. The mask in Reynolds's *Portrait of Kitty Hunter* of *c.*1760 could have a similar meaning (see exhibition catalogue *Reynolds* (London, Royal Academy (1986), p.212).

Mengs chose the same type of portrait for *Maria Luisa of Parma* in 1765 (Prado, Madrid) and for the celebrated *Portrait of the Marquesa de Llano* of 1770 (Academia de San Fernando, Madrid), which clearly recalls his image of Arabella Swimmer.

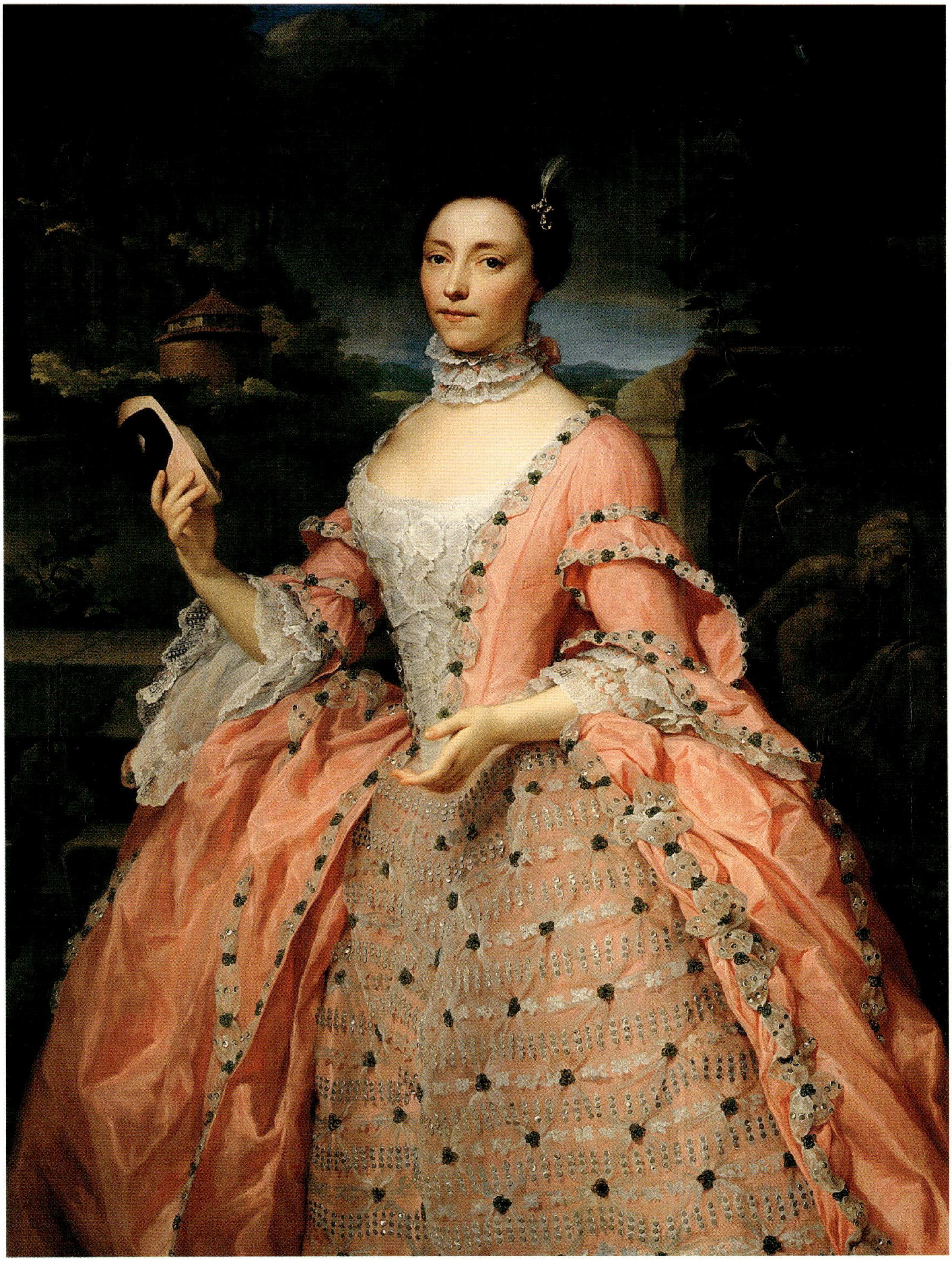

16
Portrait of Louis de Visme (1720-76)

Oil on canvas, 123.7 × 83 cm
Oxford, The Governing Body of Christ Church, inv.no.182

LITERATURE: *Catalogue of the Collection of Pictures in the Library, and Catalogue of the Portraits in the Hall* (Oxford, 1833), p.28; Mrs Reginald Lane Poole, *Catalogue of Portraits in the Possession of the University Colleges, City and County of Oxford* (1925), III, pp.70-1; Russell (1979), p.18.

Louis de Visme came from a family of Huguenots who had settled in England. He was a student at Christ Church from 1738, taking his Bachelor's degree in 1743 and his Master of Arts in 1746. As he was intended for the church he became a deacon, but then entered the diplomatic service. From 1762 to 1767 he was in Madrid; later he was a delegate to the court of Bavaria and from 1769 to 1773 he was British representative at the Regensburg parliament. From 1773 he was Special Ambassador to Stockholm, where he died in 1776.

The portrait must have come into the Christ Church collection after 1776, as it is not in the *Catalogue of the Collection of Pictures in the Library at Christ Church* which was published in that year.

De Visme made his Grand Tour from 1758 to 1759. This is evident from the profile drawing which Mengs made of him in 1759 and which is now in Otterloo (fig.20). The drawing bears the following note in the artist's hand: 'Louis de Visme/ Antonius Raphael Mengs fecit Roma Ano 1759'. We also have information on de Visme's visit to Rome from a letter from Cardinal Alessandro Albani to Horace Mann of 18 November 1758, informing him that he had received his letter of 15 October 1758 introducing Sir Wyndham Knatchbull-Wyndham and de Visme to him. So de Visme travelled to Italy with Sir Wyndham, although it is not clear in what capacity. The letter of recommendation from William Pitt for Sir Wyndham to Sir Horace Mann in Florence of 18 January 1758 speaks of 'Mr Devisme, a Gentleman of much worth' (Clark Bowron (1985), p.276). As de Visme was seventeen years older than Sir Wyndham, he was probably acting as his tutor. Sir Wyndham had his portrait painted by Batoni during his stay in Rome. It is full-length, and Winckelmann, who as secretary to Albani naturally met the sitter in Rome, thought it one of Batoni's best works (Clark Bowron (1985), no.218, Fig.199).

The portrait in Oxford must have been painted, as Russell also thinks, in the years when de Visme was in Madrid (1762-67). Unlike the portraits of the British tourists which Mengs painted in Rome, he has here used the Court portrait type, which was indeed appropriate given the diplomatic status of his client in Madrid. De Visme wears court dress, as the dagger at his side confirms, and he is shown standing in a room which can be recognized as the interior of the palace by the pilasters on the right and the red curtain on the left. The letter, which may appear to be an arbitrary choice of attribute, is appropriate to his work as a diplomat.

The portrait is distinguished by great simplicity and objectivity. The strong, glowing colours and the emphasis on the verticals provide a clear structure which is dignified but not pompous. This portrait of de Visme is an almost ideal typification of the eighteenth-century diplomat, efficient and distinguished but without vanity. A greater difference than that between this portrait and the profile head and shoulders in the classical style, which Mengs drew of de Visme in 1759, can hardly be imagined. The difference clearly reveals the gulf between the life-style and appearance of the British gentleman when in Italy, and when in his accustomed role in society.

A portrait of de Visme was in Mengs's estate after his death in 1779. It was valued at 60 scudi, so it must be the study from life.

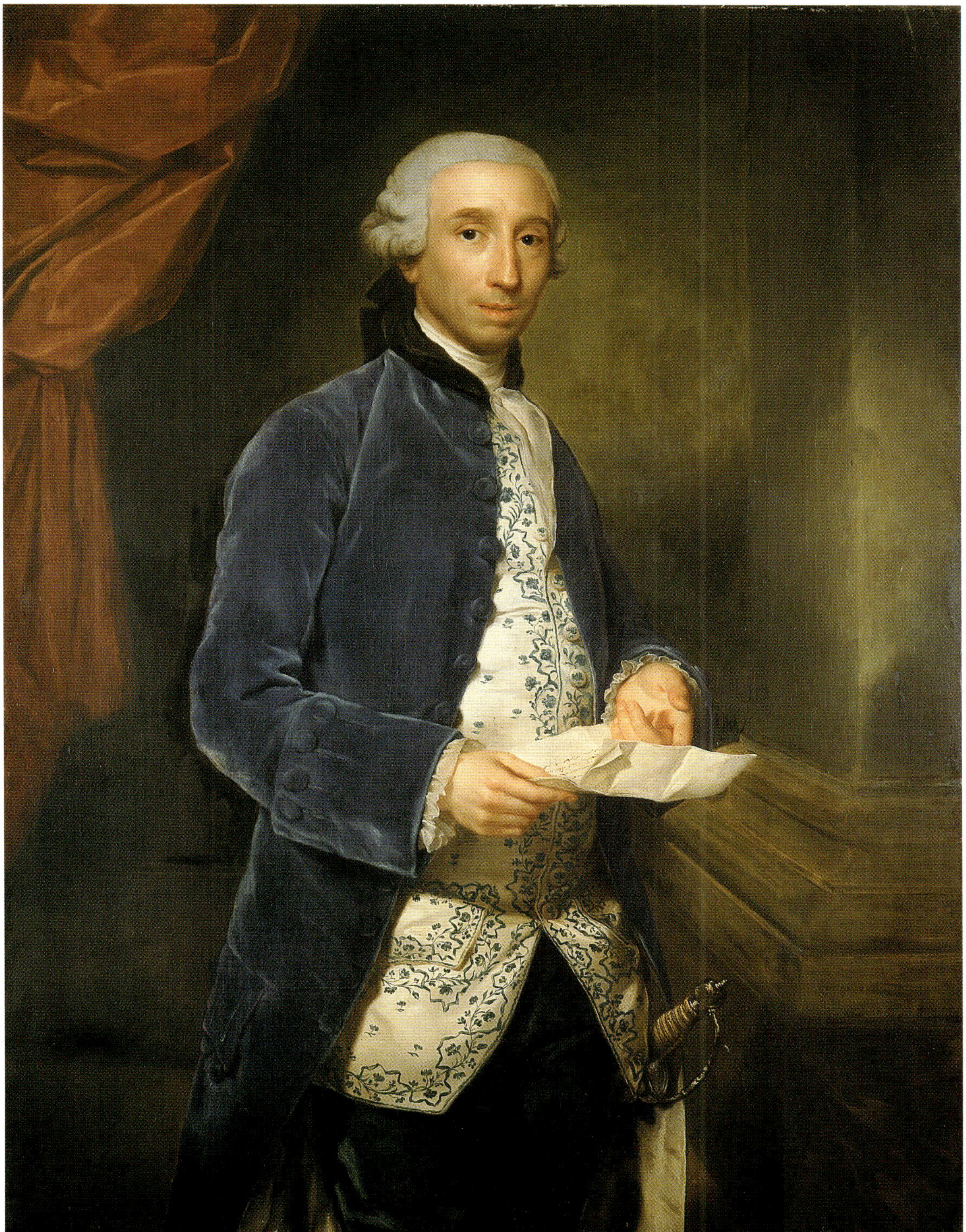

17

Portrait of Sir Charles Hanbury Williams (1708-59)

Oil on canvas, 110 × 83 cm
Inscribed on the letter held by the sitter, text largely illegible (A / M Mons / chevalie / à / Lor) 1757
Warsaw, National Museum, (Catalogue 1969, no.799)

PROVENANCE: Stanislav Augustus of Poland (1732-98); Galerie Lazienski, Warsaw (until 1939); acquired for the Museum in Warsaw in 1945

LITERATURE: Bianconi (1780), pp.29-30; Doray de Longrais (1782), pp.36-7; Prange I (1786), p.161; Azara-Fea (1787), p.XLII; S. Iskierski, *Catalogue Galeriji obrazow palacu w Lazienkach w Warszawie* (Warsaw, 1931), no.88; T. Mankowski, *Galeria Stanislawa Augusta* (Lvov, 1932), no.736; Honisch (1965), no.97 and p.19; (Exhibition Catalogue; *Angelika Kauffmann und ihre Zeitgenossen* (Brengenz & Vienna), 1968-9), no.336; *Muzeum Narodowe w Warszawie, Catalogue of Paintings, I, European Schools* (Warsaw, 1969), no.799 (with further literature); Russell (1979), p.19.

Sir Charles Hanbury Williams was already a well-known and highly-regarded writer, poet and satirist, when he decided, after the death of his friend Thomas Winnington in January 1746, to embark on a second career as a diplomat. He had been educated at Eton and made his Grand Tour in about 1730. In 1744 he was made a Knight of the Bath and built a stately home in Coldbrook, south of Abergavenny.

Sir Charles's first diplomatic mission was in 1746, to the court of Dresden, and it was during this time that he wrote a volume of letters on Germany. In 1748 Henry Fox vainly attempted to obtain the post of British Ambassador to Turin for him, and in July 1749 he went to the court of the Margrave of Ansbach-Bayreuth and then in 1750 to Berlin. Here he was posted back to Dresden; he reached the city in February 1751 and soon made the acquaintance of Mengs, who had just been appointed Principal Painter to the Court of Saxony. In 1753 Sir Charles left Dresden again, going first to Vienna and then back to England. In 1754 he returned to Dresden for a brief period, but after a dispute with Count Brühl left the court to move to St Petersburg in 1755, where he remained, until 1757. On his return from St Petersburg he collapsed in Hamburg, and died, apparently by his own hand, on 2 November 1759 in that city.

Sir Charles's intense activities as ambassador were not only due to what his own contemporaries called his 'restless spirit'; they were dictated by the changing pattern of European alliances on the eve of the Seven Years' War. Saxony was allied with Austria, Russia and France against Prussia and England, who then formed an alliance (Westminster Convention, 16 January 1756). The many verses and other writings by Sir Charles, who was friendly with many of his distinguished contemporaries, particularly Horace Walpole, came into the possession of his son-in-law, the Fourth Earl of Essex, after his death. Essex had married Sir Charles's eldest daughter on 1 August 1754. Sir Charles's eventful life and unusual character have been the subject of several biographies (*e.g.* B. Horn, *Sir Charles Hanbury Williams and European Diplomacy* (1748-1758), London, 1929). A three-volume edition of his writings, with commentaries by Horace Walpole, did not, however, appear until 1820-22.

In view of the dates that have been verified, Mengs's portrait must have been painted in the brief time between February 1751 and the painter's departure from Dresden in September of that year. Indeed, the available time must have been even shorter, for Sir Charles made his first visit to Warsaw in February 1751, where Augustus III was holding a parliament.

Regarding the more immediate circumstances of the commission, Bianconi tells us that Sir Charles felt a very warm and immediate attachment for Mengs. 'It was as if he could not live without him. This unwonted affection distracted and disturbed the artist, who was very busy, to no inconsiderable degree'. Bianconi, who probably met Sir Charles in Dresden, writes: 'Anyone who knew this particular Englishman and has seen his portrait, will be able to say whether it would be possible to paint a head more like. It seemed to me as if it were full of fire and life, like the man himself'. The tenor of Doray de Longrais's anecdote is similar. He recounts that the Irishman Hupton, who visited Mengs in his studio in Rome, was startled by the portrait, thinking for a moment that he saw the man, who was his mortal enemy, before him. Mengs's pupil Nicolas Guibal also praised the quality of the portrait: 'The portrait he made of him was admirable' (Prange).

Bianconi says that Mengs's portrait was never in fact finished, because Sir Charles unexpectedly had to leave for St Petersburg. However, he must be mistaken, for Lord Essex, later Sir Charles's son-in-law, already mentions that Mengs's portrait is in his possession in a letter to Horace Walpole in July 1752 (Walpole, *Correspondence*, Yale Edition 1937ff. p.52). Lord Essex was in Germany in 1751 and he might have taken the picture back to England with him after a visit to Dresden.

Bianconi's error may possibly be explained by the fact that he saw a portrait of Sir Charles on a later visit to Mengs's Roman studio, either the study from life or the second version of the portrait, which is also mentioned by Guibal and other contemporaries (see Introduction). The

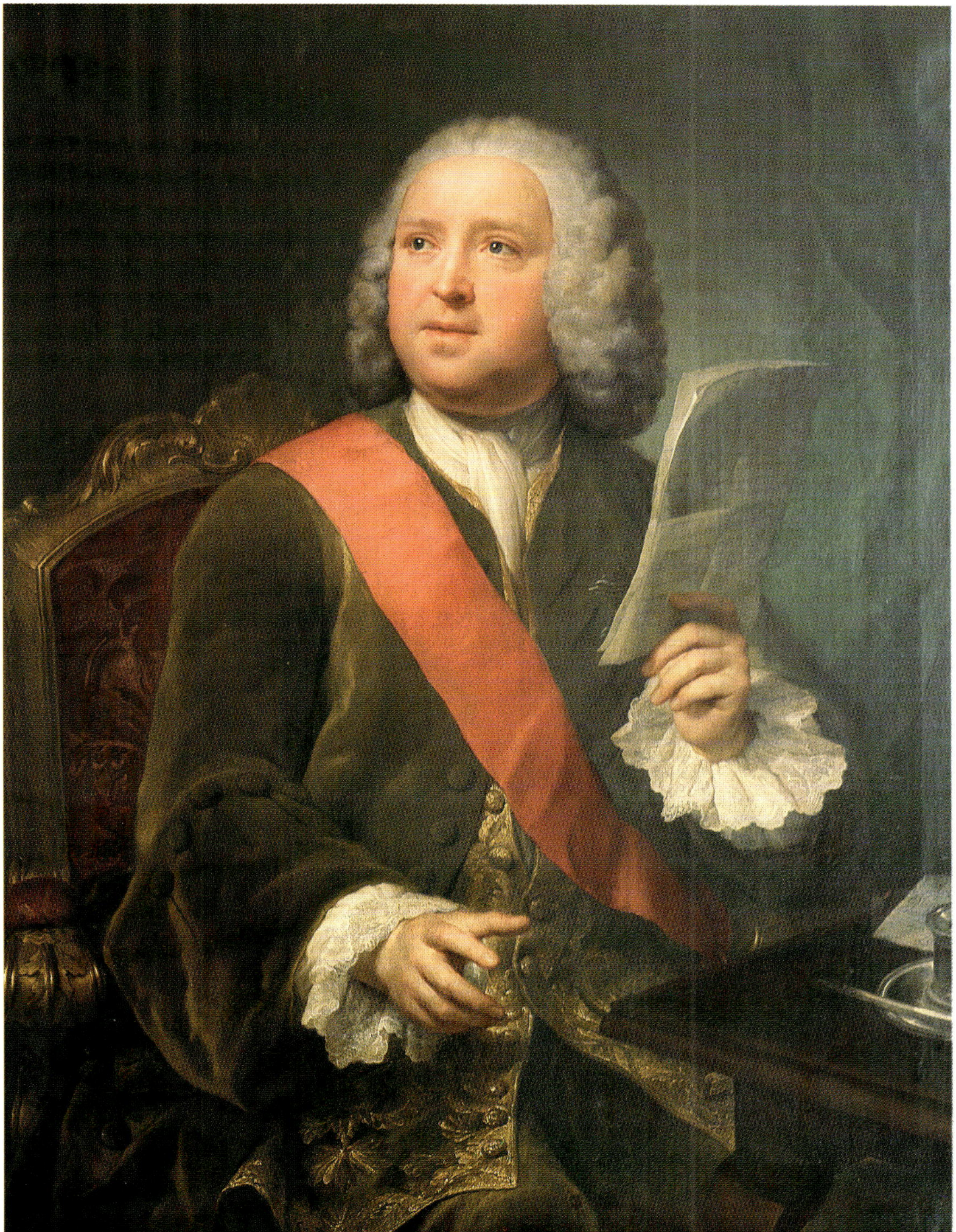

second is identical either with a version that is now in the Palazzo Colonna in Rome and which probably came from Mengs's estate, or with the Warsaw portrait, which, being from the Poniatowski collection, must have come from either Rome or St Petersburg. We know that Poniatowski was a close confident of Catherine the Great, who purchased a number of paintings from Mengs's estate in 1781, including several British portraits. Catherine corresponded with Sir Charles for a considerable time and this could explain her interest in the portrait. It is also possible that there was a connection between her great esteem for Mengs and her personal relationship with Sir Charles, as Sir Charles was one of the first great admirers of Mengs (see Introduction).

The Warsaw painting certainly cannot be the version that was in the possession of Sir Charles's heirs, as we know from the well-documented history of the original, which was in the possession of Sir John Hanbury Williams from 1922 and was lost in an air raid during the Second World War (see John Kerslake, *Early Georgian Portraits* London, National Portrait Gallery (1977), p.311). This version has come down to us in an engraving by R. Rhodes from a drawing by J. Thurston, used as the frontispiece to the first volume of Sir Charles's writings, published in 1820. The engraving bears the text: 'From the picture by Mengs in the Collection of the Right Hon. the Earl of Essex'. The portrait is apparently the same as the Warsaw picture. A miniature copy of this portrait was in the possession of Lord Malden in 1794, and it was used by W. N. Gardner for an engraving in Harding's 'Biographical Mirror'. Possibly the miniature was the one by Serre mentioned in the letter from Lord Essex to Horace Walpole mentioned above (see Kerslake (1977), p.311).

Guibal says that Mengs, although he refused Sir Charles's offer to go to England out of loyalty to his King, 'always spoke of the Cavalier with great warmth'. The mutual affection between the painter and his subject finds vivid expression in the portrait, for although Sir Charles is shown in the official court dress of a diplomat and has struck a dignified pose, the picture is lively and natural. The type is unusual for Mengs, showing the sitter seated and down to the knees. This pose was used in British portraiture for dignitaries, as in William Hogarth's *Portrait of Captain Coram*, and it is possible that the sitter chose it, being familiar with that tradition. The red sash and letter indicate Sir Charles's activity as diplomat.

Kerslake mentions several other portraits of Sir Charles, including one by J. G. Eccardt in the National Portrait Gallery in London of about 1746, which was formerly erroneously ascribed to Mengs, and other portraits by James Worsdale of 1733 and Vanloo of 1744. A copy by Sir Joshua Reynolds of Mengs's portrait of 1757 is mentioned by Graves and Cronin in *A History of the Works of Sir Joshua Reynolds* (1899-1901), p.1055 (see Kerslake (1977), p.311).

A half-length portrait by Giuseppe Maria Crespi, showing Sir Charles in front of a landscape with a letter in his hand, was auctioned by Sotheby's in London on 24 June 1970 (lot 102). It was identified by A. M. Clark and it is clearly similar in physiognomy to the Mengs portrait. It was probably painted when Sir Charles was in Italy on his Grand Tour, in 1730.

18
Portrait of Richard Wilson (1713-82)

Oil on canvas, 101.5 × 81.3 cm
Cardiff, National Museum of Wales

PROVENANCE: Sir Watkin Williams-Wynn, Wynnstay; auctioned at Christie's, London, 5.2.1947, lot 45, bought by Renwick; purchased for the Museum in Cardiff in 1947 with funds from the National Art Collections Fund.

LITERATURE: Dorey de Longrais (1782), p.37; Prange I (1786), p.120; Azara-Fea (1787), p.XLII; W. H. Hodges, 'Life of Richard Wilson', *European Magazine* (June 1790); Benjamin Booth, MS of the last decade of the 18th century (Brinsley Ford, London); Edwards, *Anecdotes of Painters* (London, 1808), pp.78-9; Collected volume: *The Fine Arts of the English School* (London, 1812); Farington's Diary, 21.6.1823 (MS Royal Library, Windsor); Wright, *Life of Richard Wilson Esq. R. A.* (London, 1824), p.75; *Catalogue of Art Treasures of the United Kingdom collected at Manchester in 1857*, British Portrait Gallery N.311; D. Cooper, 'The Iconography of Richard Wilson', *Burlington Magazine*, 90 (1948), pp.109-116; H. Granville, 'A Portrait of Richard Wilson', *Connoisseur*, CXXII (March 1948), p.54; Brinsley Ford, *The Drawings of Richard Wilson* (London, 1951), pp.14, 22; G. Constable, *Richard Wilson* (... 1953), pp.67-8; Honisch (1965), no.413, p.148; exhibition catalogue *Gifts to Galleries* (Liverpool, Walker Art Gallery, 1968), no.59, p.29; Denys Sutton and Ann Clements, *An Italian Sketchbook by Richard Wilson* (London, 1968), p.10; Russell (1979), p.19.

EXHIBITIONS: 1857 Manchester; 1876 Wrexham; 1924 Bangor; 1949 Birmingham; 1961 Manchester; 1968 Liverpool.

Richard Wilson commenced his journey to Italy from London in 1750, and in October or November of that year he reached Venice, where he remained until towards the end of 1751. On Wilson's stay in Venice see M. Levey, 'Wilson and Zuccarelli at Venice', *Burlington Magazine* (1959), pp.139-143. From Venice Wilson travelled on to Rome in the company of Thomas Jenkins and William Locke. He arrived in the city before 13 January 1752. In 1753 he was staying with Thomas Jenkins in a house on the Piazza di Spagna 'verso Propaganda Fide'. He is known to have been in Rome until 1756, and probably he remained there until 1757, for it was not until 1758 that he returned to London.

Circumstances in Mengs's biography suggest that the portrait was painted around 1752. It is uncertain whether his stay in Venice coincided with Wilson's (see Introduction), but certainly the two artists were in close contact in Rome. From a letter written by Wilson to Ralph Howard on 28 August 1752 it is clear that Wilson was hoping to be elected a member of the Accademia di San Luca and to be awarded a professorship there. Mengs was elected a member in the same year (see Introduction).

The portrait was engraved twice by W. Bromley (in 1785 and 1790) and twice by W. Bond (1812 and 1824). Bromley's plate of 1790 gives the date of the portrait as 1752. Cooper thought that the exact dating on this plate derived from information given by William Hodges, who published an article on Wilson in the European Magazine in 1790. Bromley's engraving was used to illustrate the article. As Hodges was a pupil of Wilson, and as Benjamin Booth also gives 1752 as the date of the portrait in his manuscript of the 1790s, referring to the engraving and to Hodges, who gave him the engraving, the date can be taken as verified.

Wilson is shown in a richly patterned coat and silk turban. he is seated in a relaxed pose in an armchair, the arm of which, with his lower arm resting on it, forms the lower edge of the picture. The back of the chair and the picture on the easel give the composition a firm inner cohesion, and the head is optically centred although it is not in the middle of the picture.

The painter is seated before his easel, on which we see a landscape, and in his left hand he holds his palette and several brushes or pencils. The impression is that he has just broken off from his work for a moment and turned to the portraitist, and this gives the picture almost the character of a self-portrait. Mengs used the same type of composition in his own self-portrait of 1774, now in Liverpool, placing himself in a very similar position before his easel (cat.no.1).

The gentle colouring, with its muted browns and greens from which only the strong pink of the flesh tints and the specks of paint on the palette stand out, strengthens the sense of calm composure which the picture as a whole conveys. The unpretentious bourgeois apparel, combined with the evident self-confidence and understandable pride of the artist – the chair is like a throne separating him from the viewer – are the characteristic features here. This is a professional portrait, the depiction of a reserved middle class artist's view of himself.

According to Prange, Wilson painted two landscapes for Mengs in return for the portrait, but Walmsley's *Physiognomical Portraits* states that according to Edwards Mengs painted the work in return for one of Wilson's landscapes. It may have been the landscape at which Wilson is working in the portrait. The portrait was copied by Cooper and Constable, and there are numerous derivations and graphic reproductions. This was no doubt due to Wilson's enduring fame as one of the leading British landscape painters, which continued throughout the nineteenth century.

Nevertheless, Peter Cannon-Brookes has doubted that the Cardiff portrait is by Mengs's hand (in a conversation). He regards the painting as a copy by Wilson of Mengs's original, now supposedly lost, and no doubt he had in mind a similar chain of events as occurred with the work from which Bond made his engraving in 1812. The inscription on Bond's engraving states that it is from a copy of the painting made by John Taylor from the original under Wilson's supervision (Cooper (1948), p.110, Constable (1953), p.68). Bond's engraving is indeed closer to the Cardiff picture in its handling of the lozenge-shaped pattern on the turban than the copy by Edward Penny (National Portrait Gallery, inv.1803, see Cooper (1948), p.113) and an engraving by Pye of 1822 (Walmsley, *Physiognomical Portraits* (London 1824), vol.II). The similarity is not enough however to confirm that the picture in Cardiff, the style and quality of which are absolutely convincing and authentic, is a copy. Taylor's copy was probably a miniature, and this would explain the fidelity to the original of Bond's engraving.

Of all the painted copies in the National Portrait Gallery Penny's is the best (see also inv.383, 1305). The copy numbered 1305 in the inventory bears on its reverse the inscription 'A correct likeness of Richard Wilson after Mengs of Rome 1756', so it must be by an English artist who could have copied the portrait in Rome in 1756.

The drawing in the British Museum (inv.1881-6-11-201) which Cooper and Constable thought was a preliminary drawing by Mengs, is certainly a copy. It is not only dependent in every detail on the executed painting, it is also largely in the same format (464 × 301 mm). That means that it was probably traced from the original by a copyist, to serve as the basis for a copy of the portrait. It may have been Penny's tracing for his copy. Finally, we should point out that Bond's engraving of 1812 proves the provenance from the collection of Sir Watkin Williams-Wynn, the patron who commissioned but never owned Mengs's painting of *Perseus and Andromeda* (see Introduction).

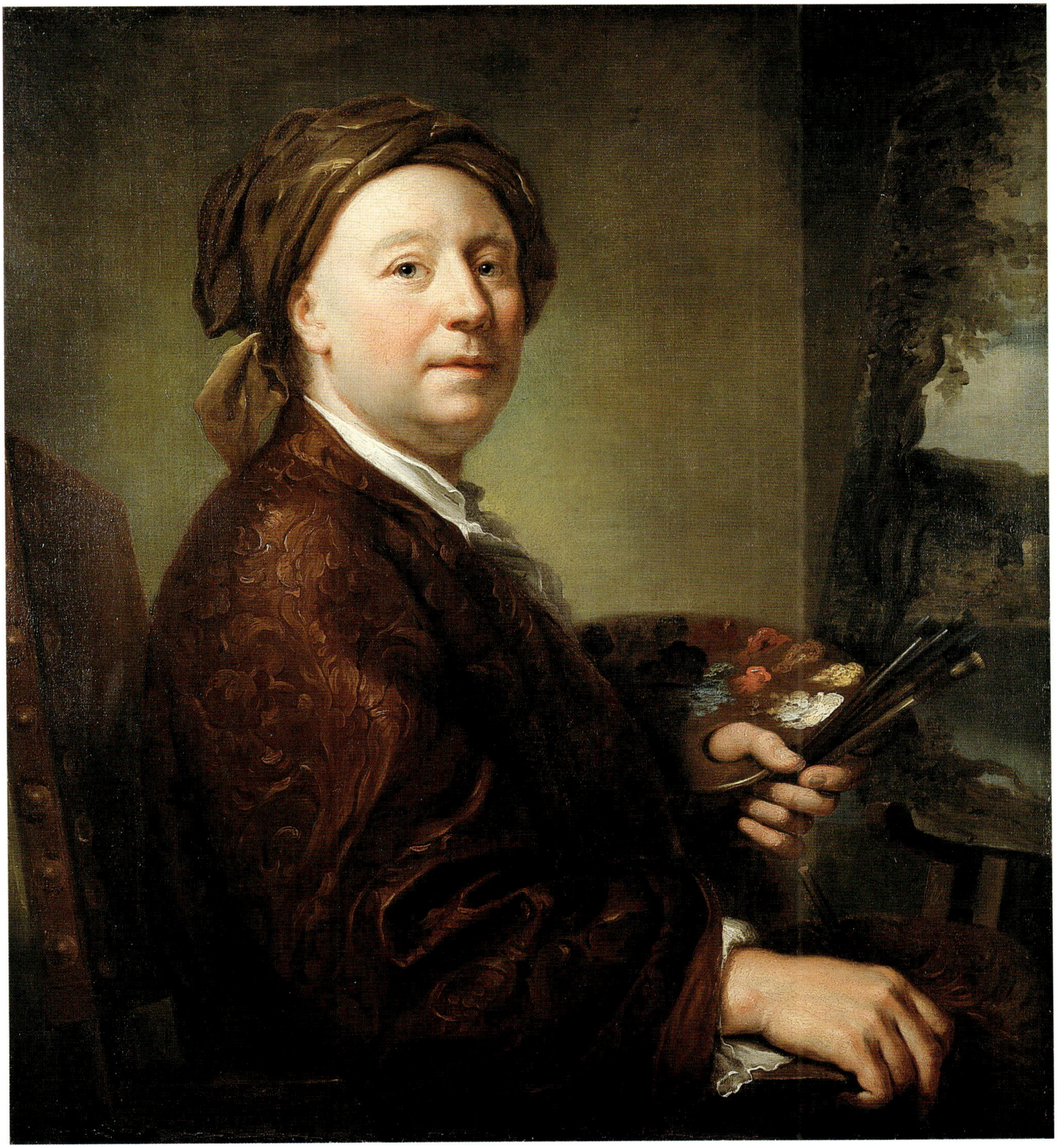

19

The Holy Family with St Elizabeth and St John the Baptist

Oil on canvas, 186.7 × 143.8 cm
London, Chaucer Fine Arts

PROVENANCE: Thomas Jenkins 1761-65; Sir William Weddell 1765-92

LITERATURE: Ratti (1779), p.II; Bianconi (1780), p.15: Doray de Longrais (1782), p.6; Prange I (1786), pp.35, 148-9, 152, 223; Azara-Fea (1787), p.XVII, XLII; Ponz, XIV (1788), Carta II; Azara (1796), p.6; Honisch (1965), p.128; Woodbridge (1965), p.106; Finke (1981), p.71; Exhibition catalogue, *Paintings, Mannerism to Romanticism 1550 to 1850*, London, Chaucer Fine Arts, 1986, no.29; Roettgen (1990), pp.628-9.

This painting must be identified as a work which Mengs painted towards the end of his second period in Rome, that is, in 1748-9, for Augustus III, Elector of Saxony and King of Poland. The picture is in large format and it was the first he displayed to the Roman public who warmly applauded him for his work.

We have information on the subsequent history of the picture in a letter from Thomas Jenkins to Sir Henry Hoare of 29 July 1761. Jenkins speaks of the acquisitions he made from Mengs's studio before the artist's departure for Spain: 'I am now Master of his finest work, being if I may be allowed the expression, his Price Picture, it is the Holy family that he painted for the King of Poland and on account of a few Cracks in it occasioned by an uncommon body of Colour least it should displease the Court, he intends to paint the same Subject over again the King pays him 700 zecchins, I got this for half price'. On a visit to Jenkins in May 1764 the Englishman James Martin saw the picture, as he recounts in the diary of his tour, which Brinsley Ford has studied (Ford (1974), p.419). A short time later the picture was bought by William Weddell, who purchased a large part of Jenkins's collection of antiquities on his visit to Rome from 1765 to 1766. These are still in Newby Hall.

Weddell had certainly had his portrait painted by Batoni, and it is known that he possessed this painting from the inscription on a signed copy by Nikolaus Mosmann in the British Museum (see cat.no.46). However, Mosmann's drawing was not based on the painting in Weddell's collection, but either on the cartoon or the second version made for Augustus III, which never came into his possession. A similar set of circumstances can be observed in other cases as well, namely, that a painting originally intended for Augustus III was acquired by a British visitor to Rome (Ratti (1779), p.II). Other sources confirm this pattern.

On 27 May 1802 a painting of this subject was auctioned at Christie's, and according to the catalogue it was a copy of a work by Mengs. The picture was purchased by a Mr Bentley for 20.17 guineas, and it came from the collection of 'Count Wedell' (see Fredericksen (1988), p.455). It may in fact have been the original, for the painting does have a certain timidity in the handling of the paint and an almost miniaturist attention to detail, so that it could have been taken for a copy. Certainly a copy of the painting has not as yet been positively identified. The proof that the exhibited painting is in fact the original can be seen in the face of the Madonna, who, according to Mengs's biographer Bianconi, bears the features of Margherita Guazzi. She was a Roman girl praised by many contemporaries for her beauty who sat for the Madonna, only to have Mengs fall in love with her. He married her the same year. The similarity of the Madonna's features with those of Margherita Mengs is only evident in the first version, not in the second, as we see from a comparison with other paintings for which the painter's wife acted as model.

Both the cartoon and the second version of the painting were purchased by Catherine the Great of Russia from the artist's estate; the painting is now in Pavlovsk and is attributed to Anton von Maron. The signed copy by Mosmann is very similar to the painting in Pavlovsk, particularly in the face of the Madonna, and this suggests that it was based on the cartoon or the second version. There is a design sketch for the composition in the Cabinet des Dessins in the Louvre, but a second sketch has only survived in a counterproof (Philadelphia, Museum of Fine Arts). The Albertina in Vienna has a chalk study for the head of St Elizabeth which is executed in great detail, and gives an idea of how extensive and careful the young artist's preliminary work for this first major painting was.

The condition of the painting also confirms what Jenkins says of its subsequent history. In many places, and especially in the flesh tints, the paint has been applied so thickly and mixed with so much oil that cracks have formed, greater than would normally be expected. There may have been some retouching and overpainting in places, on the head of the infant John the Baptist, for example. These technical defects show how difficult it was for the young artist, who was only twenty when he executed this work, to start out as a subject painter and tackle a format as large as this.

It was inevitable that Mengs would turn to his inspiration Raphael for both the thematic and formal elements of his composition. Mengs presented himself to Augustus III

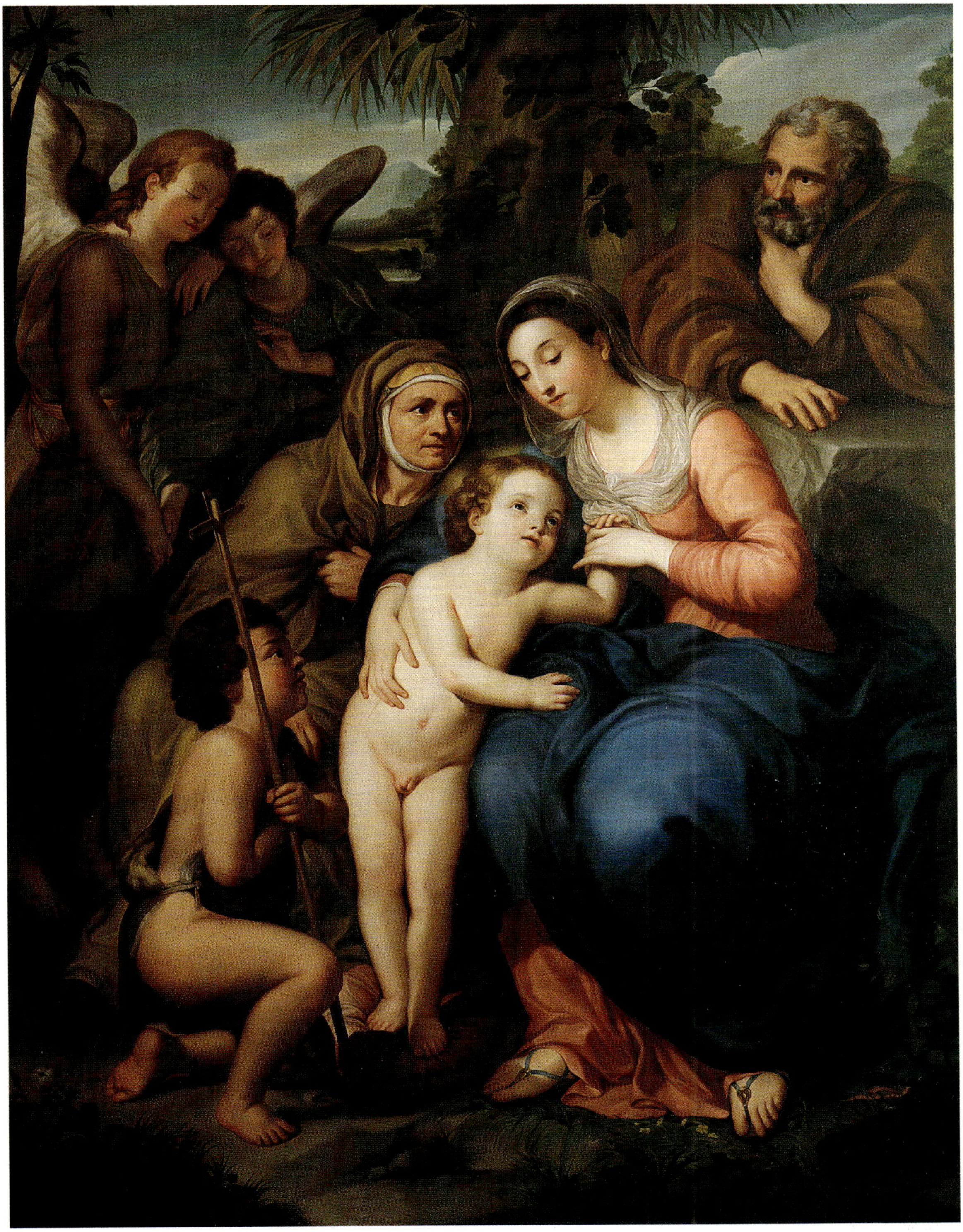

with this painting as a German Raphael, a future he had almost been specifically trained for. The King had sent him to Rome twice to study Raphael, and it may be assumed that the intention was already present when the artist was given his name. Certainly it corresponded to the political and religious tendencies at the court of Dresden, which had been an island of Catholicism in the midst of a Protestant state since the union of Saxony and Poland in the person of Augustus the Strong. Augustus III greatly esteemed Raphael and Correggio, and this was evident in the pictures he purchased for the gallery in Dresden. He had a particular fondness for the *Holy Family* by Raphael which had once belonged to Francis I of France (Paris, Louvre). Mengs was largely influenced by that composition, but he was also inspired by the *Madonna del Divino Amore* (Naples, Museo Nazionale), which he had copied in miniature.

In its rather naïve character and the lack of skill evident, for example, in the foliage on the trees and the foreground, Mengs's painting is a vivid illustration of how the young artist was moving in a new direction in his interpretation of Raphael. He was turning away from the watered-down version of Raphael's art practised by his contemporaries in Rome, and an episode that has been recorded in connection with the picture underlines this. A Roman prelate praised the picture by comparing it with works by Maratti. Mengs was not particularly pleased at this, as he was trying to approach Raphael in a different way from the Roman seventeenth- and eighteenth-century schools. He was endeavouring to restore some of Raphael's original child-like spirit, as the Nazarenes were to do later. The result was bound to appear as a striking novelty in Roman painting around 1750.

However, Mengs soon abandoned this approach to Raphael, presumably because it seemed too primitive and artificial to him. This was probably the reason why he repeated his composition in a more mature style closer to the Roman tradition. It was however the first version with which he made his name in Rome in 1749 as the successor to Raphael, and so Jenkins was right when he called this work Mengs's 'price picture'.

20
The Glory of St Eusebius

Oil on canvas, 73.3 × 36.5 cm
Manchester, City Art Galleries

PROVENANCE: Count de Saint-Saphorin, Vienna; Czernin Collection, Vienna (inventory of 1844); auctioned at Christie's, London, 2.7.1965; Alfred Brod Gallery, London, from whom bought March 1966

LITERATURE: Prange (1786) I, p.121; Karl Gustav Waagen, *Die vornehmsten Kunstdenmäler in Wien* (Vienna, 1866), p.307; K. Wilczek, *Katalog der Czernin'schen Gemäldegalerie in Wien* (Vienna, 1936), p.293; Honisch, (1965), no.349; auction catalogue, Christie's, London, 2.7.1965, lot 24; Thomas Poensgen, *Die Deckenmalerei der italienischen Kirchen* (Berlin, 1969), p.93.

This oil sketch is unusually spontaneous and colourful for Mengs, and it documents the earliest phase of the work on the fresco for the church of Sant' Eusebio in Rome, on which Mengs was working from 1757 to 1759. It shows the apotheosis of the Roman Bishop Eusebius, who suffered martyrdom under Pope Liberius between 352 AD and 366 AD. The attributes of the chain and chalice, which Mengs added in the fresco to identify the saint clearly, have not yet been added in the sketch, and this may explain why in the older literature it is referred to as depicting the apotheosis of St Erasmus.

The Sant'Eusebio painting is the first fresco which Mengs painted and the first major commission he received in Rome. The main part of the work was finished by the summer of 1757, but it went on until the summer of 1759. In the execution Mengs was assisted by Maron, who already had practical experience of the difficult technique of fresco painting. Another assistant was James Byres (see Introduction, p.16), who was a friend of Mengs and Maron. As he did not yet have any experience of painting his assistance was presumably limited to fetching and carrying.

Frescos are painted directly on to the wet plaster, and the work requires not only extensive preparations in drawings and cartoons but also a particular kind of paint. The artist also needs a number of assistants and persons to hand when executing a fresco, and for that reason scarcely any of the painters in Rome were still practising the genuine fresco technique by 1760. Generally wall and ceiling paintings were executed in tempera, which was much less elaborate and much faster. Tempera can be applied to dry plaster and the colours are more luminous than in pure fresco painting.

In view of the labour involved the fee of 200 Scudi plus expenditure on scaffolding and plasterers and board and lodging was extremely meagre. The painter probably only

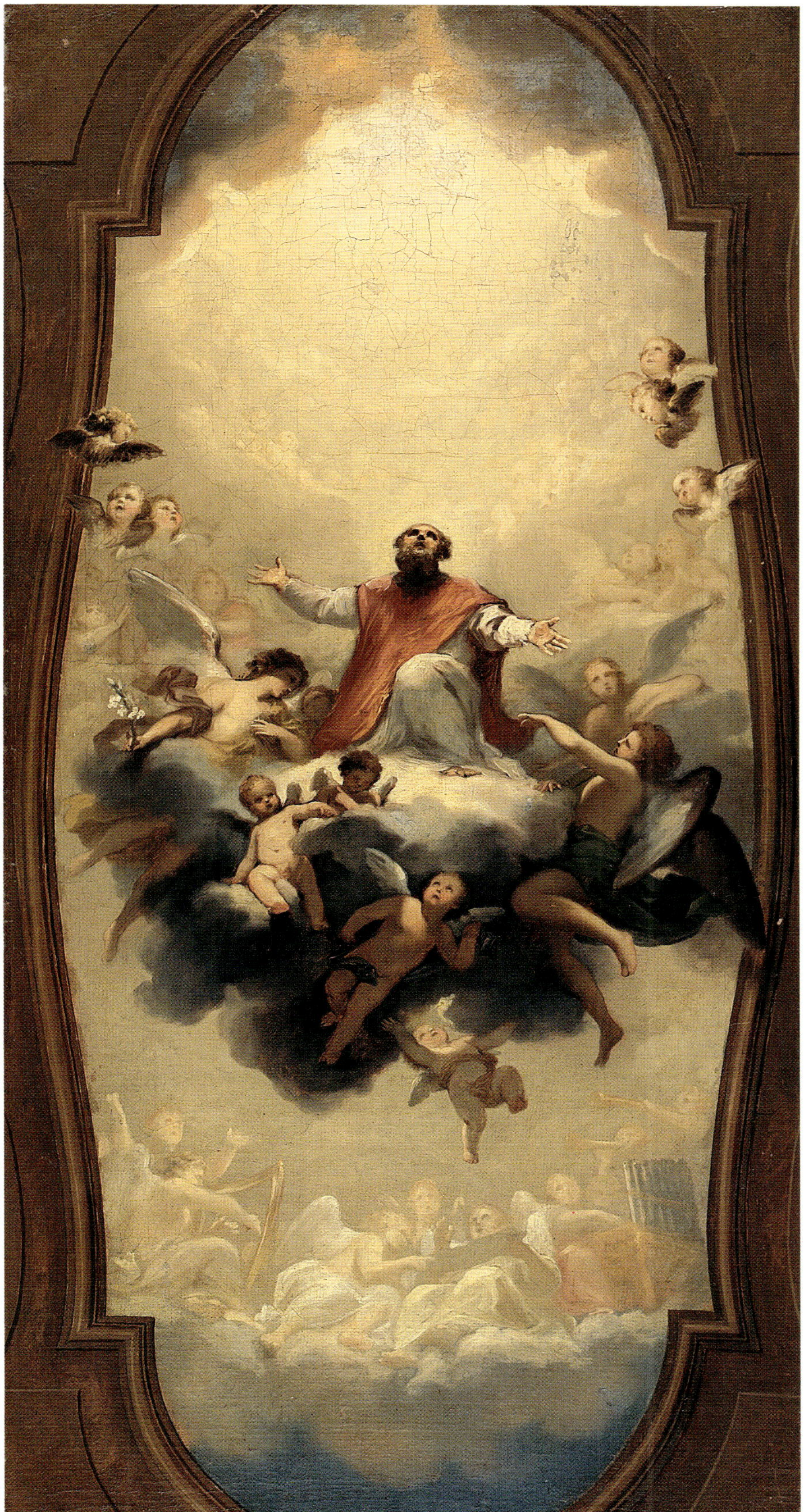

accepted the commission because his salary from Dresden had not been paid owing to the Seven Years' War.

In executing this work Mengs was placing himself in the tradition of Roman ceiling painting, and he was fully aware of the standards he had to meet. Shortly before, the Director of the French Academy, Charles Natoire, had completed his ceiling fresco in the church of San Luigi dei Francesi in Rome, and Mengs had been one of his sharpest critics.

In his composition Mengs looked to Correggio, whose frescos in Parma he had studied as a young man; in particular the depictions of the Evangelists in the pendentives of the cupola in the cathedral served him as models. But he was also influenced by Roman ceiling painting of the seventeenth and eighteenth centuries (Giuseppe Chiari and Marco Benefial). It was clearly Mengs's ambition in this work to show his Roman contemporaries how a foreigner could enter the Italian tradition of monumental fresco painting in the wake of Correggio.

The success of the composition, the mastery of perspective with its foreshortening of the figures (known as 'sotto in su'), and the accuracy of the drawing were the elements with which his fresco convinced the critics. A particular virtue was seen to be his colouring; this was so powerful and saturated that it looked like oil painting. Mengs himself was certainly pleased with the reaction, as his biographers tell us. The sketch in Manchester differs considerably from the executed composition, but it does give an idea of the strong and glowing colours which the fresco must originally have had. Sadly, they have suffered from the passage of time and bad restoration work.

The central group with the saint ascending in the midst of an angelic host is even more isolated in the first sketch, which may have been the presentation piece, than in a later one (Madrid, Azara's heirs) and in the final work. The highlights and the strong contrasts of light and shade give the picture an almost Rococo character; in the fresco this gives way to a monumental academic approach, although this was partly the result of the scale. A design for the composition based on this first sketch is in Rouen (see exhibition catalogue *La Rome baroque*, Paris, Louvre, (1990-1), no.145).

21
The Penitent Magdalen with a Cross

Oil on canvas, 111 × 89 cm
London, Chaucer Fine Arts

PROVENANCE: Colonel Joseph Weld, Lulworth Castle; Sotheby's 12 December 1980, lot 101.

LITERATURE: Bianconi (1780), unpag.(95); Doray de Longrais (1782), p.37; Jansen (1786), I, p.68; Prange (1786), I, p.122; Azara-Fea (1787), p.XLII; Azara (1796), p.6; H. Blunell, *An Account of the Statues... and Paintings at Ince* (1803), no.XXXVIII, p.223; Honisch (1965), no.253; auction catalogue Sotheby's 12.12.1980, pp.200-1; catalogue *Collecting in the 18th Century*, Chaucer Fine Arts (London, 1981), no.12.

EXHIBITION: Paintings from Lulworth Castle, Bournemouth, Rund-Cotes Art Gallery and Museum, 1967, no.81.

This is presumably the first version of a painting of which two other versions by the artist's own hand exist. One is also shown in this exhibition (cat.no.22). A third, now in El Pardo and formerly in La Granja, was painted shortly after Mengs arrived in Spain and was commissioned by the Queen Mother, Isabella Farnese. This Spanish version differs from the two shown here, which were painted in Rome, mainly in the less vivid colours and softer modelling. The differences in the motifs of the two English works are minimal and are mainly on the picture frame edges, in the facial shading and in the modelling.

The *Penitent Magdalen* repentent that is known to have been in England in the eighteenth century must be one of the three half-length figures which Mengs painted for British clients in 1761, according to Azara. A further indication that at least one of the two versions shown here was already in England in the eighteenth century is a print by an engraver named Chambers, about whom nothing else is known; the print must have been made during Mengs's lifetime. The text on it reads: 'Anthony Raphael Mengs / painter to his Majesty the King of Poland. Chambers sculpsit'. So far I have only found one of these prints, in the Albertina in Vienna.

A *St Mary Magdalen* by Mengs was offered as lot 32 in the auction sale in London on 16.5.1776 of the collection of paintings owned by Consul Smith, who died in Venice in 1770. It is uncertain whether this is a picture from the Consul's collection (see Frances Vivian, *The Consul Smith Collection, Masterpieces of Italian Drawing from the Royal Library, Windsor Castle*, exhibition catalogue (1989), p.91). However, it is very probable that the painting auctioned in 1776 was one of the two exhibited here, as so far no other Magdalen by Mengs is known to be in an English collection. The assumption is also supported by the fact that this is the most successful version of the subject which Mengs produced.

After Mengs's departure from Rome a version of the painting in his own hand remained in his studio, where it was copied by Nikolaus Mosmann (London, British Museum, Department of Prints and Drawings, Mosmann Drawings, vol.VI, no.212). It is identical to the second painting shown here (cat.no.22).

The subject of St Mary Magdalen repentant played a large part in Italian seventeenth-century painting, and it was still very popular in the eighteenth century, particularly among the Bolognese school, which went back to Guido Reni. The style and motif of Mengs's *Magdalen* derive directly from a famous and much copied work that was then believed to be by Guido Reni. It was in fact by Giovan Gioseffo dal Sole, a Bolognese painter and follower of Reni, and is now in the Palazzo Bianco in Genoa.

We know from contemporary sources, such as the memoirs of Giacomo Casanova, that the mixture of sensuality and pious repentance was felt to be particularly attractive in this subject. Mengs's *Magdalen* from the collection of King Charles III of Spain is a vivid example of this (cat.no.29). In this earlier picture the artist's interest is focussed on the decorative and voluptuous drapery, while the facial expression is somewhat contrived. The expressive possibilities of the subject certainly appear to have interested Mengs far less than the elaborate drapery, where he could display the full range of his technical ability. As with the Sibyl (cat.no. 23), the painter's main concern seems to be to show a richly dressed idealised female figure in the appealing posture of a Magdalen, and this probably explains the success of the composition, which was frequently copied.

The two versions show the artist's great technical ability, and the sustained high quality which one comes to expect from Mengs's own replicas due to his academic training. Nevertheless, the attentive observer will notice that the picture from Lulworth Castle does have greater technical and painterly finish than the other version.

22
The Penitent Magdalen with a Cross

Oil on canvas, 108.7 × 86.8 cm
London, Chaucer Fine Arts

PROVENANCE: auctioned at Sotheby's, 28 October 1987, lot 163 (as Trevisani).

LITERATURE: Catalogue *Paintings and Sculpture, Works of Art* (London, Chaucer Fine Arts, 1988), no.19.

The provenance of this painting, which is a largely identical copy by the artist of the painting from the Lulworth collection (cat.no.21), can only be surmised. In 1803 and 1804 a *Penitent Magdalen* by Mengs was twice put up for sale (see Fredericksen (1988), p.455), and it is possible that these sales refer to either or both exhibited here. Presumably the version which reappeared in 1987 attributed to Trevisani is the picture which remained in Mengs's studio in Rome when he went to Madrid (cat.no.21) and on which the copy by Nikolaus Mosmann was based (London, British Museum, Department of Prints and Drawings, Mosmann Drawings, vol.VI, no.212). A barely perceptible detail also provides evidence for this. In the Lulworth version St Mary Magdalen has a large tear on her nose, which is not to be seen either in the versions discussed here or in the Mosmann copy.

In colouring and modelling a number of other small differences can be found between the two works. In this version, the pink tone of the cloak contains more white and so appears more plastic and more sharply modelled. This and other harsh areas of modelling suggest that what is here hypothetically called the studio version does not yet have a commissioned work's degree of finish. It can cautiously be concluded from this that Mengs kept second versions of paintings to hand in his studio and only did the final work on them when a purchaser appeared. The hypothetical 'Roman' version is rather smaller than that in the Lulworth collection, and this is particularly evident at the edges of the picture frame. The picture which remained in the studio in Rome must, however, have been the basis for the many copies that have survived of this composition.

21 *The Penitent Magdalen with a Cross*

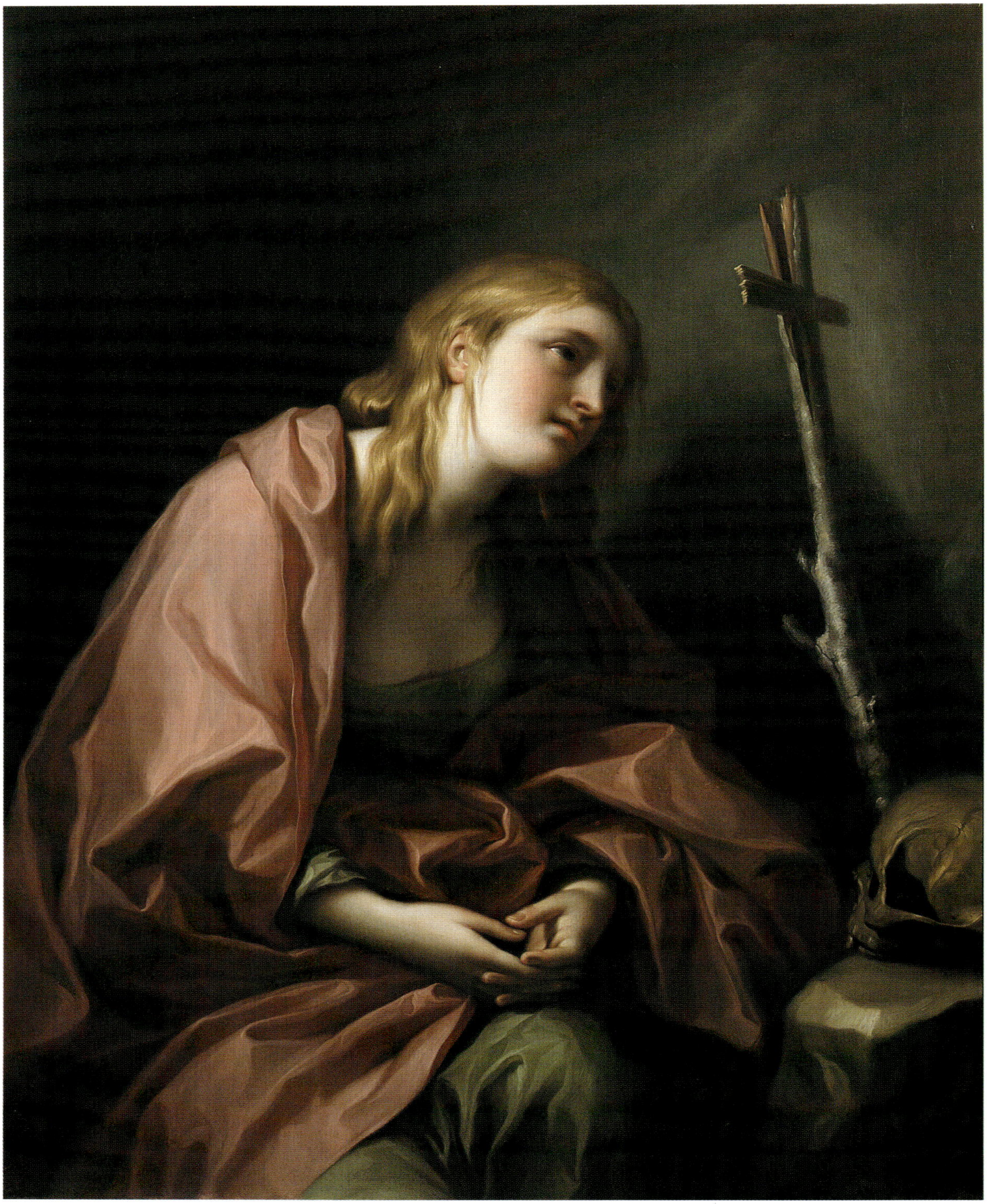

22 *The Penitent Magdalen with a Cross*

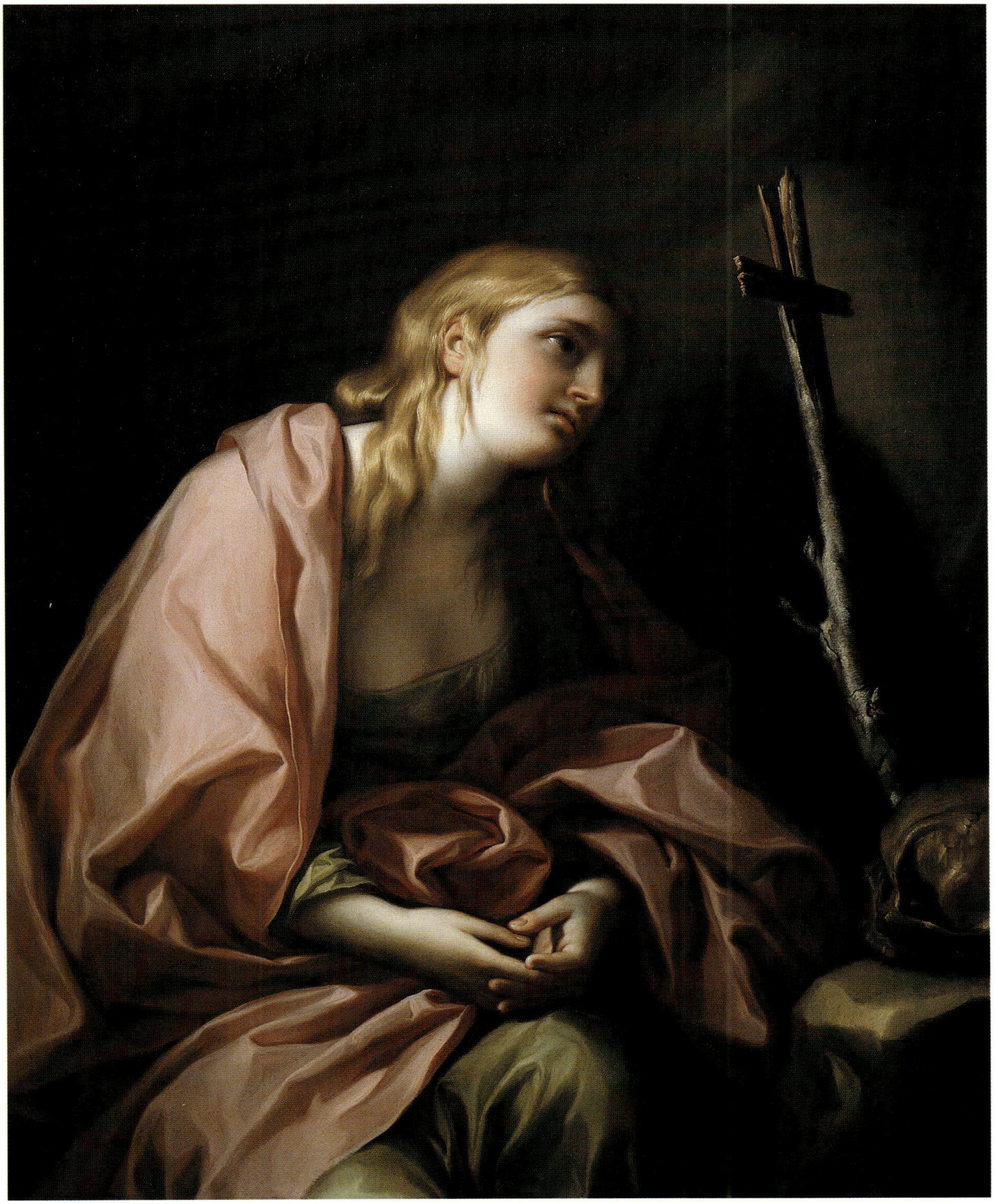

23
A Sibyl

Oil on canvas, 119 × 93 cm
London, Private Collection

PROVENANCE: auctioned at Sotheby's, London 12 May 1976, lot 29

LITERATURE: Bianconi (1780), unpag.(94); Doray de Longrais (1782), p.37; Prange (1786), I, p.121; Azara-Fea (1787), pp.XIX, XLII; auction catalogue, Sotheby's 12 May 1976, p.7; catalogue, *Neoclassical Paintings and Drawings* (London, Chaucer Fine Arts, 1979), no.1; exhibition catalogue, *Herinneringen aan Italiën*, s'Hertogenbosch (1984), no.105; Erffa/Staley 1986, pp.444-5; exhibition catalogue, *Artisti in Roma nei Sei-e Settecento*, Rome, Galleria Gasparrini (1988), p.56; exhibition catalogue, *Guido Reni und Europa*, Frankfurt am Main (1988), no.D40.

According to biographical sources Mengs painted three pictures with half-length figures for British clients in 1761, after his return from Naples in the spring and before he left for Madrid in August, but we have no information on who these clients were. For stylistic reasons, the other two paintings can be identified as a *Penitent Magdalen* (cat.no.21) and a *St Cecilia*, which is now in an Italian private collection. As Benjamin West began his copy of the *Sibyl* (cat. no.31) after Mengs's departure from Rome, it must be assumed that the original was still in his Roman studio at that time. Nikolaus Mosmann's undated engraving was probably not made from the painting, to judge from the inscription (del. et pin.) but from a drawing or cartoon.

The direct antecedent of the depiction, in both motif and theme, is Guercino's *Persian Sibyl*, which has been in the Museo Capitolino in Rome since about 1750. Stylistically, however, the influence of Domenichino was decisive, particularly in the facial type and the drapery. Colouristically the secondary hues predominate, with violet, golden yellow, light green and cream. The soft plasticity and economical use of decorative motifs (the golden border and brooch) recall the works of Guido Reni's mature period. One almost has the impression that Mengs was aiming for a synthesis of the qualities of those seventeenth-century Bolognese masters to whom he felt the greatest affinity. Possibly, however, the synthesis was at the client's request; certainly the choice of style for the painting shows how greatly the British collectors' preference for the Bolognese style influenced Mengs.

It is striking that the Sibyl is not identified by any iconography. Her only attributes are the turban and book, and so, unlike in the versions by Guercino or Domenichino, her identity cannot be exactly determined. This throws a characteristic light on the eighteenth-century approach to the subject of the Sibyl, which had been very popular since the Renaissance. The interest now seems to focus rather on depicting a richly robed female figure before a classical background than on the specific iconography. One can easily imagine that such a figure could also be an idealised portrait; certainly, the pose and direction of the gaze suggest such an association. The fluted columns on the left edge of the picture and the landscape background are used to create a corresponding mood or atmosphere.

The *Parnassus* in the Villa Albani (see cat.no.45), completed in the spring of 1761, is stylistically closely related to this work, especially in the strong colours and shimmering materials. It is one of Mengs's major works, crowning ten years of activity in the Eternal City.

The atmospheric idealised female portrait in the classical style was an important starting-point for the work of Angelika Kauffmann, although she did not come to Rome until Mengs had already left the city. It can however be assumed that while she was in Rome (1763-67) she had access to his studio, where she must have seen pictures like the *Sibyl*. During Mengs's absence his studio was managed by Anton von Maron, and it was open to visitors and artists. Gavin Hamilton's pictures of idealised female turbaned figures, which date from rather later, could also derive from a knowledge of this new type of classical half-length female figure, which Mengs evolved in the years after 1755 and of which the *Sibyl* is a particularly fine and impressive example.

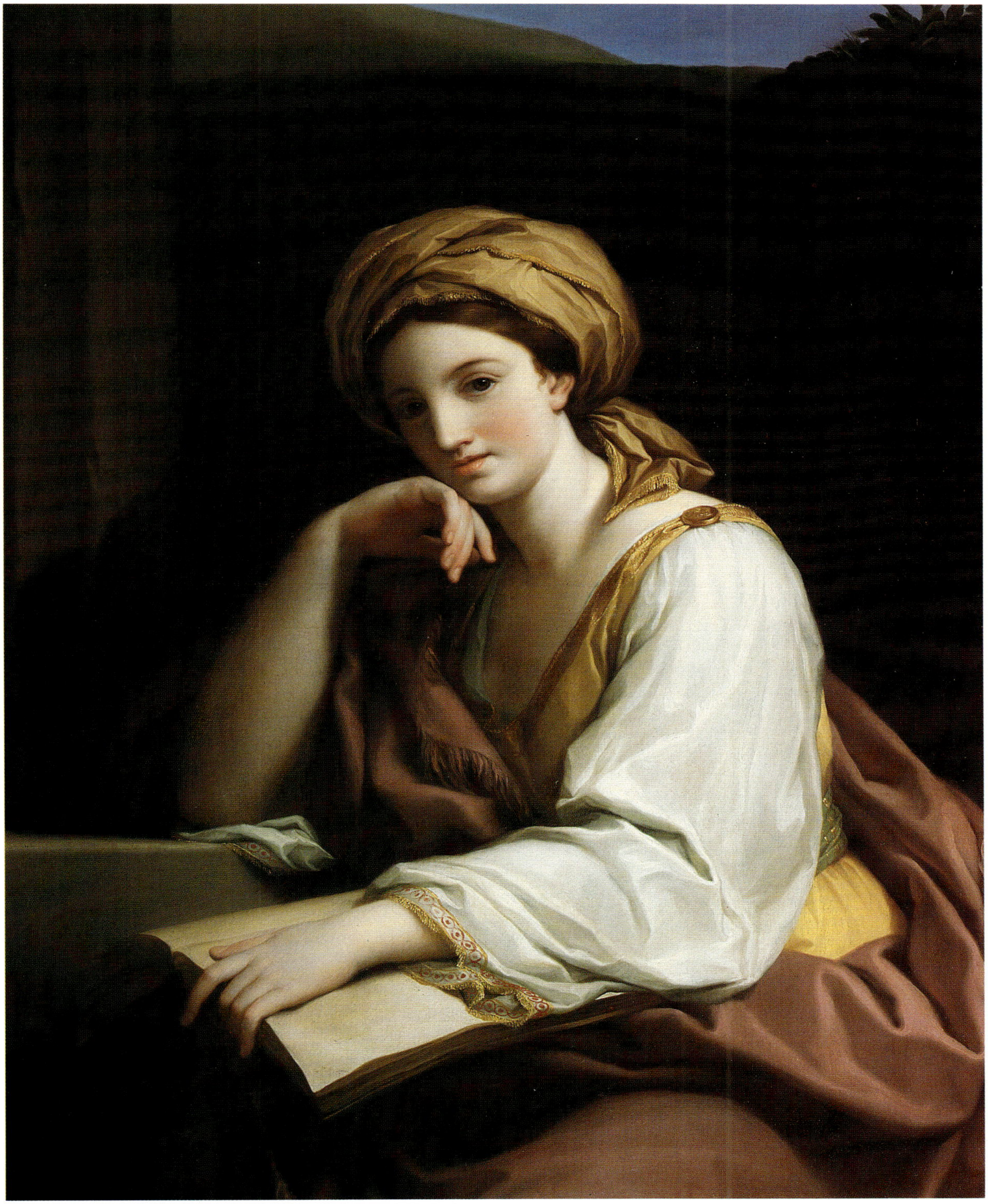

24

The Holy Family with St John

Oil on canvas, 175.6 × 125.1 cm
Inscribed on the Madonna's footstool: Antonius Raphael Mengs Sax. faceb. MDCCLXV
London, The Board of Trustees of the Victoria and Albert Museum

PROVENANCE: Royal Spanish Collections (until 1812); Joseph Bonaparte, taken by Sir Arthur Wellesley, later Duke of Wellington, on 21.6.1813 as spoils of war; confirmed as property of the Duke of Wellington by the Spanish crown on 29.11.1815.

LITERATURE: Ponz VI second edition (1776), third editiion (1793), p.33; Azara, (1780), p.XLIV; Bianconi (1780), unpaged (89); Doray de Longrais (1782), p.30 (stated to be in the possession of the Infanta Don Luis); Cumberland (1782), p.50; Prange I (1786), pp.90-1; Fabroni (1789), p.327; Conca I (1793), p.117; Céan-Bermudez III (1800), p.131; N. de la Cruz y Bahamonde, Lib.XXI, tomo XII (1812), p.110; exhibition catalogue (London, 1963-4), no.13, p.7; J. A. Gaya Nuno, *Pintura europea perdida por España* (Madrid, 1964), no.207, p.62; Honisch (1965), no.66, p.82; exhibition catalogue (Madrid, 1980), no.44.
Catalogues of the collection: Apsley House (1901), no.48, p.110; catalogue of the Wellington Museum (1982), no.105, p.93.

EXHIBITIONS: London, 1963-4, Royal Academy, *Goya and his Times*, no.13; Madrid, 1980.

The picture was painted for Charles III of Spain, and its dating constitutes a valuable fixed point for the chronology of the other religious paintings, most of which are undated, which Mengs produced during his first stay in Madrid between 1761 and 1769. It was one of the first easel paintings he made for the King in Madrid, where he was mainly occupied with the design and execution of the ceiling frescos for the Palacio Real.

It was unusual for Mengs to sign and date a subject painting and this was no doubt due to the importance of the commission. Mengs made a large number of sketches and drawings for the painting, and the composition finally emerged from numerous variants. The last preliminary drawing, which is now in the Metropolitan Museum in New York, where it came from the collection of William Esdaile (L.2617), shows the composition in reverse, a frequent feature of Mengs's sketches. Other sketches are in Madrid and on a sheet of studies in the Uffizi, which was one of the works copied by Richard Cooper shortly before 1769 in Madrid (Edinburgh, National Gallery of Scotland). The Florentine sheet also contains sketches for the *Lamentation* which Mengs was painting at about the same time for Charles III (see cat.no.27).

This composition derives from the earlier formulations of the theme of the *Holy Family* with which Mengs concerned himself in his early youth (see cat.no.19), and which he took up again around 1760 when he was painting the *Holy Family* for Lord Cowper (Introduction, fig.23). This was copied a year later by Benjamin West (Hull, Ferens Art Gallery).

The theme and composition of the Cowper *Holy Family* clearly look back to Mengs's model Raphael. However, the *Holy Family* of 1765 represents a stylistic development in that the figures have greater depth and plasticity. The change is also evident in the handling of space. The diagonal arrangement of the group of figures in a room, which is given depth by being seen from above and by the foreshortened perspective of the floor, introduces a sense of narrative, as does the inclusion of the tools of a carpenter's workshop. This is complemented by the intimate and lyrical mood, underlined by the view into a landscape. It is reminiscent of Murillo's *Holy Family* in the Prado. Mengs highly esteemed Murillo as one of the great masters of the Spanish school, as is evident from his writings. Moreover, he was concerned to draw the attention of the Spanish painters of his time to their own tradition, and to revive it. Murillo's affinity with Raphael made him one of the models whom Mengs wished to reinstate with his contemporaries. Some measure of his success can be seen in the *Holy Family* by Goya of around 1780 in the Prado, which is an interesting mixture of the influences of Mengs and Murillo.

Mengs's painting achieved great fame in Spain. Several copies of its exist and it was already mentioned in 1791 by Joseph Townsend in his *'A Journey through Spain in the Years 1786 and 1787 with Particular Attention to the Agriculture, Manufactures, Commerce, Taxes and Revenue of that Country'* (I, p.292).

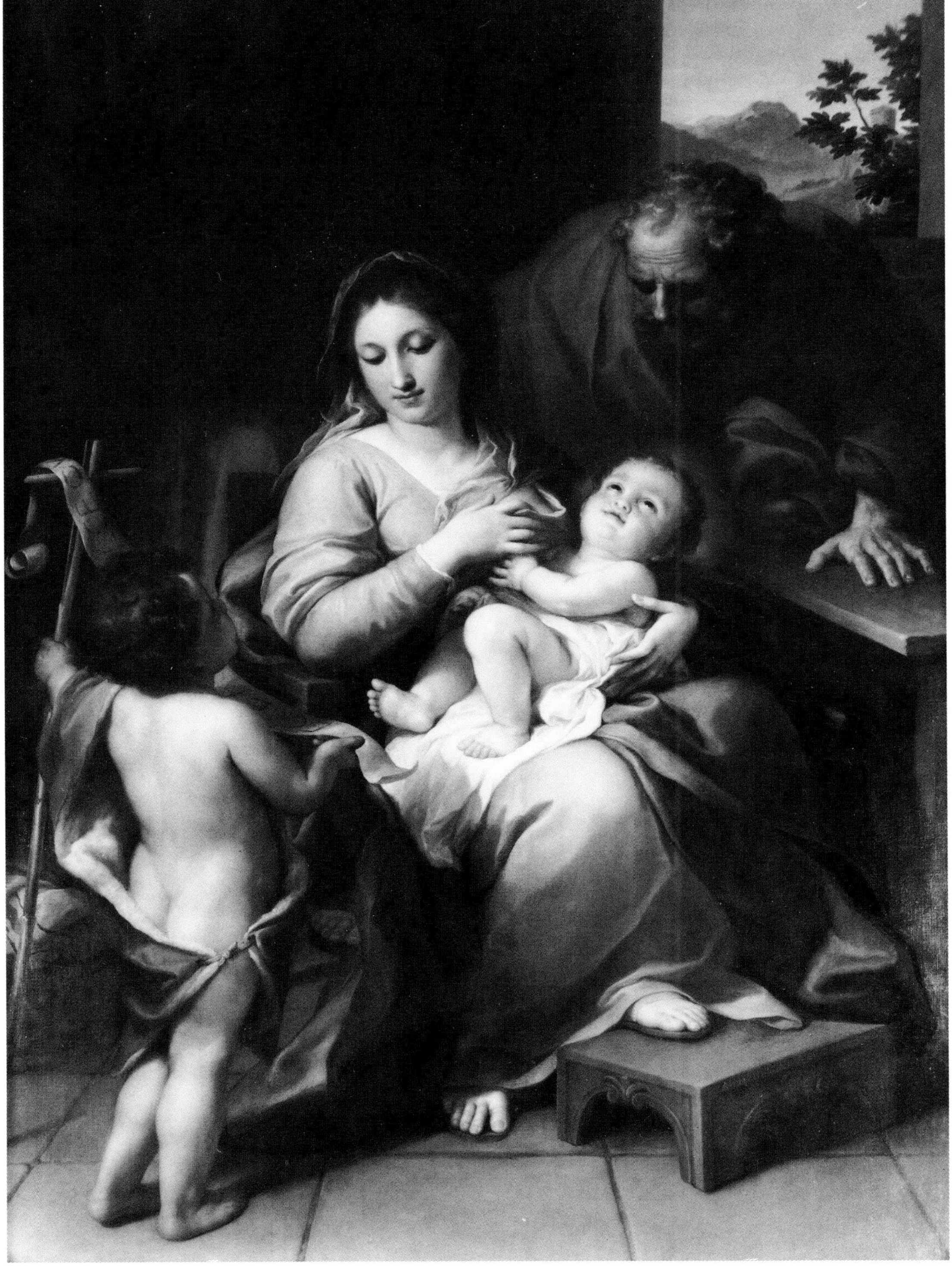

25

The Madonna and Child with the young John the Baptist

Paper mounted on canvas, black chalk, diameter 68.9 cm
London, The Trustees of the National Gallery, inv.no.1099.

PROVENANCE: Rome, Mengs's heirs, 1779; legacy of Miss Harriet Kearsley, 1881.

LITERATURE: Bianconi (1780), unpaged (93); Prange I (1786), p.120; *Bryan's Dictionary of Painters and Engravers*, III (1904), p.322; Honisch (1965), no.350, p.136; *Catalogues of the National Gallery* (1898), no.1109A, pp.347-349; 1929, no.1099, p.232; 1959, no.1099, p.97.

From a copy by Richard Cooper in Edinburgh we know that this cartoon was for a painting which was in Mengs's possession in Madrid. Cooper's copy also provides a rough indication of a 'terminus ante quem' by which the painting can be dated; it must have been between 1761 and 1769 in Madrid, that is, before Mengs left for Italy. It seems rather doubtful that the copy by Nikolaus Mosmann in the British Museum (Mosmann Drawings, vol.VI, no.211) was taken from the painting, as the inscription claims, for if so, Mengs must have taken the picture, which is now lost, back to Rome with him. That is unlikely, as it was on wood panel. Instead, it is conceivable that Mosmann used the cartoon to make his copy. This remained in the painter's possession, as can be seen from the description in the inventory of his estate. Since Mosmann knew there was a painted version he wrote under his copy 'Cavaliere Antonio Raffaele Mengs pinxit'.

According to Cooper the picture was half life-size, so presumably smaller than the cartoon. It is very possible that the cartoon was intended to be used for a larger version of the picture. However, as it shows no sign of having been used, we may take it that the actual function of this drawing, which is very highly finished, was to provide a *modello*, which would be available at all times in the studio to serve as a basis for any kind of reproduction, from a replica by the master's hand to a copy by pupils and visitors. In particular the distribution of light and shade, which played a large part in Mengs's theory of art, could be precisely determined in so detailed a drawing. This was invaluable for the execution in paint, as it made the task very much easier.

As the direct model for his composition Mengs used a painting by Sassoferrato, which is now in the Prado in Madrid and was owned by King Charles IV. The picture belongs to a category of religious painting that was particularly prevalent in Roman art, and Raphael's *Madonna della Sedia* (Florence, Galleria Palatina) also served as a model. Mengs had made a miniature copy of this work in his youth (Dresden, Old Masters Gallery) and he copied it again when he was in Florence in 1770. The way the figures are fitted into the round form, the Madonna's raised knee and the full soft features of her face all strongly recall Raphael.

A sheet of sketches in the Philadelphia Museum of Fine Arts (inv.no.1978-70-363) contains a number of designs, including a rapid sketch that could have been used for this composition. The same sheet also contains a design for a composition engraved by Cunego and entitled 'Refugium Peccatorum'. This was also copied by Cooper in Madrid, and it proves that the two compositions, which are stylistically very closely related, were made at about the same time, that is, towards the end of Mengs's first sojourn in Spain.

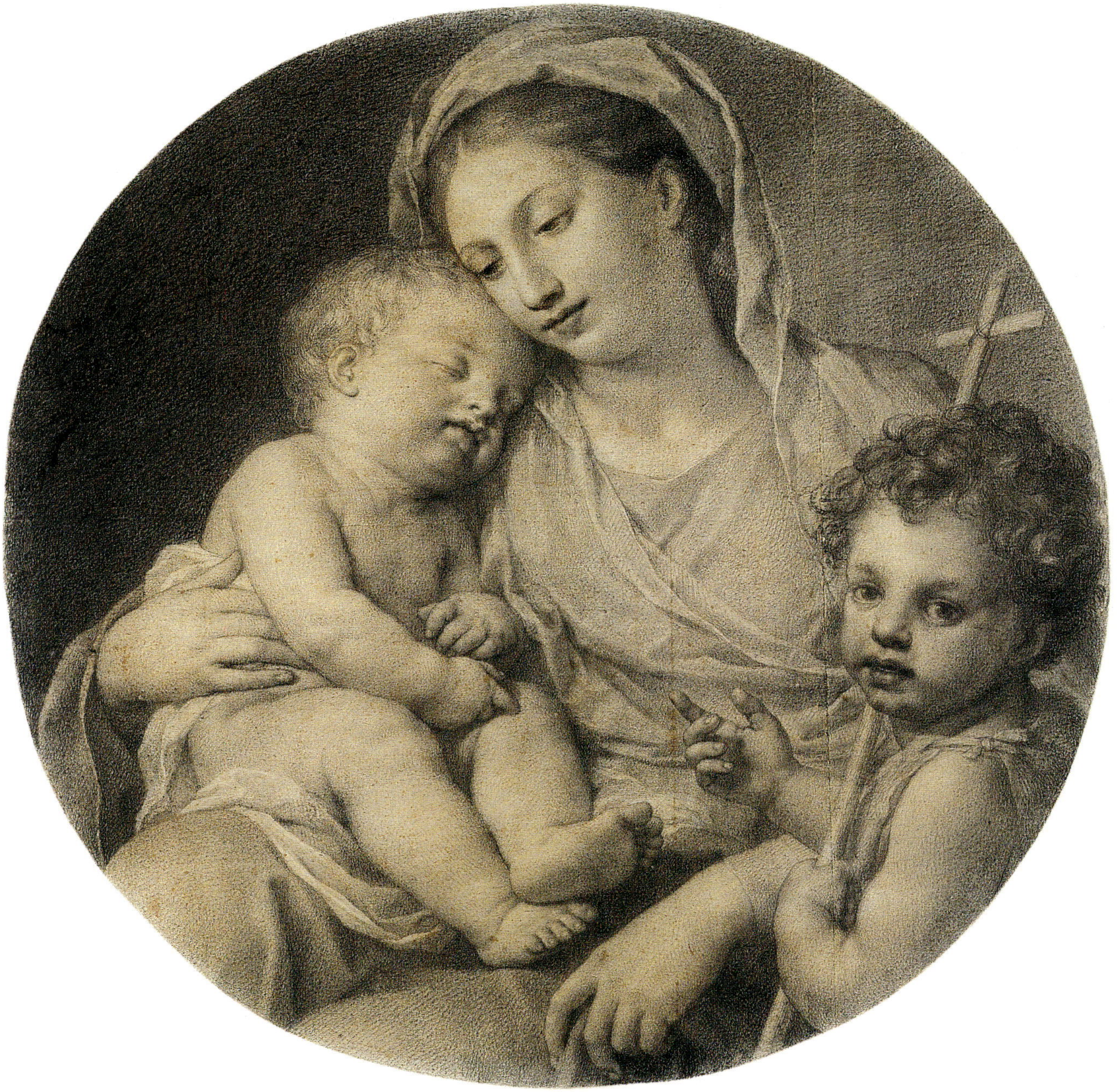

26
The Annunciation

Oil on canvas, 78.1 × 43.2 cm
Inscribed on the reverse: 'D. G. Ratti'
Trustees of the Weston Park Foundation

This painting was formerly attributed to Carlo Maratti, probably due to an erroneous interpretation of the inscription on the reverse (Photo: Courtauld Institute, B83/152). However, the inscription refers to the Genoese painter and writer on art Carlo Giuseppe Ratti, who from 1770 was in close contact with Mengs whom he regarded as his tutor. Ratti used drawings and sketches by Mengs for many of his altarpieces, but despite these academic models his manner and technique remained very sketchy and imprecise and thus of course differed totally from Mengs's. Although it is possible that the inscription on the reverse refers to an old attribution to Ratti, this therefore cannot be his work.

The painting is a carefully executed *modello*, and it is comparable to an altarpiece which Mengs painted in 1767 for the Colegiata of Castrogeriz near Burgos. This altarpiece forms the centrepiece of a magnificent retable which fills the entire front of the Gothic choir in the church. The commission for the work was given by Don Diego Sarmiento Conde de Castro y Rivadaria.

Later Mengs made an almost identical replica of this composition, although the format is more slender. It passed from the estate of his son Alberico to the Kunsthistorisches Museum in Vienna in 1816. Today the picture has been folded by about 30 cm at both top and bottom, and it should be very much higher than the picture in Castrogeriz, like the modello at Weston Park; presumably it should also be semicircular at the top. Whether the curving incision at the bottom was intended to fasten the picture to the altar can no longer be ascertained as the work in Vienna is in very bad condition.

The *modello* at Weston Park's purpose was therefore to adapt the older composition to the more slender proportions of the new altarpiece. First the artist used the sketch, but he changed some details when executing the work, again in accordance with the painting in Castrogeriz (the landscape in the background, the angel's robe). Unfortunately it is not known who commissioned the Vienna Annunciation. At any rate, it was left incomplete at the artist's death, as is evident from many details.

A largely identical sketch in St Petersburg can clearly be identified from its frame and wider proportions as the one used for the painting in Castrogeriz, and so must date from before 1767. Apart from that, it is exactly the same as the painting in Weston Park in its details, which differ from both the Spanish and the Viennese versions (the motif of the basket and the cat, the trees in the background, the angel's robe). The difference between the picture in Weston Park and that in St Petersburg is mainly to be found in the execution. The English painting is more exact in the drawing and more accentuated, particularly in the delicate folds of the angel's robe.

In his handling of the subject Mengs used the less familiar type of the triumphal Annunciation, enhancing it with an image of God the Father descending surrounded by angels. Presumably this was to adapt the subject, which normally contains only two figures, to the height of the altarpiece.

Among the Christian subjects which Mengs painted more frequently the *Annunciation* clearly predominates, with the *Adoration of the Shepherds* (cat.nos.35, 36). and the *Entombment of Christ* (cat.nos.27, 38). The compositional models are to be found in Counter-Reformation Baroque painting, like that of Guido Reni (Rome, Chapel of the Quirinal) and Titian.

The study shown here with several sketches for an *Annunciation* (cat.no.37) is one of the preliminary works for a further formulation of this subject, with which Mengs concerned himself until the end of his life. The last picture he painted for Charles III and which he completed shortly before his death, was an *Annunciation* for the palace chapel in Aránjuez (now Madrid, Chapel of the Palacio Real).

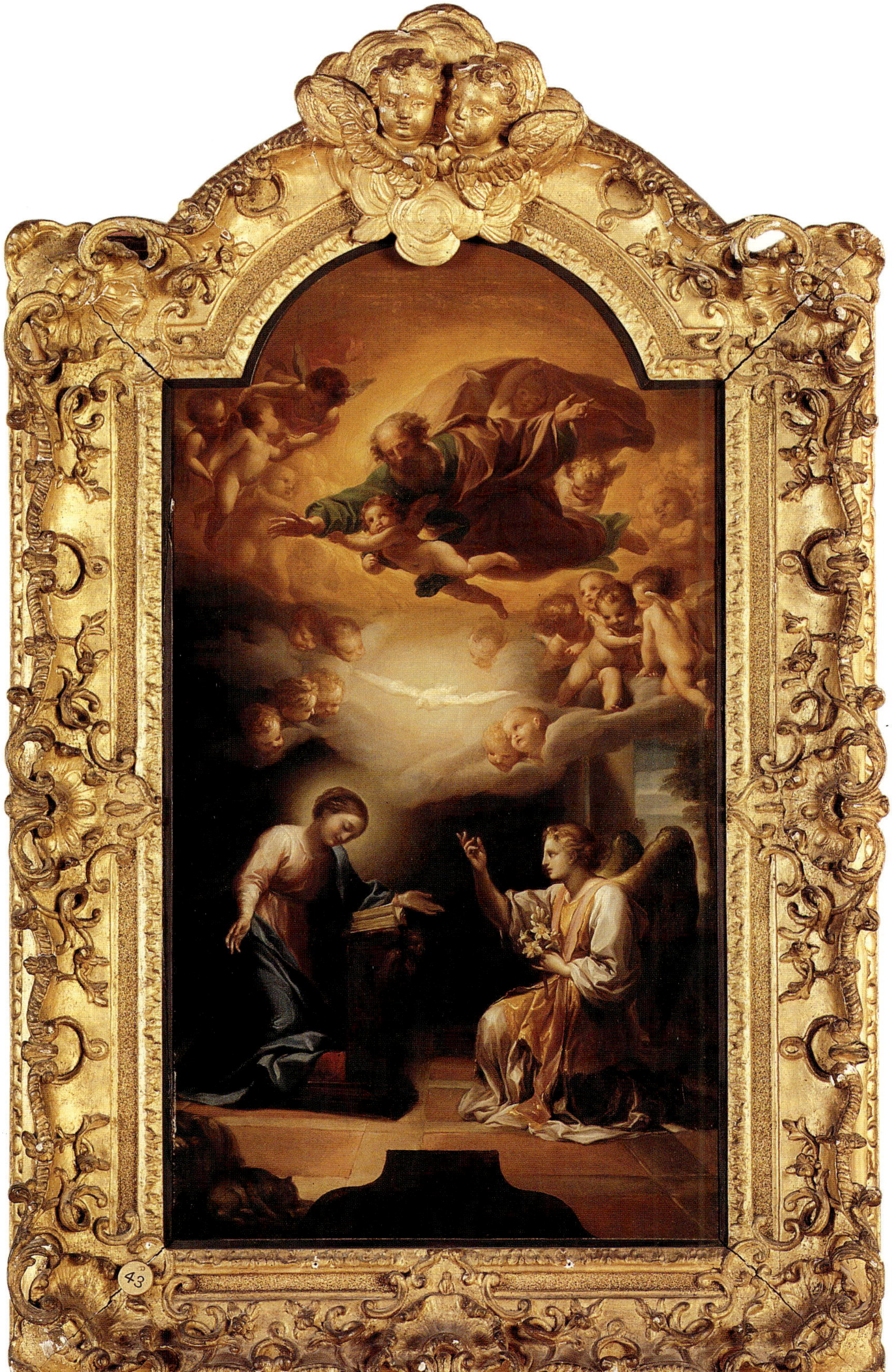

27

The Lamentation

Oil on canvas, 338.6 × 274.3 cm
Cambridge, Master and Fellows of St John's College

PROVENANCE: Legacy of the Rt Hon Robert Henry Clive, 1844

LITERATURE: Christopher Wright, *Old Master Paintings in Britain, An Index of Continental Old Master Paintings executed before c.1800 in Public Collections in the United Kingdom* (London, 1976), p.133; *St John's College, A Guide for Visitors* (Cambridge, 1976), p.13.

This painting, so far neglected by critics, is a second version of the *Lamentation* painted by Mengs between 1765 and 1769 for King Charles III's bedchamber in the Palacio Real in Madrid.

Sources give almost no indication of the provenance of the Cambridge work. Evidence that the picture may have been commissioned can be seen in that Robert Clive, Governor of Bengal from 1757-60 and again from 1765-67, was in Rome in 1767, where his portrait was painted by Mengs's pupil and brother-in-law Maron. He may conceivably have ordered a second version of the painting, which Mengs was working on at that time. Maron could have been the intermediary, since he was in constant correspondence with Mengs.

The Cambridge painting lacks the original Madrid version's angelic host with God the Father, which was painted on a separate panel and formed the upper part of the first version, now in the Palacio de Pedralbes in Barcelona. Another difference is that the second version is on canvas, while the first was on wood panel.

The Madrid panel was copied several times (see exhibition catalogue (Madrid, 1980), p.98), but the copies, like the copperplate engraving by Giovanni Volpato of 1791-2, and the preliminary work for the painting, do not include any sketches of the upper section, either (see cat.no.38). One possible reason for this may be that the painting was originally intended as a companion piece to Raphael's famous 'Spasimo di Sicilia', *Christ bearing the Cross*; it has about the same dimensions and proportions. Mengs's adherence to this model is clear from the arrangement of the figures and the inclusion of Golgotha in the background. How intensively Mengs studied Raphael when composing his picture is also clear from the fact that he made use of a drawing he owned by Raphael for the main group. This drawing was engraved in 1770 by Sante Pacini, but it is now considered to be a pupil's work rather than Raphael's. This clearly shows how seriously Mengs took the fact that his work was to form a pair with Raphael's painting. He devoted a detailed discussion to it in his 'Lettera a Antonio Ponz'. The offer was probably a welcome opportunity for him to demonstrate how close he felt himself to be to Raphael. The offer soon came to nothing, however.

The dramatically raised head of John the Baptist, as he supports Christ's body, differs from the original drawing and is not at all like Raphael's figure. According to Cumberland, Mengs based it on a study of a head by van Dyck which he owned and which Richard Cumberland later acquired (see cat.no.57). Finally, we should include the description which Cumberland himself left of the original painting in the Palacio Real in Madrid, the first version of the work: 'There are seventeen easel pictures in the palace of Madrid, exclusive of the Annunciation lately arrived from Rome; ... The picture of the Dead Christ is, in my opinion, the best of the above number; the figures are of natural size: The Nativity, which is covered with a single plate of glass, is nine feet ten inches by seven; that of the Dead Christ is considerably bigger: These three pictures of the Death of Christ, The Nativity and The Annunciation, composed at different periods in his life and at difference places, the first being painted at Madrid and the two last at Rome, are the compositions that must decide his reputation.'

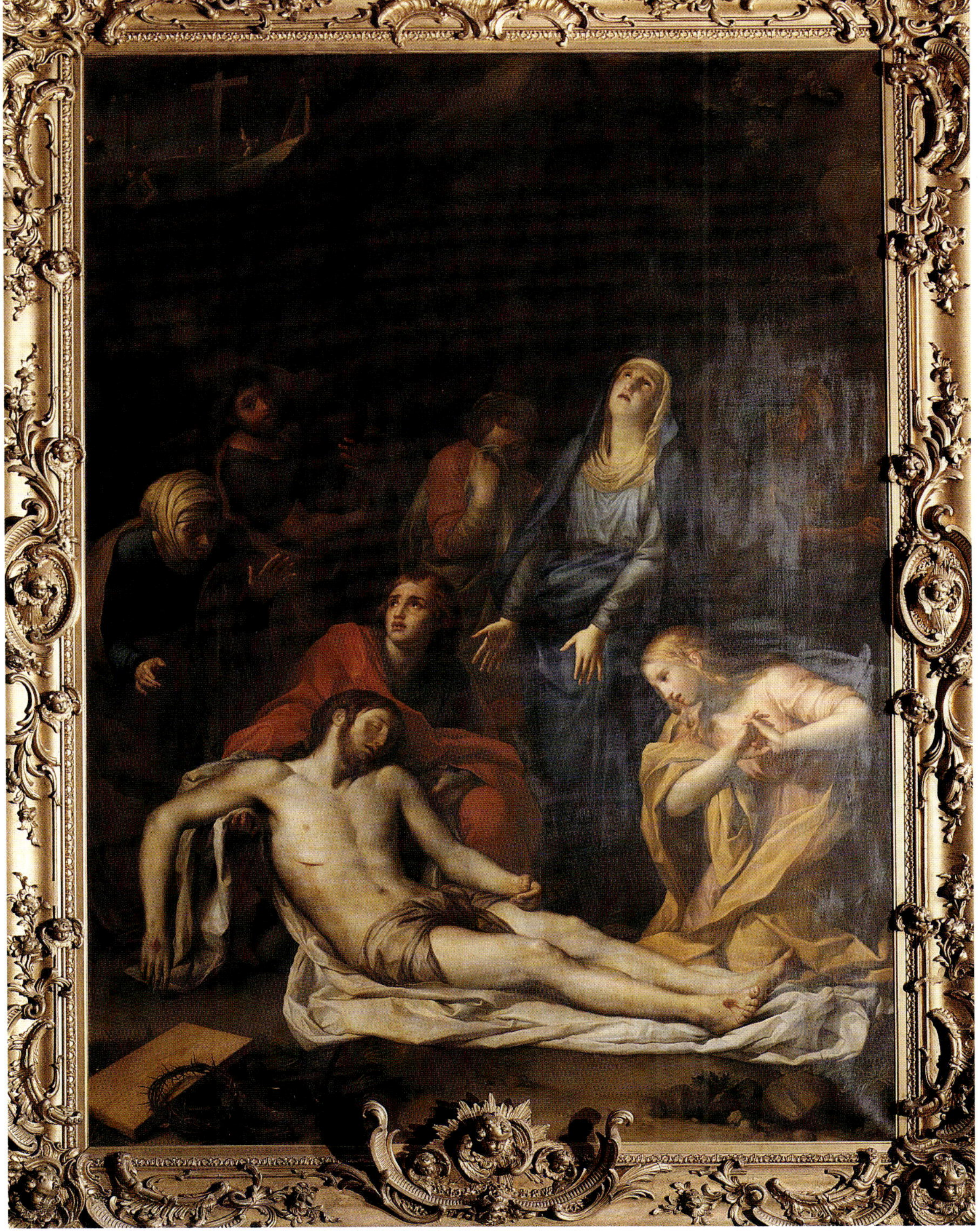

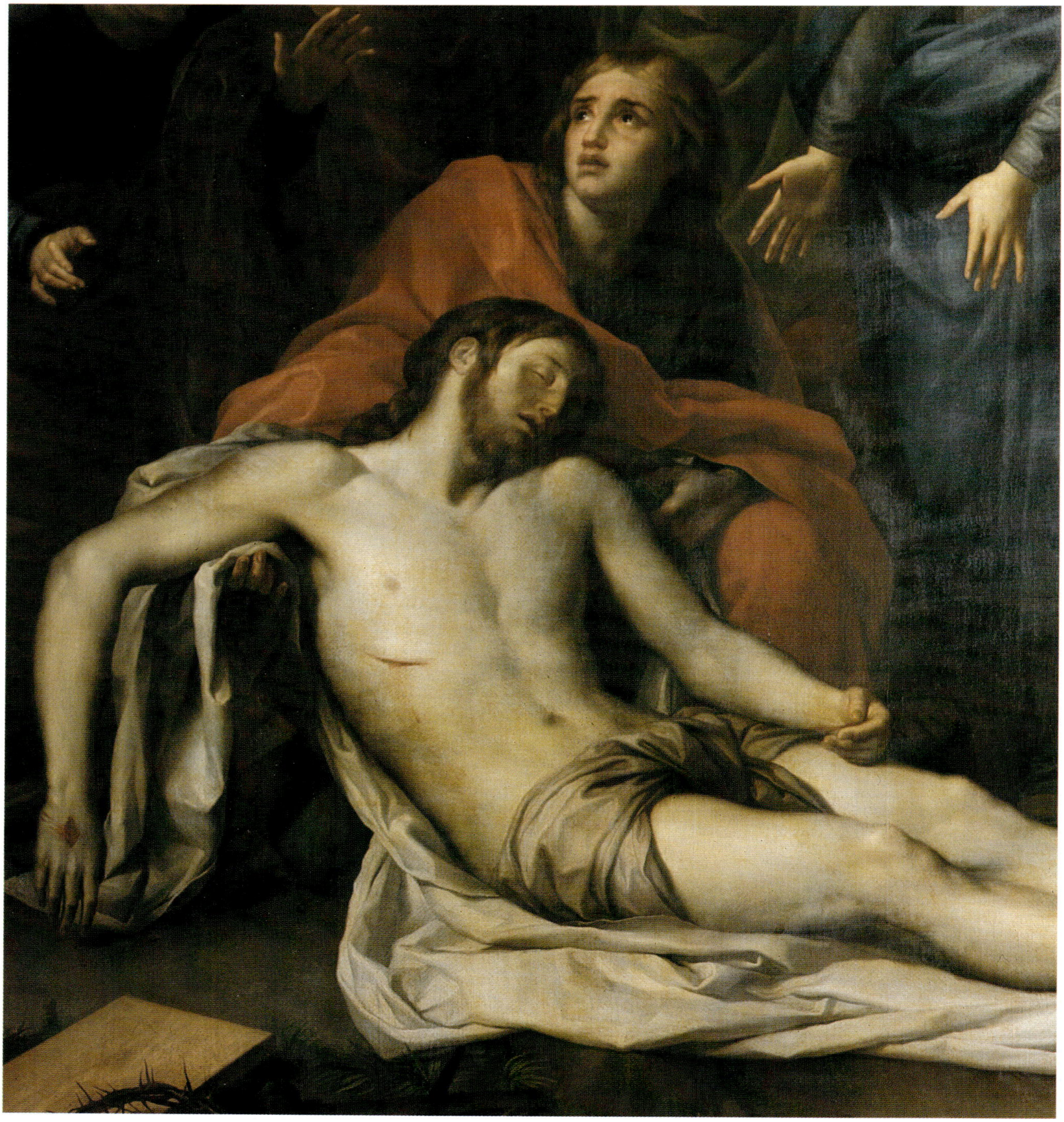

27 *The Lamentation (detail)*

28
St John the Baptist
29
The Penitent Magdalen

28: Oil on copper, 29.1 × 37 cm

29: Oil on wood, 29.3 × 37.7 cm
Both Stratfield Saye, The Duke of Wellington

PROVENANCE: Madrid, Royal Collections (until 1812); Joseph Bonaparte (1812-13); taken by Sir Arthur Wellesley, later first Duke of Wellington, on 21.6.1813 at the Battle of Victoria; confirmed as in his possession by the Spanish Crown on 29.11.1816.

LITERATURE: Ponz (1776), VI., p.34; Ratti (1779), p.v, VIIIff., Azara (1780), p.XLV; Bianconi (1780), unpag.(89); Cumberland (1782), pp.53-4; Doray de Longrais (1782), p.31; Prange (1786), I, p.90; Jansen (1786), I, pp.23, 59; Azara-Fea (1787), pp.XXII, XLII; Conca I (1793), p.117; Céan-Bermudez III (1800), p.131; de la Cruz, vol.XII (1812), p.110; Honisch (1965), nos.64, 65; C. M. Kauffmann, *Catalogue of the Paintings in the Wellington Museum*, London (1982), nos.121, 129 (with refs to the older catalogues).

Together with a *Lamentation* (cat.no.27) and four Passion scenes, both these paintings adorned the Kings bedchamber in the Palacio Real in Madrid. That Charles III wished to have so many works by his Principal Court Painter in his bedchamber shows how greatly he esteemed Mengs. Thematically these two works belong in the range of Christian subjects which were usual in the sleeping quarters of Spanish rulers. The reference to Christ can be seen on the banner held by John the Baptist bearing the legend ECCE AGNUS DEI. That the two paintings were intended to form a matching pair can be seen from their composition. However, *The Penitent Magdalen* is painted on wood, while *St John the Baptist* is on a copper panel. This was very rare in Mengs's work.

The combination of Mary Magdalen and John the Baptist was popular in eighteenth-century painting, probably because of the possibilities for the formal arrangement of both figures lying before a landscape, as seen here.

So far it has not been possible to date the two works exactly, and different biographers have given different information on where they were painted and when. Ratti and Azara state that *St John the Baptist* was painted in 1769 in Madrid, and *The Penitent Magdalen* not until 1771 in Rome. However, that cannot be correct, as Richard Cooper had already copied both works on his stay in Madrid, which must be taken to have been between 1767 and 1769. Cooper noted on his copy of *St John the Baptist* (cat.no.44) that the picture was intended to be a companion piece to a small *St Mary Magdalen* by Correggio, but then Mengs provided his own version of the subject. The work then ascribed to Correggio was probably in fact by Carlo Maratti, and can be regarded as the compositional basis of Mengs's *Penitent Magdalen.*

Although Cooper's commentary does not solve all the open questions, his information does at least make it clear why *St John the Baptist* was painted on copper. Apparently Mengs believed that the glazing technique which copper required would make his work resemble Correggio's, and the technique he used for *St John the Baptist* does differ considerably from that in the *Penitent Magdalen.* The shading in the modelling and the outlines has an undeniable similarity with the work of Correggio, who after Raphael was the artist whom Mengs most admired.

For the composition of his *Magdalen* Mengs was also influenced by a painting in the gallery at Dresden, which in the eighteenth century was attributed to Correggio. Maratti's painting in Madrid, which Cooper mentions, uses the same model. In the arrangement of the two figures Mengs also recalled the two large pictures on this subject painted by Pompeo Batoni around 1742-3 for Augustus III of Poland and Saxony (see Clark Bowron (1986), nos.60, 61).

As it is clear from Cooper's copies that the two paintings must have been executed before Mengs left for Italy, we can identify the *Magdalen* as the picture which Giacomo Casanova saw in Mengs's studio in 1768. Casanova, who had already met Mengs in Rome in 1761, lived in Mengs's house during part of his sojourn in Madrid in 1768, and he has left us so vivid an account of his conversations with the painter that it is worthwhile repeating the passage that refers to this painting here. Mengs had worked for twelve days on the *Magdalen,* and announced every morning that he would finish the work that evening. When Casanova finally asked him whether he was deceiving himself each day on the stage he had reached in the work, the painter explained: 'To ninety-nine connoisseurs who look at it, it may well look finished, but I am concerned with the hundredth, and I look at it with his eyes. You should know that there are only approximately finished paintings anywhere on earth. This Magdalen will be finished when I stop working on it; but it will not really be finished, for it would certainly be more perfect if I spent another day on it. Even your Petrarch has not written a single sonnet that one could really call perfectly finished. Nothing is perfect on earth that springs from the hand or mind of man, except a mathematical calculation' (Casanova, vol.XI, p.75-6). The passage illustrates the exacting demands Mengs made of himself, and also shows the metaphysical concept of perfection taken to the point of destruction which Mengs

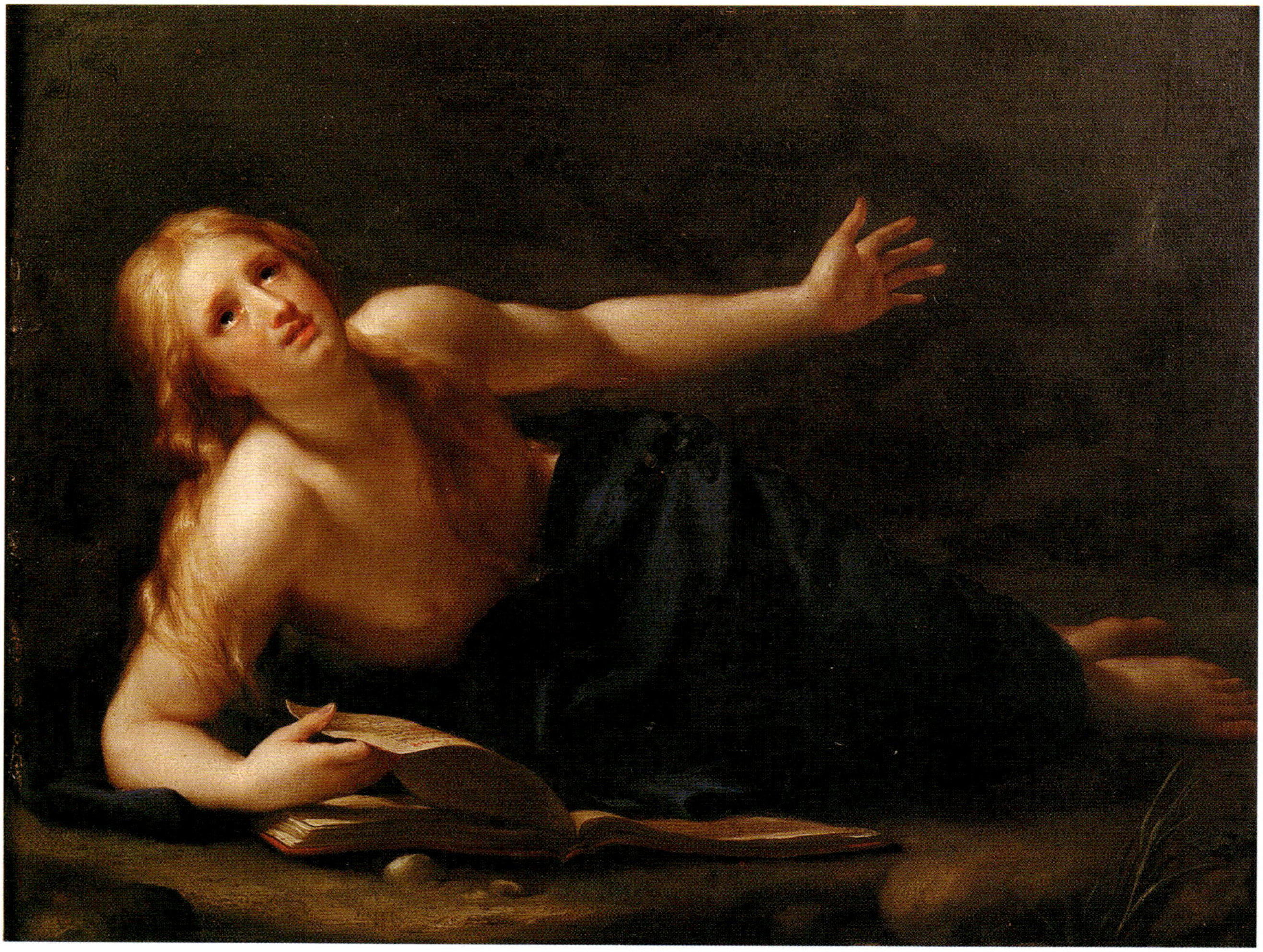

29 *The Penitent Magdalen*

expounded in his theoretical works.

Both these paintings were highly praised by almost all commentators for their great beauty and finish. Even Cumberland, usually so critical, falls into line with other critics on these. In 1784 Mengs's son-in-law Manuel Salvador Carmona produced two masterly engravings the same size as the originals. The state proof of the *Magdalen*, which was later owned by Azara, was retouched by Mengs himself, as is evident from a letter from his pupil Bonaventura Salesa. Several copies of the *Magdalen* are still extant. They include a drawing by Nikolaus Mosmann (London, British Museum, Mosmann Drawings, T.5-9, no.213).

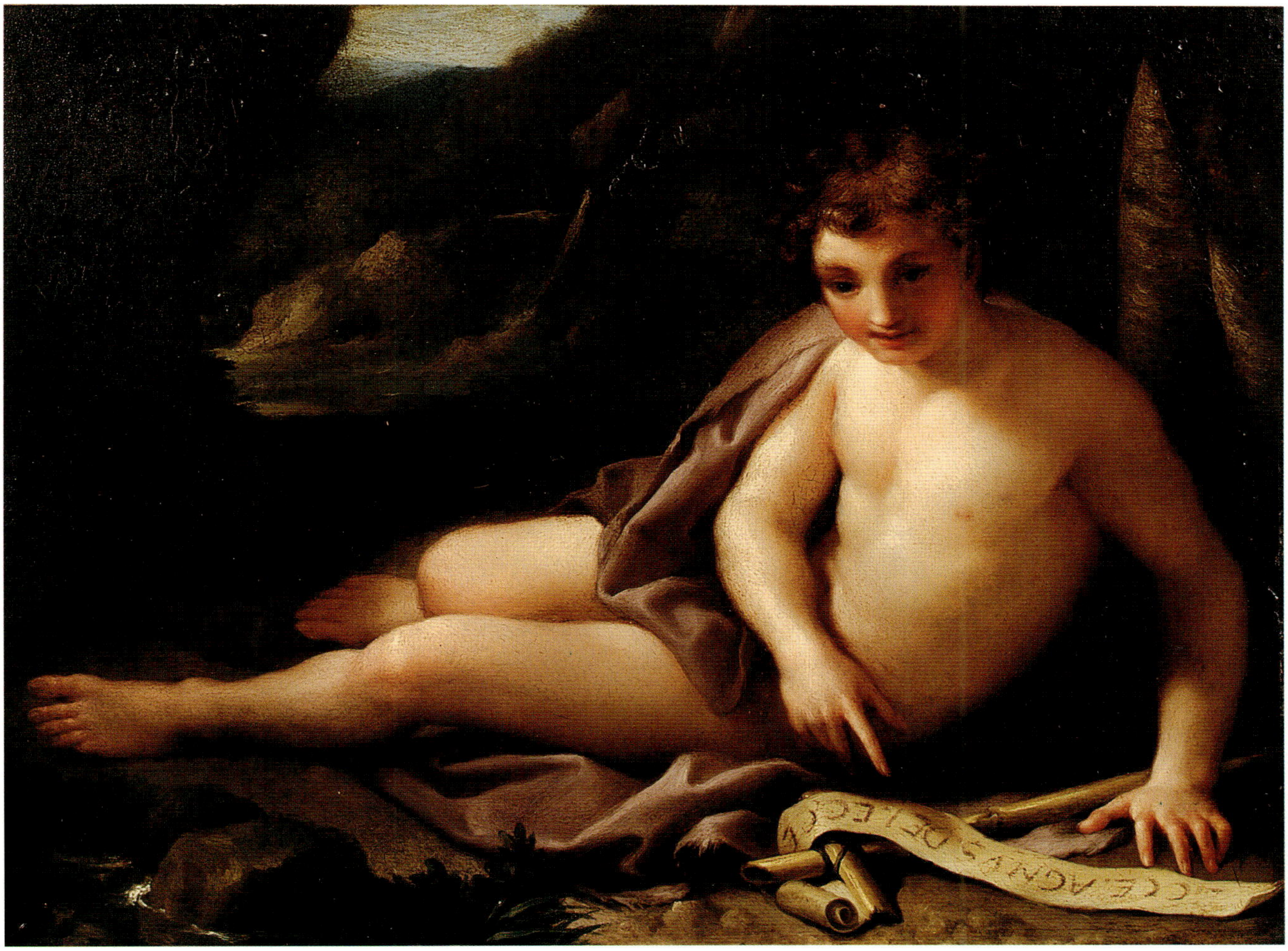

28 *St John the Baptist*

30
Head of Christ for 'Noli me tangere'

Oil on canvas, originally board, 47.2 × 37.8 cm
Labelled on the reverse: 'Mengs made this sketch for his great Picture of Christ in the Garden in All Souls Chapel, Oxford, bespoken at 300 gs.
Given to Sir W.am Hamilton in its present Rosewood frame it was purchased at his sale by the late Mr Lambert of the Temple for 16 Gs. of him by Mr Steers of the Temple for 23 Gs. of him by me for 40. The outer frame was (10 Gs.) procured me by Mr Seguire T. C. July 182 (?)'.
Oxford, Warden and Fellows of All Souls College

PROVENANCE: Sir William Hamilton, Naples (until 1798); Hamilton auction at Christie's, London, 27.3.1801, lot 25; auctioned at Christie's on 3.6.1826.

LITERATURE: *James Clark, Catalogue of Pictures, Marbles, Bronzes, The Property of the R. Hon. Sir William Hamilton, packed at Naples in Octr. Novr. 1798*; Parker, *Handbook for Visitors to Oxford* (1847), p.127; O. E. Deutsch, 'S. W. Hamiltons Picture Gallery', *Burlington Magazine* (Feb. 1943), p.38; Sparrow (1960), pp.9, 127.

This painting is a study for the head of Christ in the '*Noli me tangere*' which was commissioned by All Souls College, Oxford and painted in Rome in 1771. It was originally painted on board and comes from the collection of Sir William Hamilton. There was a presumably matching study for the head of St Mary Magdalen in the de Cotoner collection in Mallorca at the beginning of the twentieth century which came from the artist's estate. Presumably Sir William Hamilton also acquired his study from the artist's estate. Other sketches for the composition and some detail drawings are in Florence, Vienna and Madrid. The fact that so carefully executed a head study was made to the same size as the picture throws a revealing light on the artist's method of working. Mengs must have made an incredible number of drawings and oil studies for all his larger compositions. From the sources we know that two oil sketches existed. Lord Cowper had a grisaille in Florence, probably purchased from Mengs's estate, which later came into the Rinuccini collection in Florence. Peter Beckford had already bought another sketch in 1771, paying a high price for it, according to Thorpe (see Sparrow). The study of the head differs only slightly from the finished painting. However, in expression, brushwork and liveliness it is superior. The contrasts between the dark hair, the background and the very light and soft flesh tints in the face were weakened in the painting, and this may be due to the fact that there is a layer of gold leaf between the ground and the paint, as we know from the comment by the French painter Julien de Parme (see Rosenberg 1984, p.212). This reduced the permeability of the ground and weakened the tonal gradations of the colours.

Mengs received the commission to paint the altarpiece in November 1769, while he was in Madrid. He must have made the first preliminary studies in 1770 in Florence, for we know from the correspondence between the Roman agent James Byres (see Introduction, p.16) and the Board of the Chapter of All Souls College the exact date when the painting was finished: 19 September 1771. The painting was then taken to the papal palace to be shown to the Pope.

When the picture was displayed in the Villa Medici in October that year, Roman public opinion was divided. James Byres described his impression as follows: 'The Picture is finish'd, and I really think among the very best that I ever saw of his painting. In the Christ there is a great dignity and meekness, in the Magdalene the remains of Grief with a mixture of surprize and joy, is wonderfully express'd. The disposition of the Figures is very agreeable, the colouring strong and clear, but very harmonious and true; the background well adapted to the subject and calculated to sett off the Figures to advantage' (Sparrow (1960), p.4).

After the picture was displayed Byres had generally only positive reactions to report. He comments on them in his letter of 30 November 1771, in which he reports that the painter has been paid and the picture taken on board an English ship: 'I have the pleasure to assure you that it gave very general satisfaction, the few criticisms that were thrown out were more the Effect of Envy and Ignorance, than founded on knowledge and reason'. He was not entirely wrong, for the severest criticism, which Byres was certainly not unaware of, had come from Father Thorpe (see Introduction, p.32), who was an admirer of Batoni. He criticised mainly the posture of Christ, whom he compared with a dancing master, and the overheavy folds in Mary Magdalen's robe. Thorpe has also left us the painter's illuminating response: 'When Mengs heard of some remarks made upon his performance he allowed the justice of them, but added that he conformed himself to the taste of the nation, where the painting was to be placed. I dare not say how far this may be taken as a compliment to England but I know that he was paid above twelve hundred Crowns for his picture which he is said to have done in less than six weeks' (letter of 25.11.1771 to Lord Arundel, see Sparrow (1965), p.631).

The composition was based on a painting of the same subject which Mengs had painted shortly before for the bedchamber of Charles III in the Palacio Real in Madrid (Madrid, Patrimonio Nacional). A comparison between the two pictures could explain what Mengs meant by 'the taste of the nation'. The most striking differences between the two versions of the subject, which are related in composition and iconography to Correggio's *'Noli me tangere'* in the Prado, are in style and expression. The Oxford painting is much closer to Guido Reni than the Madrid version. Mengs was therefore not only aware of the particular preference of the British for the Bolognese school, but also knew how to respond to it. The oil study for the head of Christ shows the clear influence of Reni.

Sparrow has published extensive documentation on the commission, its execution and the preliminary work. This shows that the painter received a drawing of the Neo-Classical aedicule before the altar from the drawing master of the College, on which Thornhill had painted a fresco in 1714 showing the apotheosis of the founder of the College, Chichele. The chapel was extensively restored and renovated before the altarpiece was made, and Mengs's picture was displayed in London before it was put in place in Oxford.

Criticism of the Neo-Classical style of the altarpiece started as early as 1817, as we can see from the commentaries in the guidebooks to Oxford which Sparrow compiled. From 1869 to 1871 the chapel was redesigned in the Neo-Gothic style and Gothic wall paintings were discovered behind Thornhill's fresco. This changed the entire situation of the altar. The marble aedicule was sold and the College also considered selling Mengs's painting to the National Gallery. Finally, however, the work was hung high up on the south wall of the Ante-Chapel.

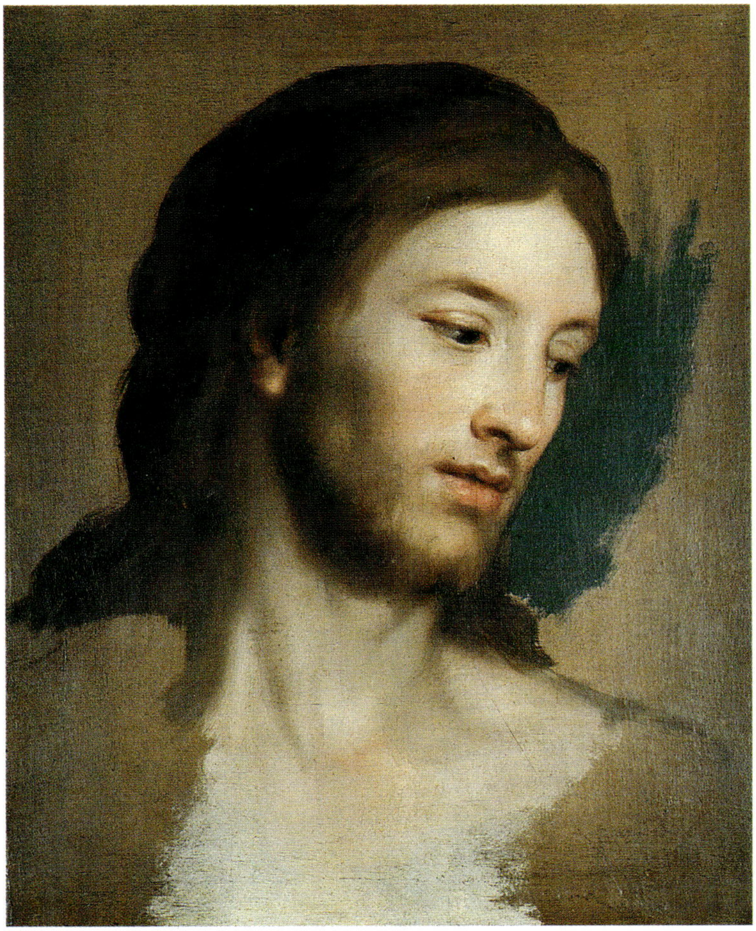

31
Benjamin West (1738-1820) after A. R. Mengs
A Sibyl

Oil on canvas, 118 × 92.7 cm
Kingston-upon-Hull, Ferens Art Gallery: Hull City Museums and Art Galleries

PROVENANCE: William Allen and James Hamilton, Philadelphia; The Hon. Margaret Hammond (Given to the Gallery from her estate by Sir George Barnes)

LITERATURE: Erffa/Staley (1986), no.510

Benjamin West said in a letter written on 11 May 1762 that he had just finished this copy and that it was already on its way to America with its companion piece, a copy of *St Cecilia* by Domenichino. The copies were for Chief Justice William Allen and the Lieutenant Governor of Pennsylvania, James Hamilton, in Philadelphia, to whom West also owed the financing of his trip to Europe. The *Sibyl* was therefore the first work by Mengs to make his name and style known in America.

It is characteristic that West chose a work by Domenichino as a companion piece; clearly he had recognised his influence on Mengs's style. He copied a *Holy Family* by Mengs presumably at the same time, that is, after Mengs had already left Rome. This had been painted for Lord Cowper and the copy is now in Kingston-Upon-Hull as well, with the same provenance (see Introduction, p.18). In sending these copies West was showing his patrons the progress he had made in subject painting, and also giving them a clear idea of the current trends in painting in Italy. Mengs was, incidentally, the only living painter whose work West copied.

The two pictures must have been accessible to young American painters in Philadelphia, together with other copies by West. On 29 September 1771 John Singleton Copley inspected the collection and remarked on the *Sibyl* after Mengs: 'I think a Niobe, I cannot be certain' (see Erffa/Staley (1986), no.510).

A comparison with the original shows that the young American painter did indeed already have considerable expertise in drawing, but he was still far from having mastered colour, which is one of the outstanding features of Mengs's *Sibyl.* Later works by West show that, like Mengs, he preferred the range of secondary colours.

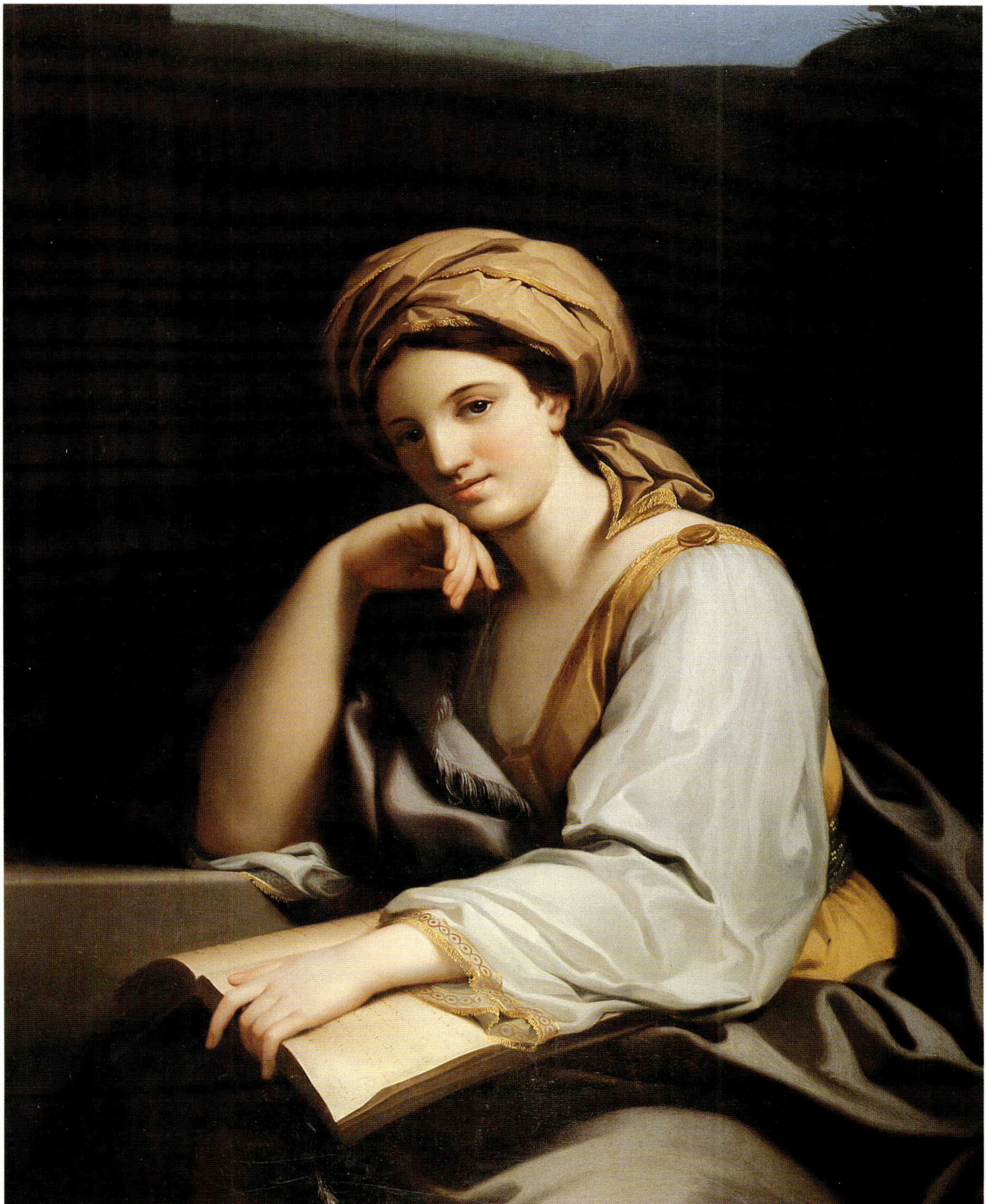

32

The Three Arts Mourning Raphael

Pen and ink in bister, wash, over grey chalk.
30.8 × 39.1 cm
Inscribed: A. R. Mengs Fec. a Roma 1741
London, Trustees of the British Museum, inv.no.1928-10-16-10

LITERATURE: Kurt Gerstenberg, 'Die künstlerischen Anfänge des Anton Raphael Mengs', *Zeitschrift für Kunstgeschichte*, II (1933), pp.77-88; Hans Ost, 'Ein Ruhmesblatt für Raphael bei Maratti und Mengs', *Zeitschrift für Kunstgeschichte*, XXVIII (1966), pp.281-98; Roettgen, pp.624/625).

As Ost showed, disagreeing with Gerstenberg, the picture is a copy of a print by Pietro Aquila which was used as the frontispiece to the series of engravings of Raphael's frescos in the Vatican loggias published in 1675. Aquila's engraving was based on a drawing by Carlo Maratti, which was once owned by Queen Christina of Sweden and was in a French private collection in 1971 (exhibition catalogue *Dessins francais et italiens du XVI et du XVII s. dans les collections privées françaises*, Paris, Galerie Claude-Aubry, December 1971, no.72). Maratti's composition is influced by the memorial to Michelangelo erected by Vasari in Santa Croce in Florence.

The Raphael bust is taken from the bronze bust by Giovanni Battista Naldini in the Pantheon. This bust was used by Mengs in 1744 for one of his first self-portraits (formerly Dresden, Gemäldegalerie), in which he showed himself as the German Raphael. The signature and the date on the copy are an important indication that even at the age of thirteen, and right at the start of his first visit to Rome, Mengs was intensely concerned with Raphael and his fame. However, he still had so little experience in drawing that he could only express his admiration for Raphael in a copy of a work by an admirer and imitator of that artist. It was to be almost ten years before Mengs regarded himself as more faithful to Raphael than Maratti (cat.no.19).

The rapid and skilful translation of the lights and darks in the print into a broad and loose wash technique shows how highly developed the boy's talent was. Indeed, to his contemporaries he appeared as something of a child prodigy.

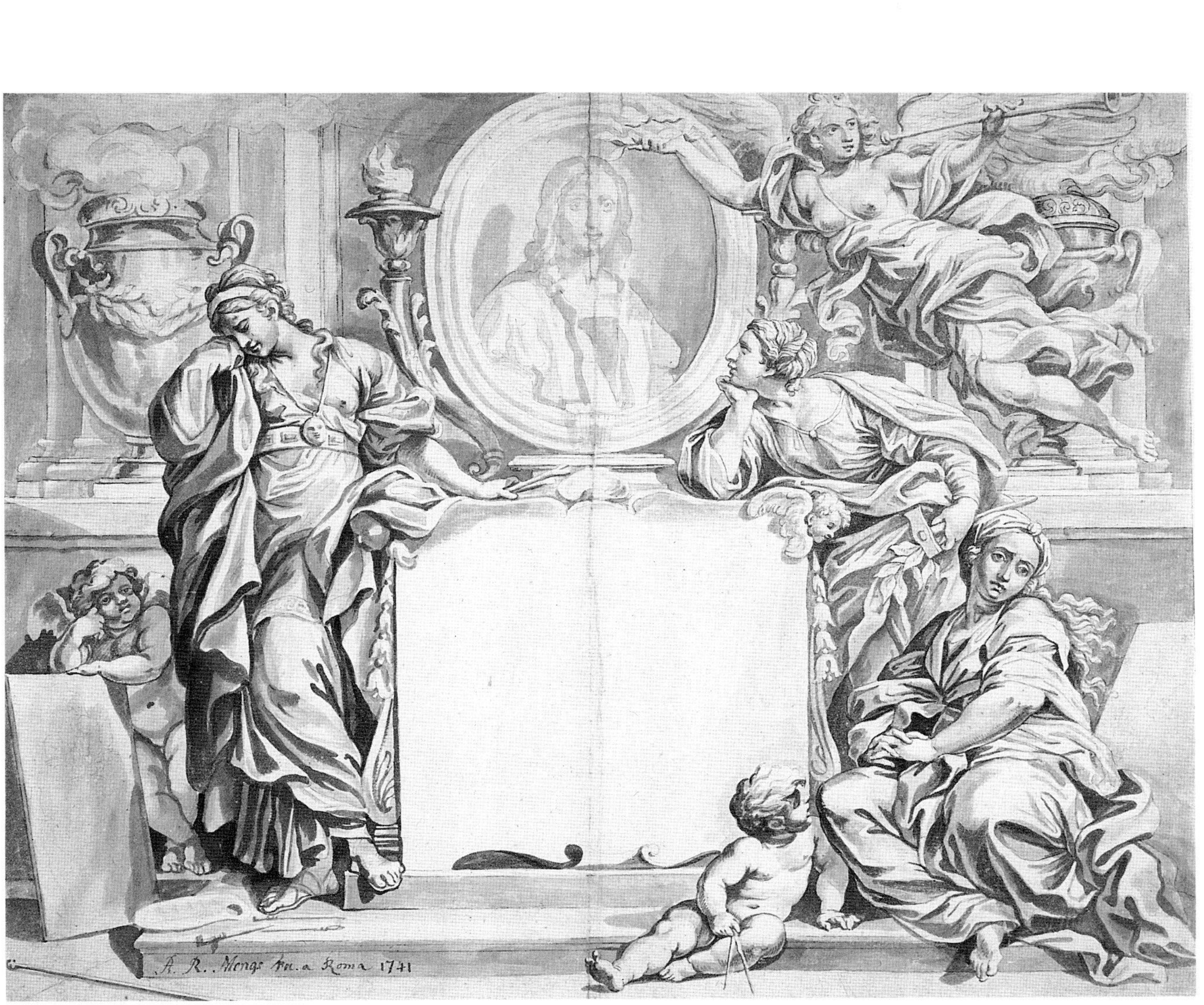
A. R. Mengs fec. a Roma 1741

33

Seated Male Nude

Black chalk, 51.9 × 38.5 cm
Inscribed, recto, bottom left, in brown ink: ... *ael Mengs Delint*; and below this, also in brown ink: ... *Rome by Robt Crone for Alex^r. Mangin Dublin;*
Inscribed, verso, top left, in ink: *Raphael Mengs procur^d at Rome for Alex^r Mangin by Rob Crone;*
PROVENANCE: Alexander Mangin; Royal Dublin Society; transferred to National Museum of Ireland, 1878; transferred to Gallery, 1966. Inv.no.3930
Dublin, National Gallery of Ireland, inv.no.3930

LITERATURE: A. McGoogan. *National Museum of Science and Art: Catalogue of Watercolour and Oil Paintings, Chalk and Pencil Drawings, etc.* Dublin, 1920, no.113; *National Gallery of Ireland Catalogue,* 1983,no.3930.

Mengs was regarded by his contemporaries as a master of life drawing, and the studies that have survived, of which there are not many, clearly show the reason for this high regard. Some of his life studies were so eagerly sought after that he made gifts of them. Some copies from his studies have also survived.

Mengs's great interest in life drawing was an integral part of his early academic ambitions, which were strengthened by his teaching work in the life class at the Accademia di San Luca in Rome, founded in 1754, where he taught from 1756 to 1760. After copying plaster casts of antique statues, he regarded drawing from life as the best means of acquiring the ability to depict the naked human form correctly. This was necessary for the painter's work, for he had to be able to handle any kind of movement, pose and perspective accurately. The ceiling design in the Victoria and Albert Museum (cat.no.43) shows the use Mengs himself made of his studies. Some of the *ignudi*'s poses are taken from his repertoire of life studies.

It was the tutor's job in all life classes to choose poses that suited his artistic aims, which would then influence the students' technique and repertoire of poses. Mengs preferred attitudes of repose, and in his drawings he paid great attention to soft and differentiated modelling of the muscles. To make the modelling as life-like as possible he used a dense system of hatching, and smudged over the harsher differences between areas with breadcrumbs. The models constituted a particular problem in that school; some were so old and unpleasant that both pupils and teacher protested.

The life study shown here, however, is from a young and well-proportioned, if not very muscular, model. The rather sunken chest seems unusual, and it is accentuated by the greatly lowered head. The pose could have been used for the youthful St John the Baptist.

There are only a few indications that might help date this sheet. It can technically best be compared with a study of a back in Florence (Uffizi, 9955s.), which could have been made before 1761.

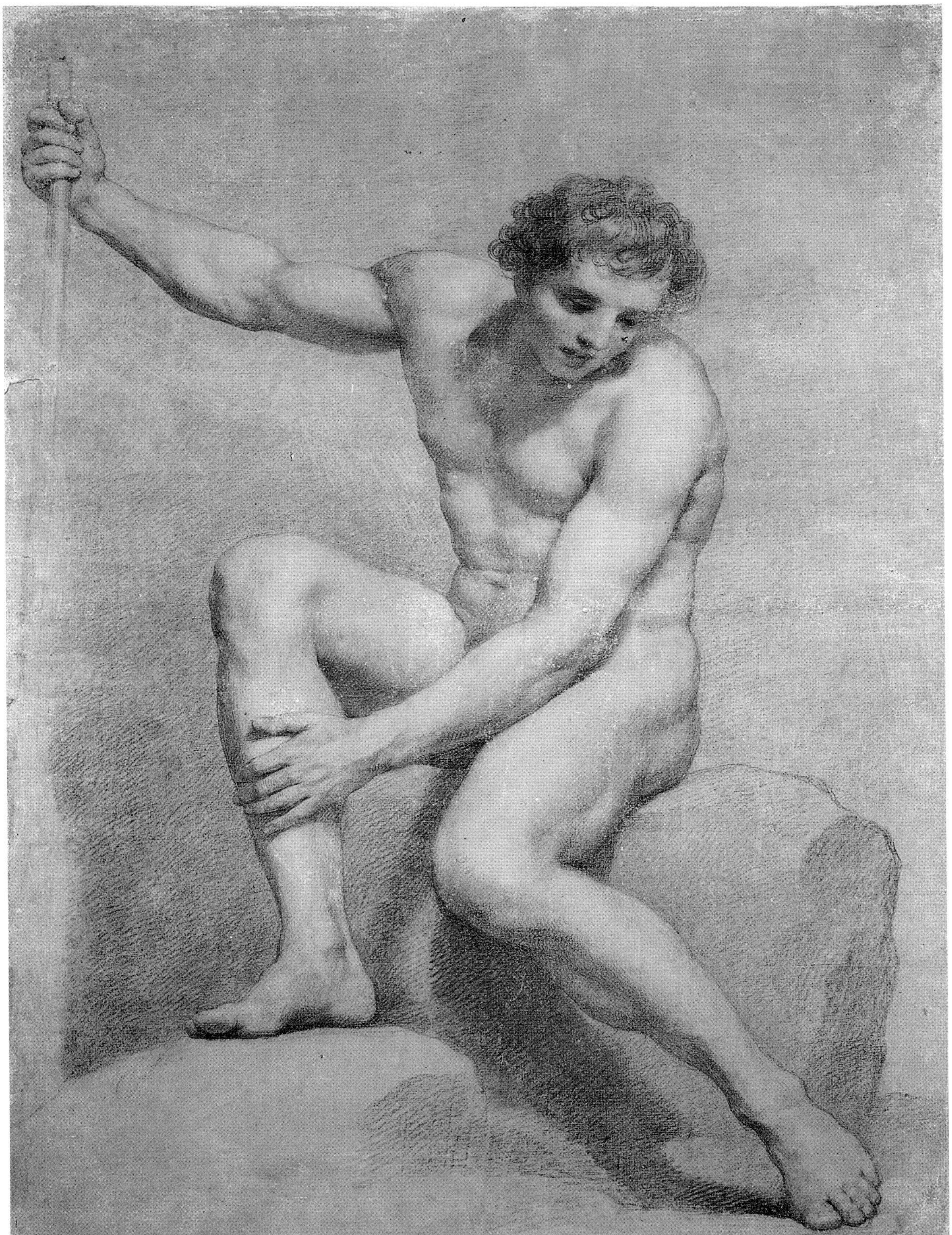

34
Augustus and Cleopatra

Black chalk, pen in grey and white on grey tinted paper
33.3 × 25.4 cm

Rotterdam, Museum Boymans-van Beuningen, inv.no.Mengs 6

PROVENANCE: Legacy of F. J. O. Boymans, 1847 (L.1857)

LITERATURE: *Catalogus van teekeningen in het museum te Rotterdam* (1852), no.1634; *Beschrijving der teekeningen in het museum te Rotterdam*, 1 (1869), no.2001; Hoetink (1964), no.87; Saabye (1976), p.22; Roettgen (1977), p.154-5.

This drawing is the only sketch for the painting in Stourhead House which Mengs produced in 1759-60 for Henry Hoare; it is largely identical with the finished work. Ample documentation has survived on the history of this second major commission for a British client (cat.nos.52, 53, 54) and the main points were clarified by Woodbridge in 1965.

The idea of commissioning a painting from Mengs may have been suggested to Hoare by Horace Mann; the picture was intended to match Carlo Maratti's *Apotheosis of Marchese Pallavicini*, which Hoare had purchased in 1758 with Mann's assistance. The two pictures are still in the Picture Gallery at Stourhead. In Mengs's work, the image is supposed to mean that Augustus, true to his principles and unlike Mark Antony and Cæsar, was able to withstand Cleopatra's charms. Plutarch describes the encounter between Augustus and Cleopatra in detail, and from the surviving correspondence between Mengs and Hoare we know that the painter reflected deeply on its psychological and historical aspects. He endeavoured to make his interpretation of the event plain while keeping exactly to the known historical facts.

The agents for this commission, which must have reached Mengs before June 1759, were the landscape painter John Plimmer and Thomas Jenkins. Mengs only appears to have been given the required dimensions of the work very much later, however, after the fee had already been agreed. This was possibly the reason why he first designed a completely different composition for the picture in a small *modello* that has survived (Augsburg, Städtisches Museum). The rejected version was much broader and included the dark, cellar-like architecture that Plutarch emphasised in his narrative. The fee agreed was for a painting with only two figures, and the painter received only 410 scudi for his work, despite the larger number of figures actually included. This suggests that when the fee was being negotiated he had not yet made definite plans for the work, and at that time he was presumably still thinking of the compositional model which Hoare apparently had in mind right from the start: Guercino's *Augustus and Cleopatra* in the Capitoline Museum in Rome, which does only have two figures.

The letters exchanged between Hoare and Mengs, or his Roman agents, show that the picture was finished in July 1760, two months after Mengs returned from an extended stay in Naples. While Jenkins greatly praised the picture and assured Hoare that it would meet with a very positive response in Rome, Hoare himself was not pleased with the way Mengs had handled the subject (cat.no.53). He thought Cleopatra seemed too humiliated, and argued that a nobler posture for the Egyptian Queen would not have detracted from the majesty of Augustus. Mengs, however, maintained that Cleopatra's defeat must be clearly evident from her attitude. (For the painting's influence on Benjamin West and Angelika Kauffmann see Introduction, p.26.)

The most important change to this preliminary work in the finished version was the opening-up of the space in the left half, which enables the Rotterdam drawing to be exactly dated. At Christmas 1759 the picture was nearly finished, but the background was closed and in the Egyptian style. Mengs was hoping that his client would accept this arrangement, but apparently he did not. The drawing documents the state of the composition towards the end of 1759. The use of a colonnade to open part of the space gave the entire composition a more grandiose effect, although it does not accord with Plutarch's description of the location, that of a dark, grave-like cell. It also meant that the niche with the figure and the lion throne visible on the left edge of the drawing had to be dropped. Instead, two servants of Augustus were added in the background, balancing, formally and numerically Cleopatra's two servants. The rectangular niche in the wall with the image of Canopus and the two servant women were moved to the right. This allowed Augustus's right arm, outstretched to emphasise his speech, to stand out more effectively against the pilaster; the distance between the two hostile protagonists was also enlarged, and the depiction as a whole gained greatly in dramatic tension. A rapid preliminary sketch showing the composition in reverse is in Besançon (Musée des Beaux-Arts, inv.no.D.842).

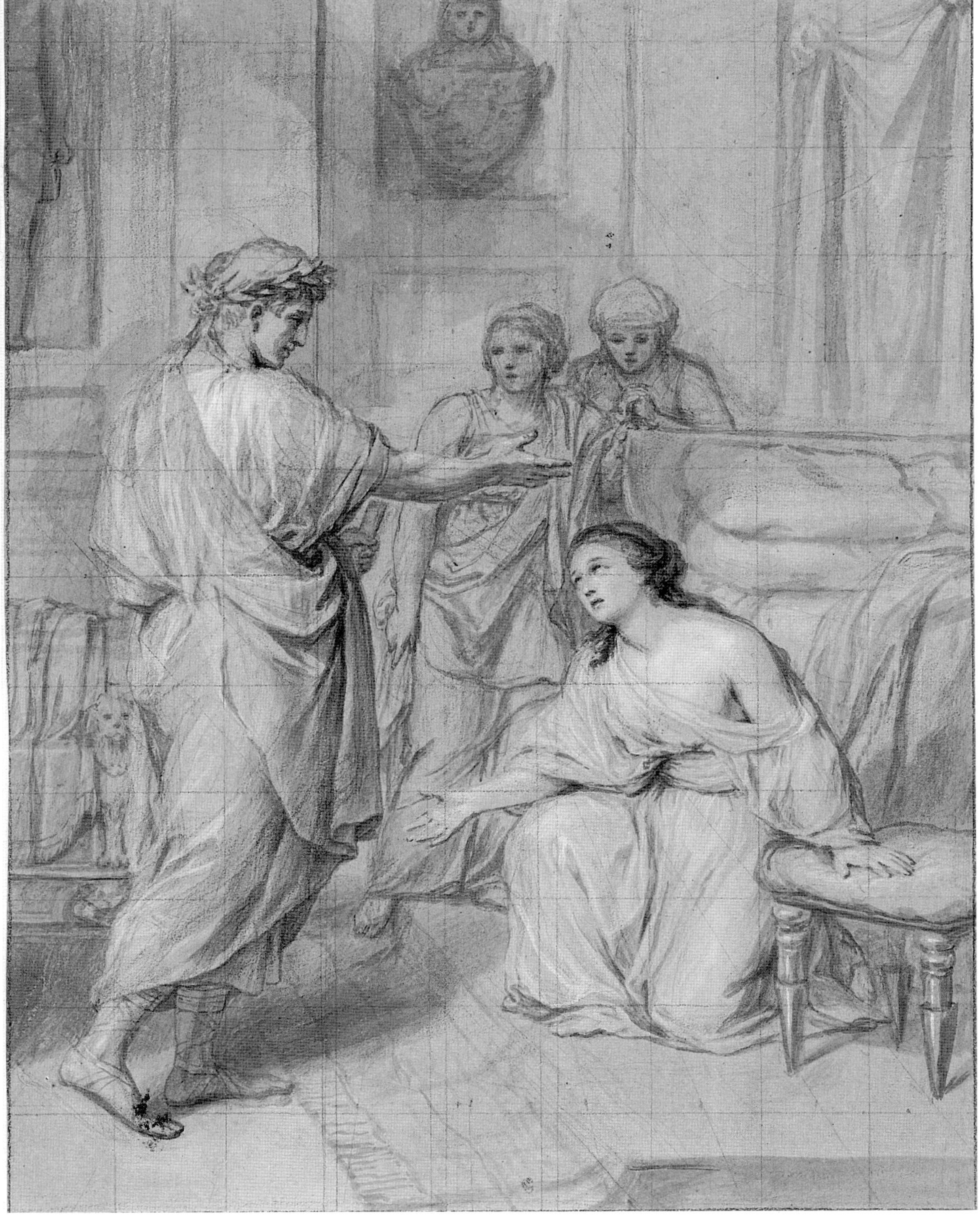

35

Hovering Angel with Censer

Black and white chalk on bluish-grey tinted paper 26 × 32.1 cm
Inscribed N.o 58 cart.a p.ma del Caballero Mengs/ 160 r.es
London, Courtauld Institute Galleries (Witt Collection no. 155)

PROVENANCE: Sir John Stirling Maxwell, Stirling Maxwell auction, London, Parsons 1926; Sir Robert Witt; Witt Bequest 1952.

LITERATURE: Exhibition catalogue: *German Art 14-1600*, City Art Gallery, Manchester 1961, no.27. Exhibition catalogue, *Goya and his Times*, London, Royal Academy (1963-4), no.323; exhibition catalogue, *German Drawings from the Collections of H. M. the Queen*, London, Courtauld Institute (December 1969–March 1970), no.40.

EXHIBITIONS: *German Drawings from the Collections of H. M. the Queen, University College, London and the Courtauld Institute of Art*, Courtauld Institute Galleries, December 1969–March 1970, no.40; *Neo-Classical Drawings from the Witt Collection augmented by Drawings and Models by Flaxman and Gibson from the Collection of University College, London and by Drawings from the Collections of Professor Sir Anthony Blunt and the Royal Institute of British Architects*, Courtauld Institute Galleries, November – December 197? no.1; *Spanish Drawings from the Witt Collection*, Courtauld Institute Galleries, March – May 1978, no.52.

This drawing is one of the few figure studies to have survived for the second *Adoration of the Shepherds*, which Mengs painted for Charles III of Spain; it is now in the Prado. The painting was executed in 1772 in Rome, so directly after the *Noli me tangere* for Oxford (cat.no.30). It was intended for the King's Dressing Room in the Palacio Real.

The angel is largely identical with the figure on the executed painting. In the study the painter has concentrated mainly on the drapery, and the face and wings are only faintly indicated. The censer is too big, and in the painting it is replaced by the smaller vessel here drawn in detail in the middle. The drawing is a particularly fine drapery study, with handling typical of Mengs. It shows the careful study of the contrasting effects of strong partial lighting which was necessary for the depiction of a form shrouded in the darkness of night. A composition drawing in Weimar (Staatliche Kunstsammlungen, HE1501), which was in the collection of John Charles Robinson in 1876, has the same characteristics.

The study shown here must, like the Weimar drawing, have come from Mengs's estate, as is evident from the inscription. The large stock of drawings in his studio after his death was catalogued by portfolios. The first contained almost exclusively drawings by other masters, and so presumably the words 'del Caballero Mengs' were added by another hand. In the nineteenth century this drawing appears to have been in Spain. This is suggested by its provenance from the collection of the celebrated historian Stirling Maxwell, who also discusses Mengs in his *Annals of the Artists in Spain* which appeared in 1848. Possibly Stirling Maxwell acquired the sheet from Mengs's Spanish heirs, that is, from the painter José Madrazo, a descendant on his mother's side of Mengs's daughter Ana Maria who had married the copper engraver Manuel Salvador Carmona. The Madrazo collection contained a study for one of the angels in the *Adoration of the Shepherds* in 1858 (catalogue Madrid, Galeria José Madrazo (1856), no.558).

Although the composition of the picture has a long iconographic tradition, going back to the seventeenth-century Bolognese painters (Lanfranco, Domenichino, Carracci), and can be traced back to Rubens, it was Mengs's declared intention to rival Correggio in this work. At any rate, this is stated by his Spanish biographer José Nicolas de Azara, but he also maintains in the same context that Mengs excelled Titian in his rendering of the flesh tints in this painting and Raphael in the expression of the figures. Such statements were, in fact, the usual way of measuring artistic quality, and until far into the eighteenth century these traditional comparisons constituted the normal practice in passing judgements on works of art. Richard Cumberland's verdict on Mengs' *Notte* was not nearly so positive, however, and what Azara had so praised, he criticised as being too dependent on the Italian tradition.

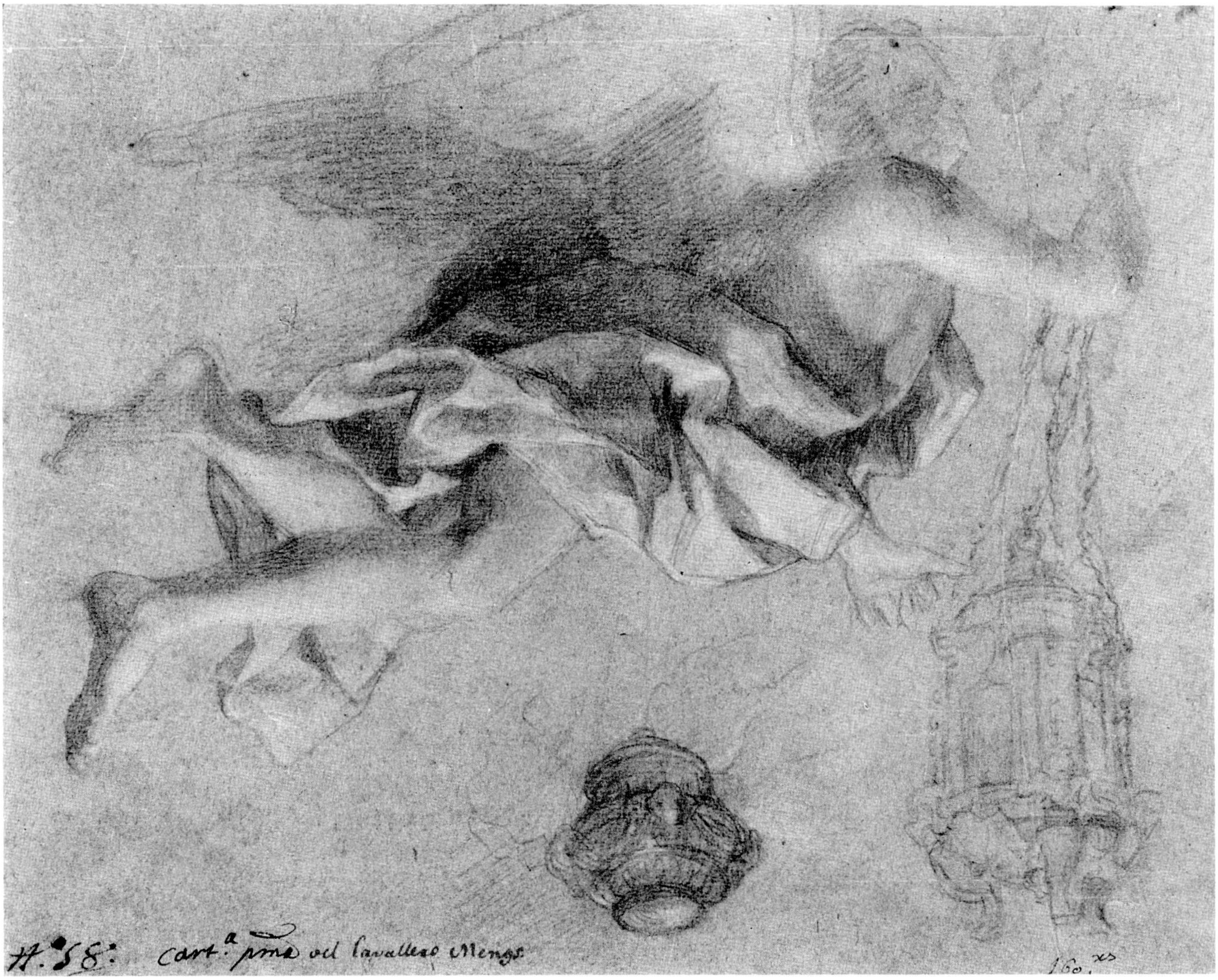

36
The Adoration of the Shepherds

Pen in brown ink, brown and grey wash over grey chalk, heightened in white, squared in the upper part, 22.6 × 14 cm
Inscribed recto by the artist: 'questo a da essere un Agnello è non un porco come pare'
Oxford, The Visitors of the Ashmolean Museum

PROVENANCE: Colnaghi, London 1965

Verso: Rapid sketch of a standing figure with wings (not identifiable)

This drawing formed part of the extensive preparatory work for the *Adoration of the Shepherds* which Mengs painted for Charles III in the first years of his sojourn in Madrid, and which has been in the Corcoran Art Gallery in Washington since 1869. The painting was originally destined for Charles III's private chapel in the Palacio Real, but soon had to be removed as light reflections fell on it, preventing a proper view. Mengs replaced it with a fresco which was later destroyed. The painting was removed from Madrid, with other works by Mengs, by Joseph Bonaparte, who confiscated it from the Spanish crown, but unlike most of the other pictures, which came into the possession of the Duke of Wellington at the Battle of Victoria, this one remained in Bonaparte's collection. He took it with him when he retired to Bordentown in the state of New York, where he died in 1844.

With the *Annunciation*, the *Lamentation of Christ* and the *Holy Family*, the *Adoration of the Shepherds* was one of the Christian themes which Mengs repeatedly depicted. For the *Holy Family* Raphael was the model against whom he measured his own achievements all his life, but the unattainable model for the *Adoration of the Shepherds* was Correggio's *Notte*, which the Elector of Saxony had acquired for Dresden in 1748 from the Este Collection in Modena. Mengs had been concerned with this subject since his first big commission for the court chapel in Dresden, but it was only in the painting that is now in Washington that he succeeded in what can really be regarded as a convincing translation of Correggio's composition into the artistic taste of the eighteenth century. Particularly the number of figures is reduced, and this improves the clarity of the composition. The nocturnal lighting is also realised in such a way that the depiction radiates the intimacy and security the subject demands.

The drawing in Oxford documents an early stage in the working-out of the composition. Ultimately only the choir of angels was used in the final version. That they were adapted in identical form can be seen from the fact that the upper part of the drawing has been squared to transfer it to canvas, but not the lower part. The postures of Mary and the shepherds went through several more major changes. The figure of the kneeling shepherd in the right half was removed, while Joseph is shown standing. As can be observed with many of Mengs's compositional sketches, the final version was worked out in a long and laborious process, with many digressions and corrections. One has the impression that the solution finally chosen was always only one of several possibilities, and that the accumulated drawings and ideas would be used again in future depictions of the theme.

In the Oxford drawing this is evident from the critical remark on the lamb on the floor in Mengs's own hand, and in the painting as finally executed the lamb no longer appears. Presumably the failure to depict the animal to his own satisfaction (he notes that it looks more like a pig than a lamb) was one of the reasons why Mengs was not satisfied with the arrangement of the figures in the lower half. He had taken the motif of the shepherds and the lamb from an earlier composition.

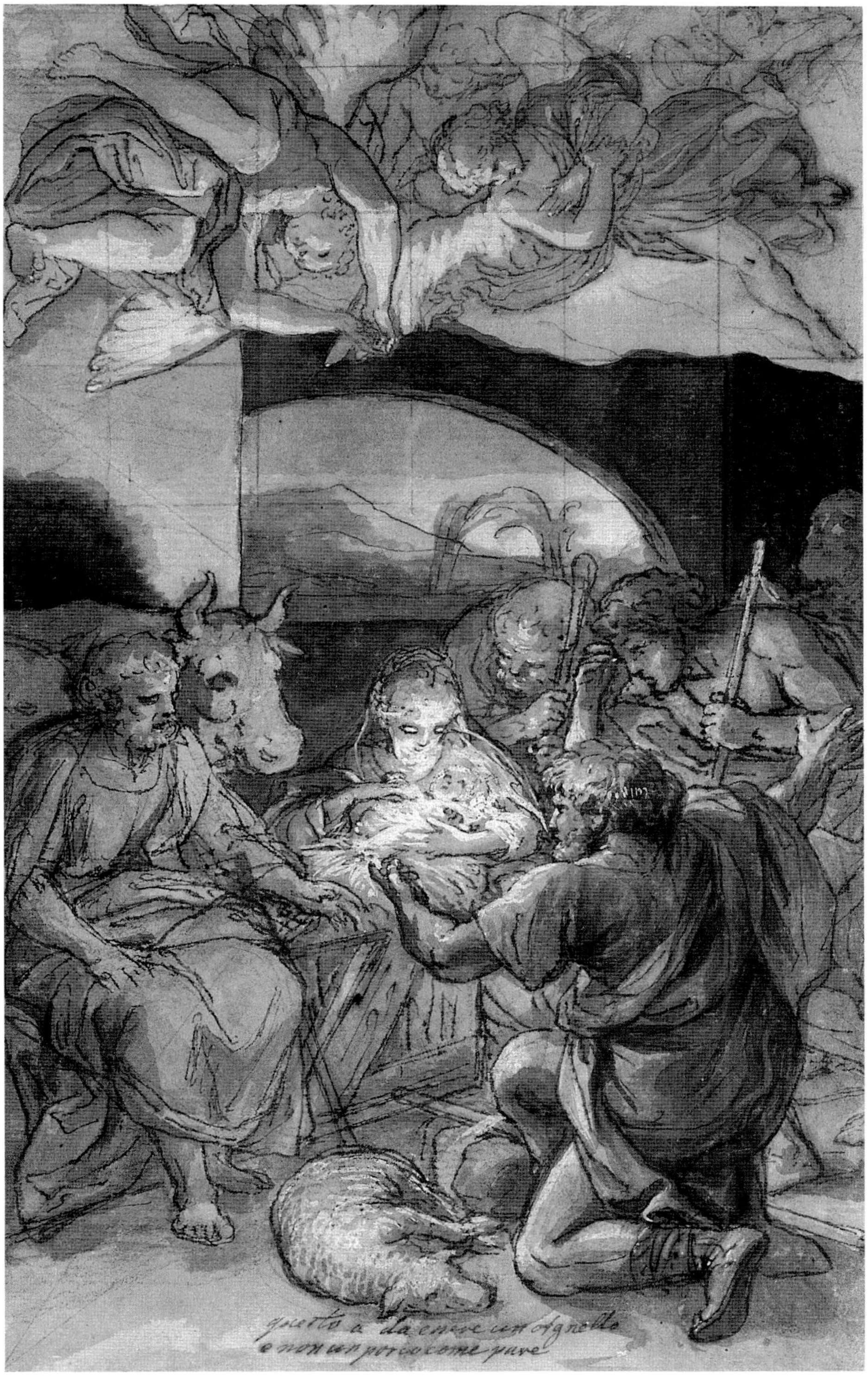
questo a da essere un Agnello
e non un porco come pare

37

The Annunciation

Pen in sepia ink over grey chalk, 19 × 25.9 cm
London, The Trustees of the British Museum,
inv.no.1960-7-16-26

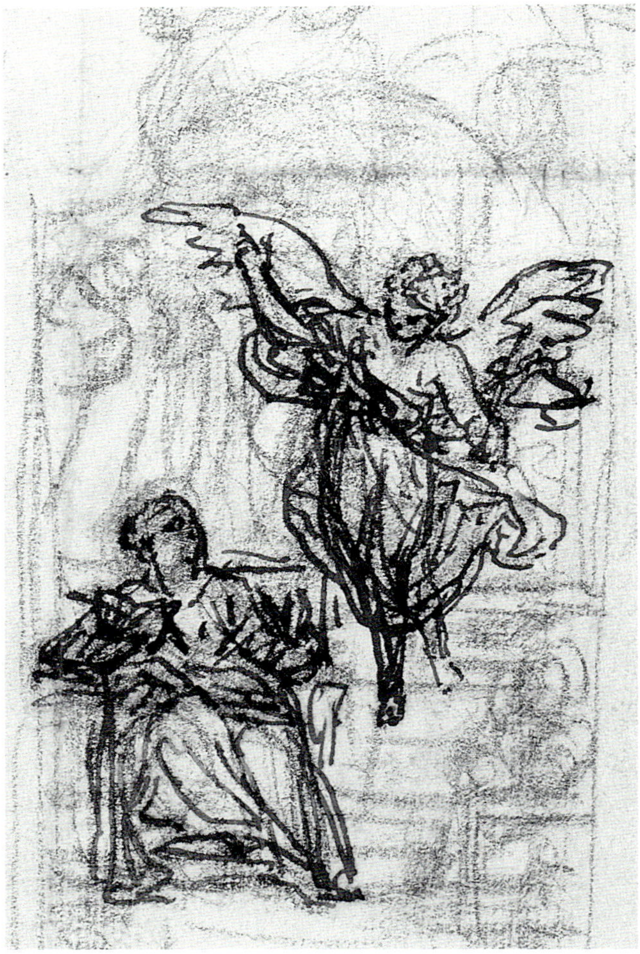

This study is a characteristic example of the sketchy drawings which Mengs used for the preliminary work on his compositions. The overdrawing of the chalk lines in sepia ink is also typical of this way of working, as is the co-existence of framed and unframed sketches in which the artist worked out a number of variants before the final solution was reached. This drawing in the British Museum shows three variants. The possibility explored in the left half of the sheet is also indicated in two chalk sketches in the right half. The compositional sketch on the left is closely related to a sketch in the Uffizi (9944.S.), which has the same arrangement of the figures and a similar frame. However, the angel is different here, no longer kneeling on a cloud.

None of the finished versions of the Annunciation has a composition directly related to any of the very sparse design material that has survived. However, the arrangement of this sketch, including the frame and proportions, suggest that the sheet is one of the preliminary works for the *Annunciation* for the Colegiata in Castrogeriz now in Vienna (cat.no.26), and could therefore be dated around 1765.

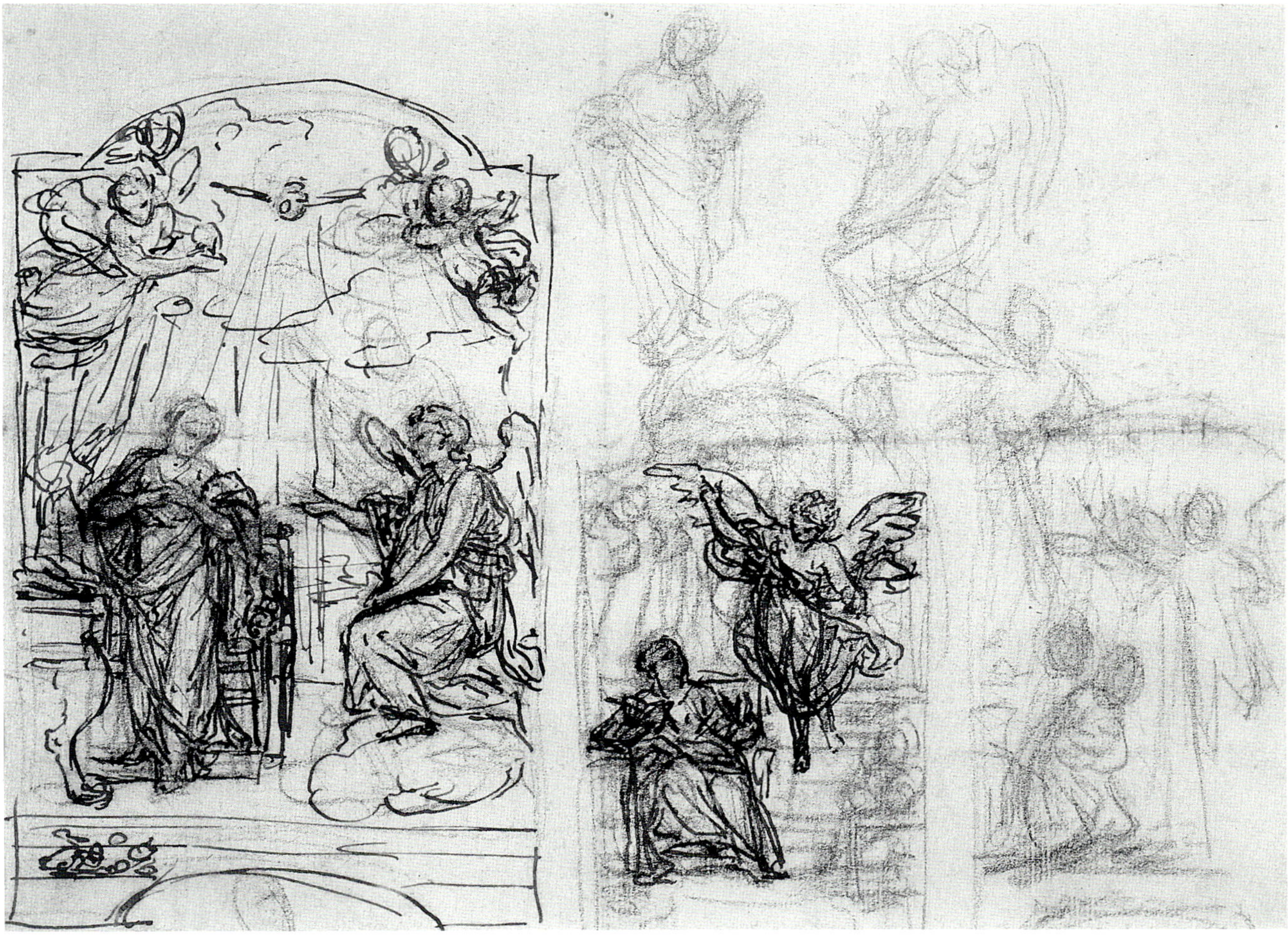

38
The Descent from the Cross and the Lamentation of Christ

Pen in brown ink, grey wash heightened with white, 26.7 × 22 cm
Rotterdam, Museum Boymans-van Beuningen, inv.no.Mengs 1

PROVENANCE: Legacy of F. J. O. Boymans, 1847 (L.1857)

LITERATURE: *Catalogus van teekeningen in het museum te Rotterdam* (1852), no.1692; *Beschriiving der teekeningen in het museum te Rotterdam*, 1 (1869), no.1996; Hoetink (1964), no.89.

This is a carefully executed and finished drawing which concluded the first phase of the prepatory work for the *Lamentation.* However, it was finally rejected for the painting, as a comparison with the version from Cambridge in the exhibition shows (cat.no.27).

Unlike the executed painting, the drawing combines the subject of the *Descent from the Cross* with that of the *Lamentation.* This is evident mainly from the presence of Nicodemus and Joseph of Arimathaea, who are not normally shown in a *Lamentation.* The scene is also set directly beside the place of crucifixion, while in the finished painting this has been moved into the distance and given way to the open grave on the right.

That this is a preliminary work for the *Lamentation* is, however, clear from the arrangement of some figures and the sheet in Florence (Uff.S.9954), which contains sketches for both variants. The first cursory design for the Rotterdam composition is a drawing in the Academia de San Fernando in Madrid (inv.no.2224). The sheet in the Uffizi, which contains a large number of sketches, shows how the two variants gradually converged.

The picture is a characteristic example of the technique which Mengs used on all his drawings where the composition had already been largely determined. The wash is applied like watercolour to show the distribution of lights and darks, and gives the drawing pictorial character.

The discarded composition on the Rotterdam drawing served as the basis for an early oil painting by Goya (Guidol II, illus.7), which is now in a private collection. Goya copied the motif of the composition exactly but in an entirely different formal language.

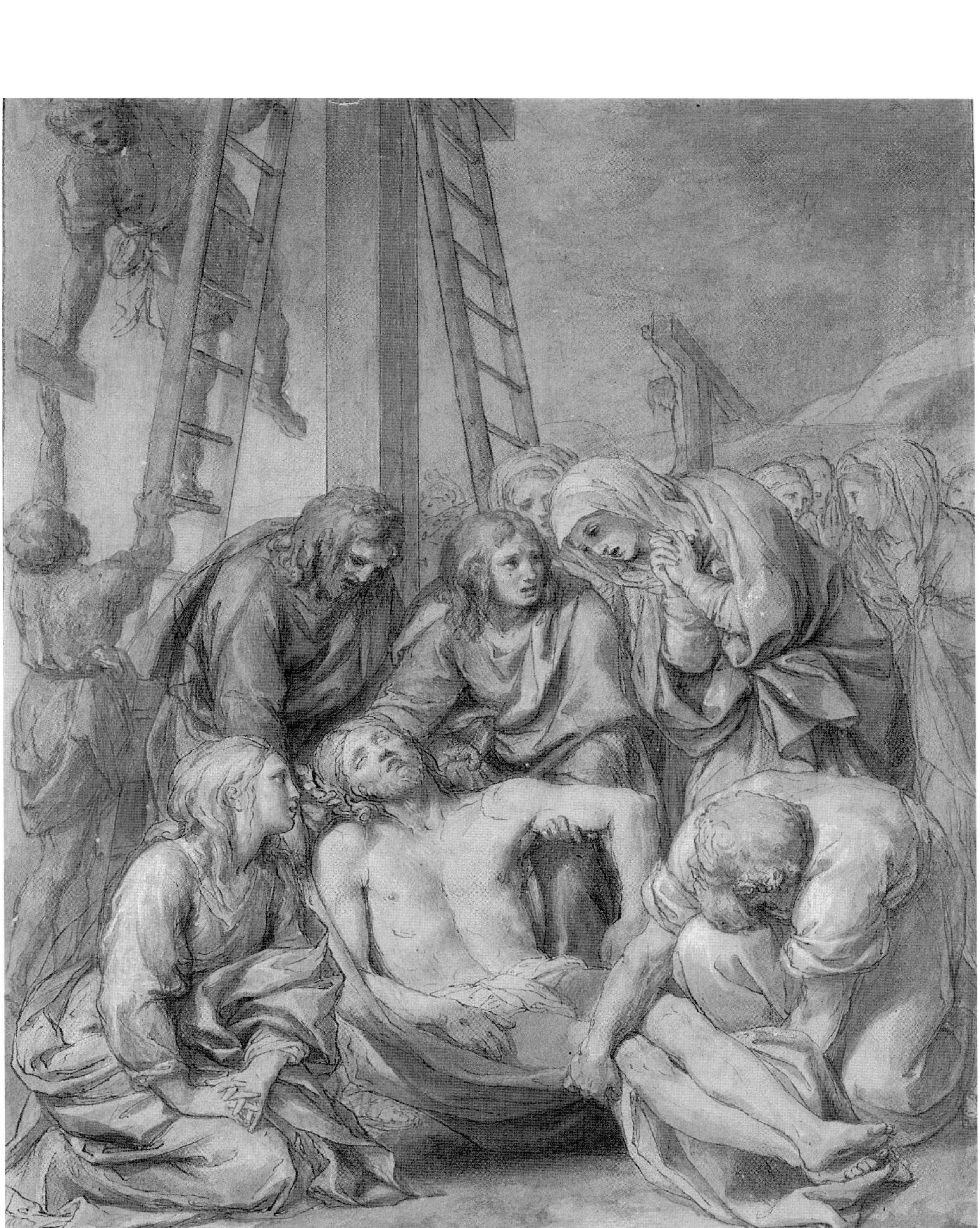

39
Oedipus at Colonnos before the Temple of the Eumenides

Pen and brush in brown ink, blue wash, heightened in white on light brown paper
18.1 × 22.4 cm
Inscribed on the verso: 'This Drawing representing Oedipus before the Temple of the Furies at Corinth was done by Mengs at Rome as an Imitation of the Antique in order to be engraved. Pichler accordingly copied it for me (who procured the drawing of Mengs himself) in 1763; upon a fine onyx. P. Montagu has its companion, Priam at Achilles feet, drawn by Mengs and engraved by Pichler'.
Inscribed on the recto: MENZ (in Greek letters)
London, Ralph Holland

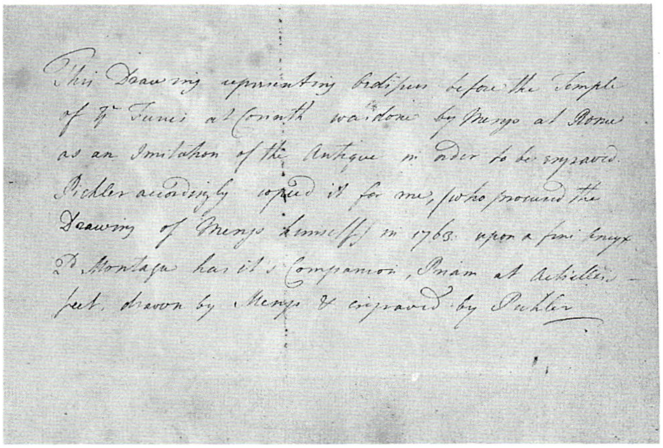
This Drawing representing Oedipus before the Temple
of ye Furies at Corinth was done by Mengs at Rome
as an Imitation of the Antique in order to be engraved.
Pichler accordingly copied it for me (who procured the
Drawing of Mengs himself) in 1763. upon a fine Onyx.
P. Montagu has its Companion, Priam at Achilles
feet, drawn by Mengs & engraved by Pichler

PROVENANCE: Collection of Robert Redford of Drummond Street, Montreal; London, Christie's 25.2.1969, lot 174.

LITERATURE: Timothy Clifford, Burlington Magazine, June 1974, p.354. Exhibition catalogue, *Italian and Other Drawings 1500-1800*, London, Courtauld Institute Gallery (1975), no.73.

This drawing is one of the most remarkable testimonies to Mengs's intensive preoccupation with the Antique, which was further fuelled by his friendship with Winckelmann and his own antiquarian interests.

The subject of the blinded Oedipus, led by his daughters Ismene and Antigone to the temple of the Eumenides at Colonnos in order to find release from his torments, is taken from Sophocles's drama *Oedipus at Colonnos.* As far as I have been able to ascertain, the subject had not been depicted in the modern era before Mengs. It was only taken up again towards the end of the eighteenth century by a few French artists. A drawing by Jakob Asmus Carstens in Weimar must have been based on a knowledge of Mengs's handling of the theme.

The composition is laid out like a relief in a horizontal oval, as was necessary for a cameo carving. The figures, in ancient robes and poses, are arranged almost symmetrically in the picture, with the main group consisting of Antigone and Oedipus, framed by Ismene and the frightened messenger, who is holding his horse by the bit. In the background on the right are two priests, guardians of the sacred grove where Oedipus sought refuge and found release.

Ancient models for Mengs's work might best be sought in carved gems, but no such composition has been found. The history of the composition is even more puzzling in that there is a drawing of the same scene and composition in Florence with some variants (Uffizi 14831 F). It has all the features of a copy, and from what is known so far it must be assumed to be a copy of an ancient drawing or at least of one which the artist thought was ancient, and which he then used for his own design for the cameo.

The cameo made from the design was in the collection of Thomas Robinson, whose portrait Mengs had painted in Rome in 1760 and who was an enthusiastic admirer of the artist (cat.no.51). This is evident from the catalogue of the Cristian Denh collection made in 1772, which contains a print of the Pichler cameo. The catalogue text comments that the gem belongs to Mr Robinson (*Descrizione istorica del Museo di Cristiano Denh… per l'abate Francesco Maria Dolce*, Rome (1772), vol.3, p.37). It is not known where the engraving is now, but at least a few prints are confirmed by the older literature (*Trésor de numismatique et de glyptique* (Paris, 1835), PL XIII/7; Lippold T.143/7)). These prints are identical with the drawing shown here.

It may be assumed that the drawing for the cameo, which was not carved by Anton Pichler until 1788, was made when Robinson was in Rome, in 1760. However, Mengs must have taken an identical copy of the drawing to Madrid with him, for the composition was copied there by Richard Cooper (cat.no.44), who commented that the drawing was made in Spain. According to the information we have so far, that cannot be correct.

Cameo carvings were a passion which seized all visitors to Rome in the second half of the eighteenth century. Their tiny size and the belief that so handy an antique could be acquired at a low price made the tourists eager to buy, and the number of forgers and their output rocketed. Pichler was the best known cameo sculptor in Rome around 1760,

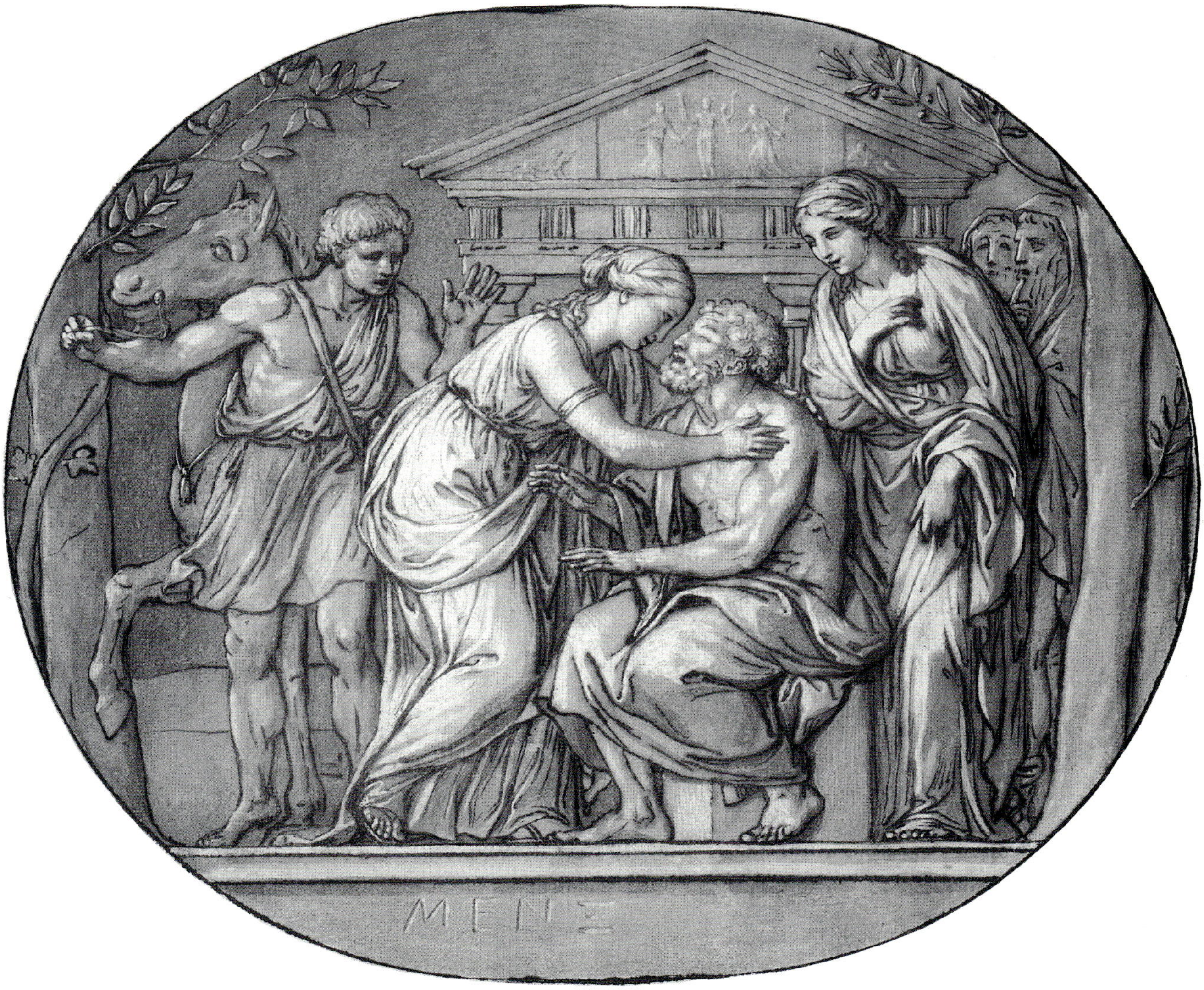
MENS

and like all his colleagues he did not draw too fine a line between forgery and his own creations. However, in this case we have a design signed, as was usual, in Greek lettering and there can be no question of forgery.

Thanks to the inscription on the reverse of the drawing, which, to judge from the circumstances described must have come from Thomas Robinson, we can also identify the matching intaglio showing *Priam before Achilles.* A print of this intaglio was described in the catalogue of the collection owned by Cristian Denh in Rome as follows: 'Questo intaglio moderno in Onice disegno del Cav. Mengs… à inciso Antonio Picler, Possessore essendo Mylord Brudenal, rapresenta l'atto, che Priamo ingionocchiato chiede ad Achille Il Corpo di ettore suo Figlio, Achille sta sedente in atto di sorpresa nel vedersi all'improviso Priamo. Questi con il manto reale prostrato stringe la ginocchia; vi sono due Famegli in piedi in atto anch'essi di ammirazione, essendovi un fanale acceso per indicare che tal dimanda vanisse fatta di notte.' ('This modern onyx gem designed by Cav. Mengs… for Anton Pichler to engrave, the owner being Milord Brudenal [sic], shows the scene in which Priam, kneeling, begs Achilles for the body of his son Hector, Achilles remains seated in an attitude of surprise upon seeing Priam so unexpectedly. The latter, his royal mantle lying on the ground, clasps his knees; there are two attendants standing by similarly dumb-struck, while a burning lamp indicates that this action takes place at night'). A print that is identical with this very exact description is known (Lippold (1922), p.186). Moreover, the description confirms the former owner of the cameo, whom Robinson also names in his notation: it was Lord Brudenell, whose portrait Mengs had painted (cat.no.2). The design for the cameo, which has not yet been recovered, was probably made around 1758.

The subject of *Priam before Achilles* became one of the most popular in Neo-classical art, unlike that of *Oedipus at Colonnos.* Gavin Hamilton's depiction of the subject, which was engraved in 1766 by Domenico Cunego, recalls Pichler's cameo and thus Mengs's design, which itself had been influenced by ancient depictions of the theme.

40
Portrait of a Man in Profile (Lord Brudenell?)

Black chalk, heightened in white, on green (formerly blue) tinted paper, 21.1 × 15.5 cm
The Duke of Buccleuch, Kt

This drawing, in a vertical oval frame, has traditionally been regarded as a self-portrait of the artist, but it does not bear a convincing likeness to the verified self-portraits of Mengs (cat.no.1), which do include one in three-quarter profile.

The sitter's hairstyle and profile are greatly idealised and the features highly individualised. It must therefore be a contemporary portrait. There are several such portraits in Mengs's œuvre, used as models for portrait cameos, as was the case with this drawing as well, although the carving is not exhibited here. There is a matching drawing, of the same size and framed in the same way, showing a bust of Cæsar in the style of ancient cameos. The Rome-based sculptor Anton Pichler made a cameo from this model (Lippold (1922), Plate CLVIII/6).

The present location of the drawings, with their implied provenance from Lord Brudenell, make it seem possible that this was an idealised profile portrait in the antique style to contrast with the social portrait (cat.no.2). There are indeed certain similarities between this drawing and Lord Brudenell's features and hairstyle in the portrait of 1758, although the subject looks older here. For a painter interested in antiquity like Mengs, there must have been a certain fascination in showing the models he had depicted in more or less fashionable dress in the costume of ancient heroes.

Lord Brudenell certainly owned the cameo of *Priam before Achilles* which Anton Pichler made from a sketch by Mengs (cat.no.39), and so was clearly interested in modern cameos carved in the ancient style. As he also loved having his portrait taken in a wide variety of forms (cat.nos.2, 3), it is quite likely that he would have wanted one of these antique profiles as well.

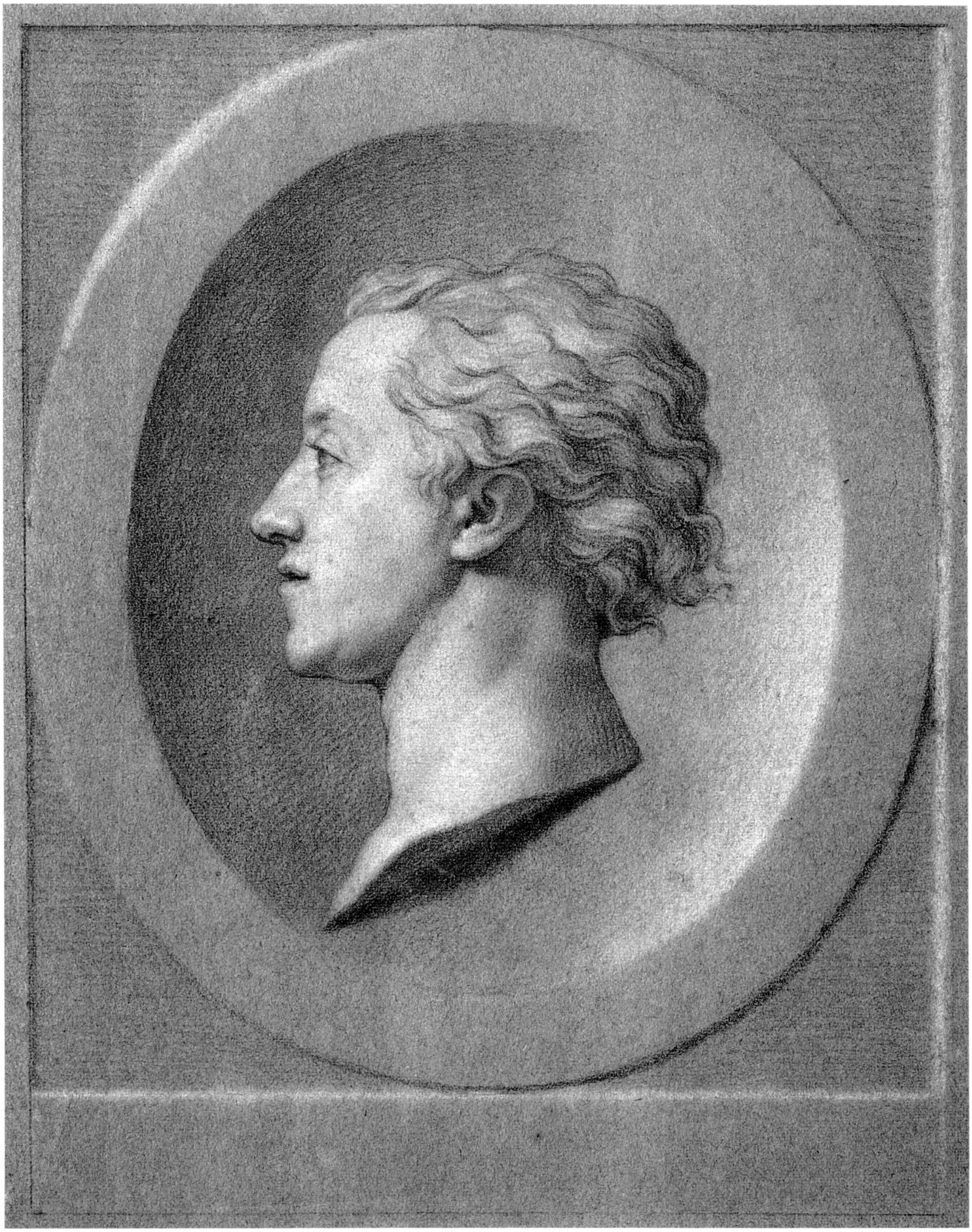

41

Sketch for 'The Apotheosis of Hercules' in the Palacio Real, Madrid

Pen on brownish tinted paper, squared in black chalk
14.7 × 42.9 cm
Edinburgh, National Gallery of Scotland, inv.no.RSA168

PROVENANCE: Dr Jackson; Present by him to David Laing 1859; David Laing Bequest to the Royal Scottish Academy; on loan to the National Gallery of Scotland since 1966.

The drawing is a sketch, largely worked out, for the west side of the fresco in the Conversation Room of King Charles III of Spain in the Palacio Real in Madrid. A relatively large number of individual studies for the fresco are still extant, but nothing has survived of the many cartoons used to transfer the drawing on to the wall surface; however, many of the cartoons were copied by younger artists, so some must have been in Mengs's studio in Rome later.

The designs for the other three sides of the room, which was roughly square, have been in a private collection in Madrid since about 1965. The dimensions, technique and script of these three sheets are so similar to this one that, despite a different provenance in the nineteenth century, it can be assumed that the Edinburgh drawing is also part of that group. The Madrid sketches have the same British provenance as the drawing for *Apollo in his Sun Chariot* for the Villa Albani (cat.no.42), which shows the same characteristics.

The style of these four sheets suggests that they date from about the same time as the painting of the gallery in the Villa Albani (see cat.no.45), and they are very similar to the only surviving design for the *Parnassus* there in the emphasis on clear outlines. That sketch is now in the Albertina in Vienna. Presumably these four drawings were made soon after Mengs's arrival in Madrid in the autumn of 1761. The many differences from the completed work also suggest an early date.

Originally, Corrado Giaquinto had been commissioned to paint the King's Conversation Room, and the stucco works had already been made to his designs. Mengs had these removed again before starting the painting in summer 1762, after Giaquinto had left Madrid. Tiepolo was working close by with his sons on the Throne Room fresco at the time. At first the work made good progress, and in May 1764 Mengs was still expecting to finish the fresco soon. But work on the preparatory drawings for the roughly sixty figures proved very protracted, owing to the many detailed studies and cartoons that were needed, and the work underwent ever more frequent interruptions from 1764 to 1768, not least because the painter was undertaking numerous other commissions. In October 1768 Mengs resumed intensive work on the fresco, but again had to break off, this time because he fell seriously ill. The scaffold remained in place during his absence from Madrid from 1769 to 1774, so that the room could not be used. When he started work again, in 1774, a few areas were already in such bad condition that the layer of paint was peeling off and had to be completely renewed. The exact date when the work was finally finished is not known, but presumably it was not until the summer of 1776.

The main subject on the ceiling is Hercules, who was regarded as the mythical founder of the Spanish monarchy. The ascension of the hero to Olympus on the north side of the room is matched on the east side by the Kingdom of Love and the Forces of Nature, and on the west side by the Muses and Inspiration (Apollo and Bacchus), while the south side is dominated by the deities and personifications of time. All three areas are closely related to the theme of Hercules.

The Edinburgh drawing is for the west side and it shows, standing close together, from left to right, Mars Victor with Castor and Pollux, Aesculapius, Vertumnus and Pomona, Apollo and the Muses in the centre, and on their right Bacchus, Comus and Silenus, with Maenads and satyrs. It is remarkable how far Mengs moved away from the *Parnassus* in the Albani here in his handling of the subject of the Muses and Apollo. This is particularly evident in the posture of Apollo, who is shown seated in the drawing while in the executed fresco he is standing, in the posture of the *Belvedere* Apollo.

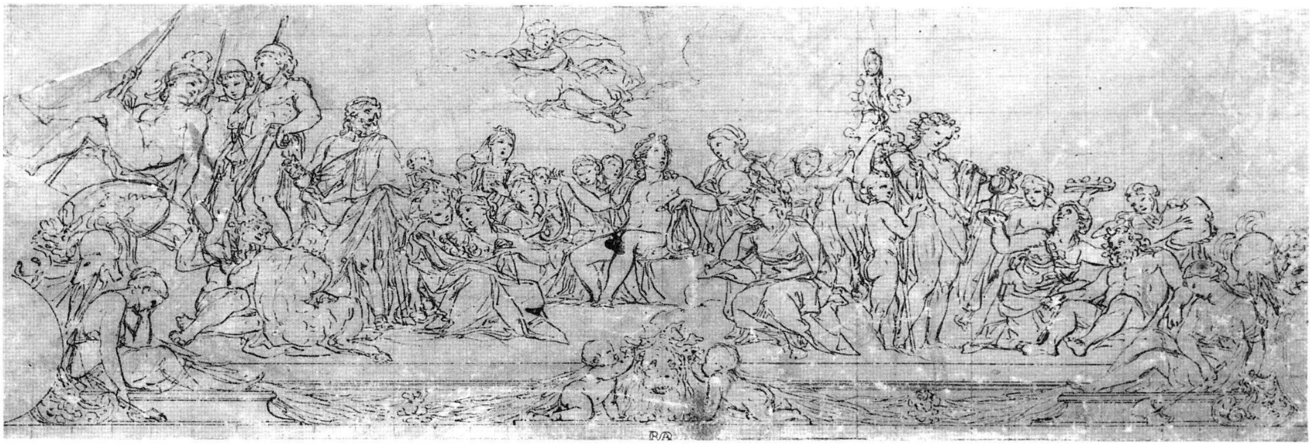

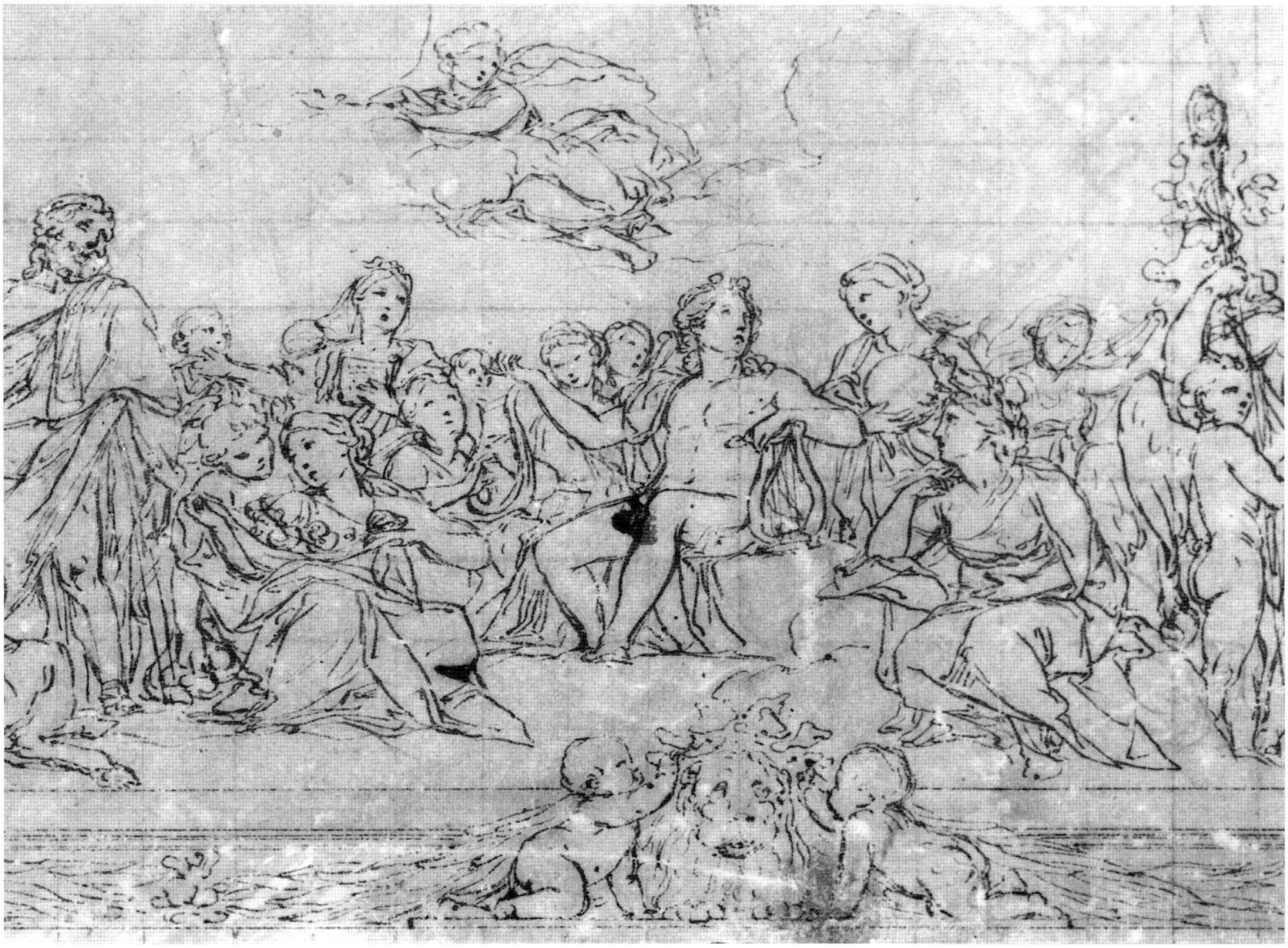

42

Apollo in his Chariot, led by Aurora and Lucifer

Design for a ceiling
Pen in brown ink, washed in grey, 33 × 32 cm
London, Sir Brinsley Ford, C.B.E., Hon F.R.A., F.S.A.

PROVENANCE: Colonel Thomas Wildman (?); William F. Webb (1817-99), his daughter Lady Cheamside, Richard Gatty Esq of Pepper and Arden, Northallerton, Yorkshire; Gatty auction at Sotheby's, London 18.3.1959, lot 67.

LITERATURE: *Catalogue of Old Master Drawings from the Gatty Collection in Temple Newsam House*, Leeds, 1954.

The drawing has the same provenance as four designs for the *Apotheosis of Hercules* in the Palacio Real in Madrid, of which three are now in a Madrid private collection and one in the National Gallery of Scotland in Edinburgh (cat. no.41). However, it is evident from some motifs in the decoration that this is not a design for a ceiling in Madrid.

The decoration framing the drawing gives some indication of the intended destination. Two winged personifications of Fame flank a coat-of-arms, which is crowned by a cardinal's hat. The empty cartouche for the coat-of-arms on the opposite side is flanked by two gryphons. This motif occurs several times in the relief decoration in the Villa Albani in Rome: for instance, in the framing of the Antinous relief and over the doors of the gallery. The combination of a cardinal's hat with hanging garlands and the two vases, one of which is certainly antique, makes it probable that this was a design for one of the ceilings which Antonio Bicchierari painted in the Villa Albani.

The design was apparently intended for one of the ceiling paintings in the *piano nobile*, which were executed by Antonio Bicchierari after 1766. Bicchierari's drawings for the ceilings in the Villa Albani (Rome, Gabinetto Nazionale di Disegni) include two designs, which were not executed, for Apollo in his chariot, with Lucifer hastening on ahead and one for Aurora in her chariot (Schröter 1982, illus.173, 59). Apparently both were rejected and Mengs supplied a drawing which combined the two. The reason why the fresco was not painted could be the painter's appointment in Madrid which came in the summer of 1761, when the painting work on the Villa Albani was not yet finished.

Formally, the design is closely related to the first design for Parnassus in the gallery of the villa (cat.no.45), now in the Albertina in Vienna and must date from 1759 or 1760. The clean and carefully executed pen and ink drawing must be regarded as a kind of presentation model, and presumably it was preceded by a large number of sketches by Mengs, although these cannot now be traced.

Mengs made similar designs for his ceilings in Madrid. The correctness of the outlines and the line work are very similar to the coloured ceiling design in the Victoria and Albert Museum (cat.no.43).

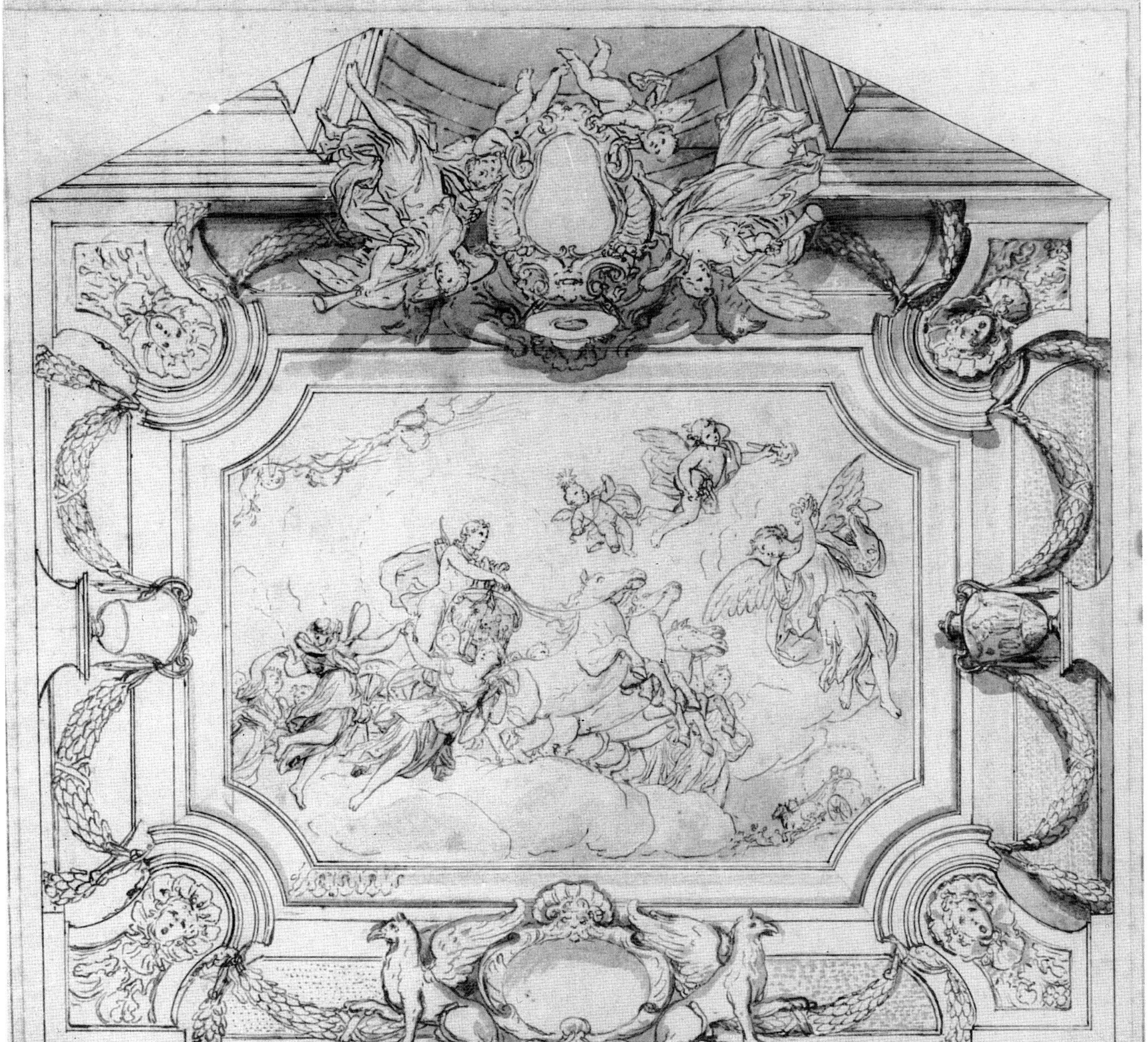

43

Apollo and Athena Rewarding the Talents

Design for a ceiling, flanked by medallions showing Mars, Venus, Hercules and Cybele
Pen and ink over grey chalk, watercolour
59.5 × 61.2 cm
London, Board of Trustees of the Victoria & Albert Museum, Mus.no.8453

This design is one of the few sheets that give a glimpse of the working methods used by Mengs after his appointment as 'primer pintor de camára' in Madrid after the departure of Giaquinto in spring 1762. It is the only presentation drawing verified to date. Mengs made it for a ceiling fresco in the Palacio Real in Madrid, which was then completed by Antonio González Velázquez. The ceiling is in the second room of the Prince's suite in the east wing. The painter who executed the design had already worked under Giaquinto, but he only followed Mengs's design loosely, both formally and in iconography, as we see from Fabre's description of the ceiling in 1829 (Fabre, pp.23-27). This fact, and the design, which is very detailed in parts, suggest that Mengs initially expected to paint the ceiling himself. The drawing obviously dates from the first years of his first stay in Madrid from, among other things, the similarities in motif and style with the fresco of *The Triumph of Aurora* made in 1763-4 for the Queen's bedchamber and with the *Apotheosis of Hercules* in the King's Conversation Room, which was started at the same time but only finished many years later. The drawing also gives an indication of what the ceiling showing *The Triumph of Aurora* may have originally looked like and how it was subdivided. Mengs used the same arrangement again in the ceiling fresco for the former theatre in the palace of Aránjuez, which he began in 1775 but did not finish.

The square central area has a complex structure. On one side is Apollo with the nine Muses in a garden landscape. To their left is a group of people led by an old man in antique robes, who may represent Homer. Nothing in this depiction of Parnassus harks back to the Assembly of the Muses in the Villa Albani (cat.no.45), but there are similarities in the motif to the two depictions of Parnassus that Mengs included in his other ceilings in Madrid.

On the opposite side of the ceiling is a helmeted Athena enthroned on clouds, flanked by two winged personifications of Fame. At her feet kneels a woman, who points to a large inscribed tablet held behind Athena by a putto. She could be Clio as the Muse of History, or the personification of History, who has inscribed on the tablet the names of those who are to be rewarded by Athena. Behind these figures two forms gesture towards Athena, presumably two poets (possibly Dante and Ariosto). A crowd of putti and the winged Pegasus fly in the air above.

The central section is supported by naked caryatids, who also flank the oval medallions in the centre. Before them are naked male figures, evidently influenced by Michelangelo's *Ignudi.* Each side also contains two square areas between the corners and the medallions, with unidentified images that were obviously intended to be freely invented reliefs. The connection between Mars, Venus, Hercules, Cybele and the ceiling subject must at present remain an open question, as the iconography of the drawing has not yet been fully explained.

In the arrangement of his ceiling Mengs clearly drew on the early seventeenth-century Roman tradition, which reached its peak in Annibale Carracci's gallery at the Palazzo Farnese in Rome. Here it becomes clear how successfully he had tackled the problems of ceiling fresco painting in Rome.

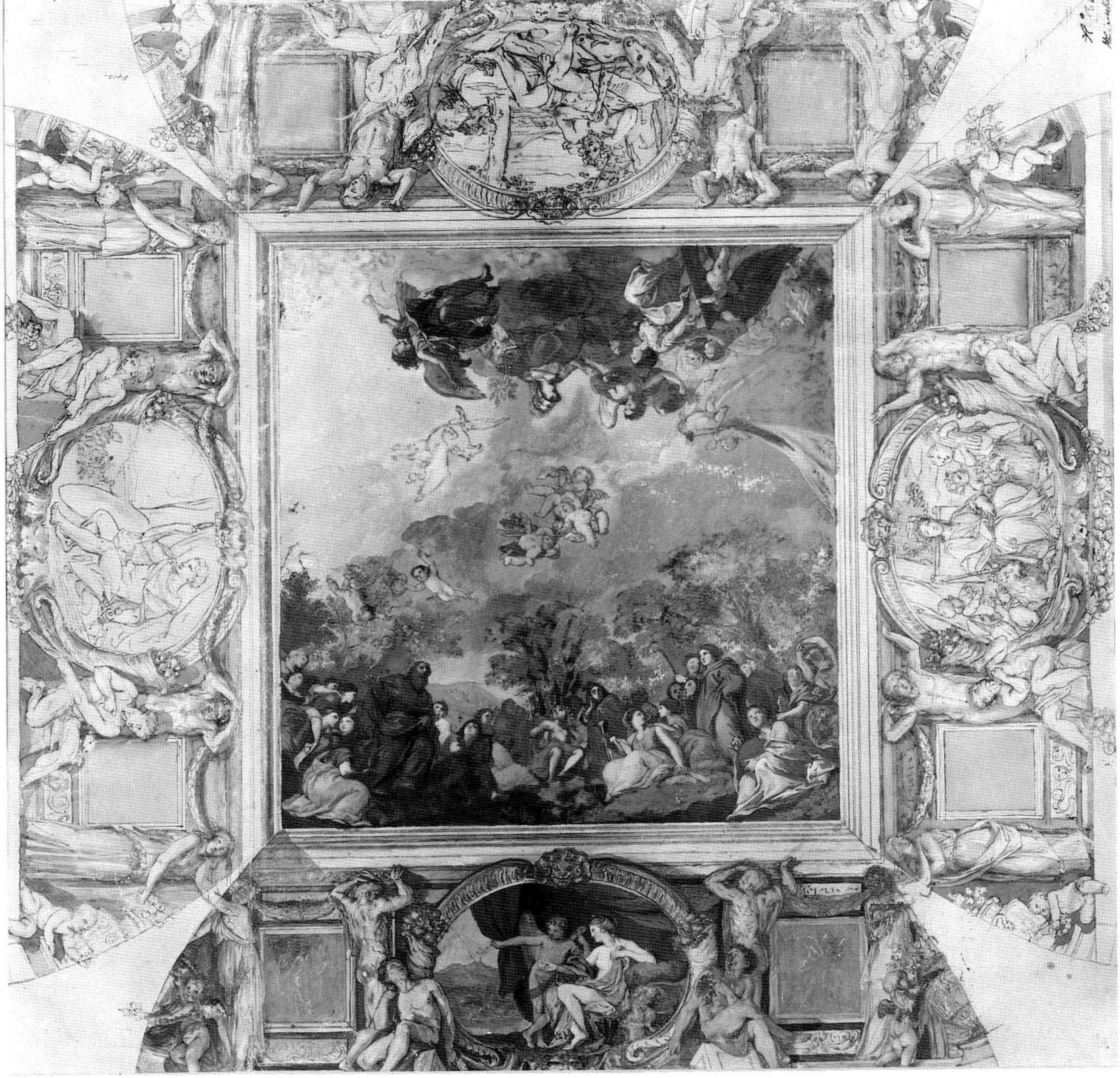

44
Richard Cooper (1740–after 1814), after A. R. Mengs
St John the Baptist

Pencil on blue tinted paper, 29.8 × 39.2 cm

Inscribed: '36' on the album leaf 'Page 32nd'/Framed/ Framed/ made a finished Drawing of this in black lead upon a reddish tinted paper /Framed/ Chevr. Mengs Pinxt a little larger than this / The New Palace Madrid / made a finished Drawing of this/ St. John / meant as a Companion to Corregio's small Magdalen / Mengs painted also a Magdalen as a Companion to this / Small board St. John Compn. Corregio Magdalen
Edinburgh, National Gallery of Scotland, D4823/II F 32

PROVENANCE: Miss M. Eyre, Gift 1959

LITERATURE: Bull/Harris, p.646

This copy of the picture which was formerly in the royal palace in Madrid was made between 1767 and 1769 in Madrid. The engraver and copyist Richard Cooper the Younger was a pupil of Robert Strange. In 1764 he embarked on an extended study tour of Italy and France, and at the beginning of 1767 he was studying in Paris. He informed his patron David Lord Cardross in a letter written on 4 January 1767 (Edinburgh, University Library Laing MSS. La.IV.26) that he intended to go to Madrid shortly to see Mengs,and that he had good recommendations from people who had known the artist in Rome. Presumably the recommendation was from Strange, whom Mengs is known to have met in Rome in 1760.

Bull and Harris have been able to establish from the letter they have published that two albums of drawings in Edinburgh contain a number of drawings by Cooper from works by Mengs. The authors have also been able to date Cooper's stay in Madrid more exactly, to between 1767 and 1769. Mengs left Madrid in November 1769, and by that time all the works copied by Cooper must have been in his studio or in the royal palace. That Cooper had access to Mengs's house and studio is also evident from a drawing from a painting by Correggio which was then in the painter's studio, as the copyist has expressly noted on the drawing (Bull/Harris, p.647).

Cooper's copies give even more precise insight into Mengs's studio stock during a relatively short period of time than Mosmann's drawings (cat.no.46). The selection which Cooper made for his copies represents the taste of his potential customers. So his selection is very characteristic of a particular kind of contemporary, and confirms the close proximity, already commented on several times, between Mengs's Neo-classisicm and the preferences of British art-lovers. All the pictures which Cooper copied are in the 'modern style', where the advantages of Italian sixteenth- and seventeenth-century painting appear in the garb of a refined academicism. The influences were recognisable, but it was also evident that the works had only just been painted.

This is particularly the case with this depiction of *St John the Baptist*. Here the style of Correggio had to be reflected in both pose and expression, as the painting was intended to serve as a companion piece to a *Magdalen* by the Italian artist. This information is noted by Cooper on his drawing, and it explains not only the style of the painting but also how great a challenge and an opportunity the request for a companion to so famous a painting was deemed by the eighteenth-century artist and his viewers. The comparison would make the work a test piece of the 'challenger's' artistic skills.

Cooper's copy is an almost pure outline drawing. As it is known that Cooper sold copies, one may assume that he kept drawings like this as a stock from which he could make further copies. In giving such prominence to the contours, however, he has lost the painterly character of the work, which is preserved in the copperplate by Salvador Manuel Carmona. Cooper has achieved a charming but probably unintended sense of refinement.

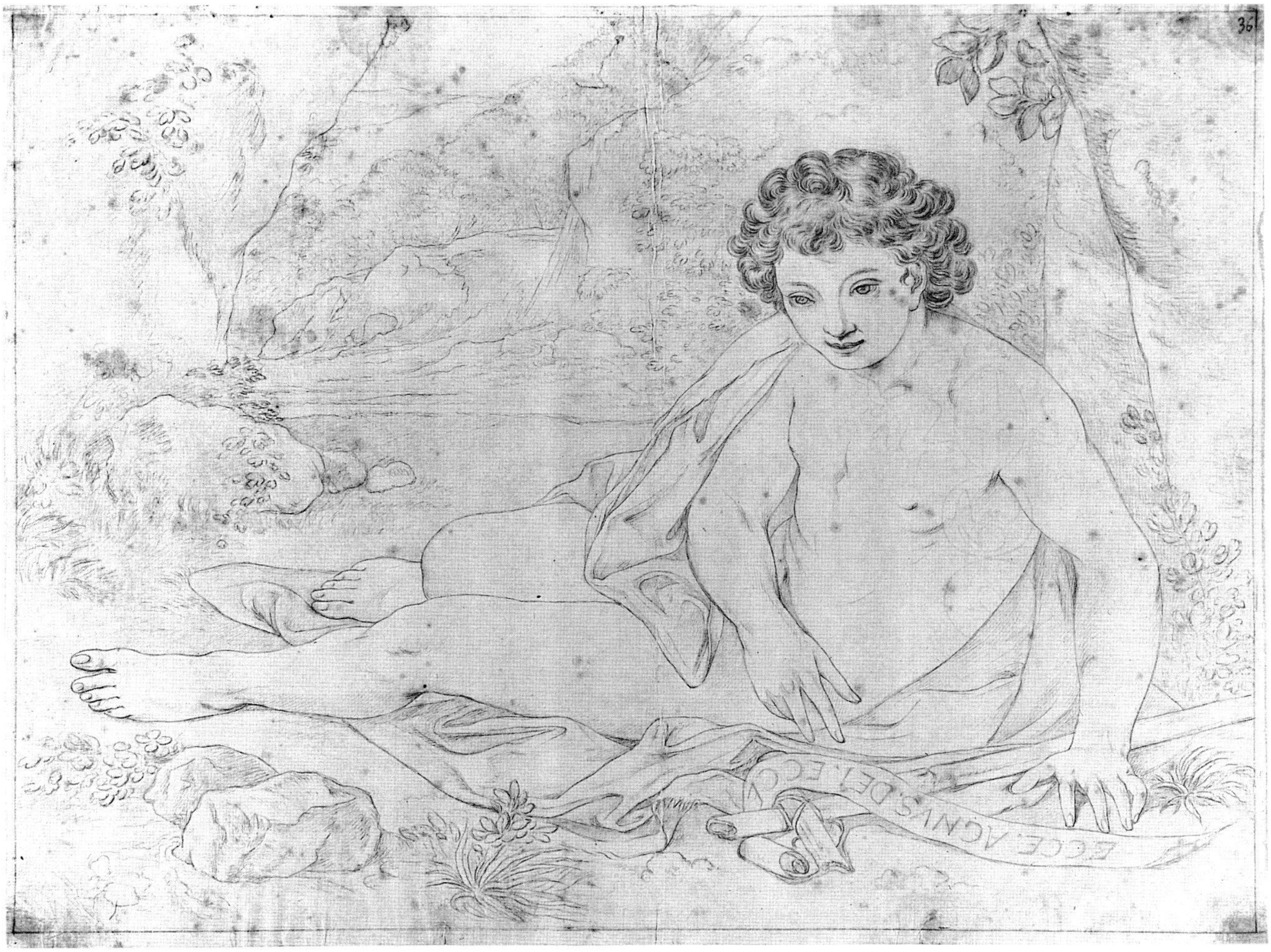
36
ECCE. AGNVS. DEI.

45

Giuseppe Mannocchi (Rome, c.1731-Rome, 1782)
View of the Ceiling of the Galleria Albani with Mengs's Frescos

Pen and grey ink, wash and watercolour over black chalk, on two sheets glued together
56.5 × 125 cm
Inscribed: Giuseppe Mannocchi Romano 1774
London, Chaucer Fine Arts

LITERATURE: Catalogue *Collecting in the 18th Century*, London, Chaucer Fine Arts (1981), no.41; *Zur Villa Albani, Forschungen zur Villa Albani, Antike Kunst und die Epoche der Aufklärung*, ed. H. Beck & P. C. Bol, Berlin, 1982.

Mannocchi was a Roman architect, copper engraver and draughtsman; he spent some time in England, where he worked as a draughtsman for the Adam brothers, and some of his ornamental drawings are in the Victoria & Albert Museum. He must have returned to Italy before 1774, as the drawing of the ceiling of the Villa Albani is dated 1774 and was certainly made in Rome from the original. However, Mannocchi also worked for British clients after his return to Rome (see Sotheby's, London, auction sale catalogue, 14 November 1991, lot 34, information from Alastair Laing).

Mannocchi's drawing is the only full depiction known of the ceiling in the gallery of the Villa Albani, which Mengs painted in 1760-1. It is understandable that as an architect and draughtsman he was interested in the whole ceiling, while most visitors and copyists concentrated on Mengs's frescos. Mannocchi's drawing gives a vivid impression of the decoration on the ceiling, which is a flat mirror vault supported by lunettes with an oval soffit from which the three fields for the frescos were marked out. While the central picture of *Apollo and the Muses* is a 'quadro riportato' (i.e. painted as if viewed straight on), the two *tondi* with allegorical depictions of *Amor Virtutis* and *Gloria et Premium* are painted as seen realistically from below. With its great rectangular central section flanked by two *tondi*, this scheme follows a very common type that occurs elsewhere in Rome in secular architecture, and presumably was modelled on the decoration of the gallery in the Palazzo Verospi by Francesco Albani.

The decorative parts of the ceiling are painted and were probably only executed after the frescos were finished, in the spring of 1761. The shape of the ceiling, and therefore of the decorative paintings, was probably determined by the architect, Carlo Marchionni; designs by him for the walls have survived. The grisaille paintings in the small fields in the lunettes and the arches, some of which are based on ancient models, are by Niccolò Lappiccola, and they were presumably also made later than Mengs's frescos. They may have been based on designs by Mengs. The gallery was finished, with all its decoration, in October 1762.

Around 1775 the owner of the villa, Cardinal Alessandro Albani, began to have drawings made of the villa, its gardens and furnishings, now completed after many years' work. It is possible that Mannocchi's drawing was made in connection with these plans, which were never fully realised. With its rich collection of Antiquities the Villa Albani came close to embodying the ideal of 'Roma æterna', and this also found expression in its pictorial works. It became justly famous, and in the second half of the eighteenth century was the Mecca of all foreign visitors to Rome. Alessandro Albani was a patron and collector, and he was the last leading churchman in the eighteenth century to be able to realise the concept and ideal of the Roman 'villa suburbana' in a completely new building. He acquired the financial means for his project by selling some items from his collection, which were valuable but not essential to his aim. They included the ancient statues which he sold to Dresden in 1728 and the major collection of drawings, which form the basis of the Royal Library at Windsor and which he sold to King George III of England in 1763.

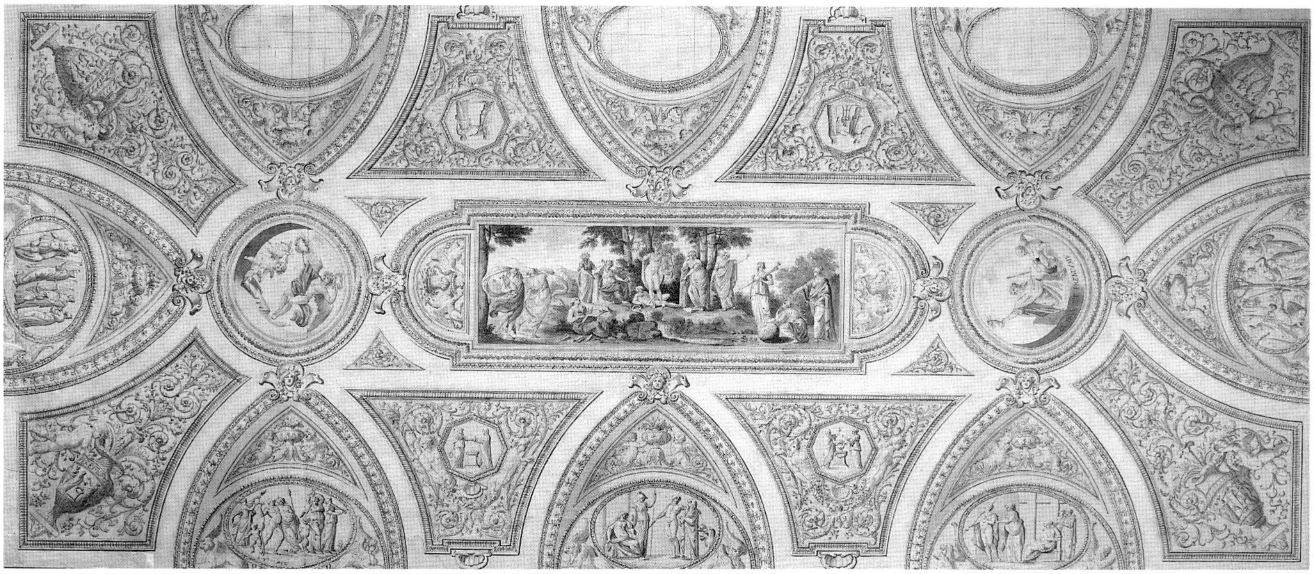

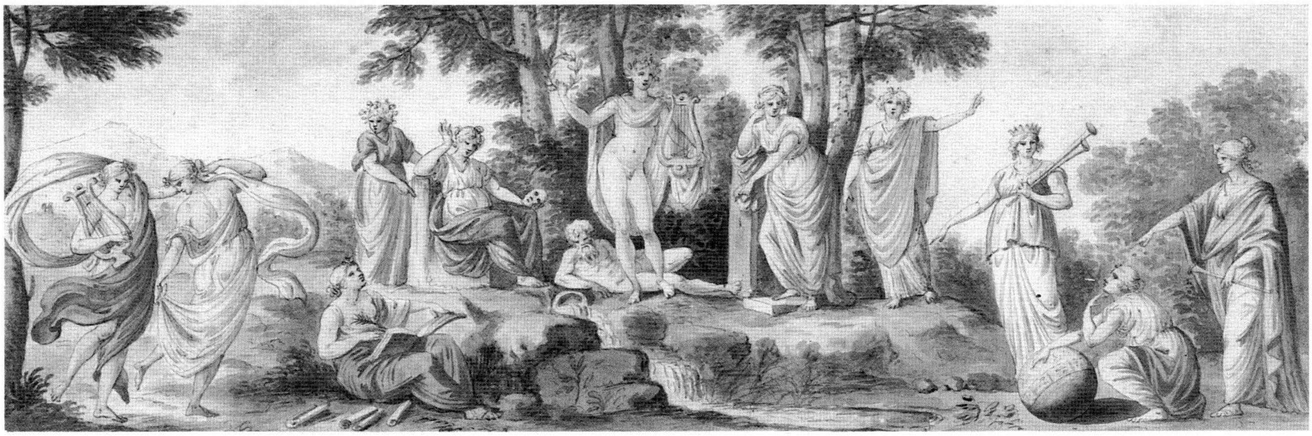

46

Nikolaus Mosmann (1717-87), after A. R. Mengs The Holy Family with St Elizabeth and St John the Baptist

Black chalk, 56 × 41.5 cm
Inscribed: Antonius Raphael Mengs invenit et pinxit/ in the Collection of Wil.m Weddell Esq.r
London, Trustees of the British Museum (T5-7, vol.VI, p.25).

This drawing is one of a set of nearly 250 which Nikolaus Mosmann, a pupil of Mengs, executed in Rome between about 1769 and his death in 1787. This is evident from a note on the first volume of the copies. Altogether they fill seven volumes, making this one of the largest as well as one of the best in quality of such sets to survive from the eighteenth century. The label bears the following text: 'Mr Nollekens Statuary in Mortimer Street, London, assured me that he was in Rome, when the drawings in this book were made by one Mosmann, a German who was recommended to Brownley, Earl of Exeter and he worked at them several years at five shillings a day, afterwards Lord Exeter gave him half a guinea. Lord Exeter told Mr. Nollekens the book cost him 2000. Mosmann was a pupil of Mengs. Annesley'.

Smith reports on the more immediate circumstances of the drawings (*Nollekens and his Times*, London 1828, I, p.233; Ashby p.498), saying that some of the drawings were copies of paintings in Jenkins's collection, while the others were mainly copies of paintings that had not yet been engraved. Whether it was the intention to reproduce the gigantic undertaking in the form of engravings as well has not so far been proven. Certainly to do so would have cost many times what the drawings had already cost. That Jenkins had something to do with the commission to Mosmann is suggested by the fact that Mosmann copied two paintings by Jenkins (see Introduction, fig.3, 4).

Little is known of Mosmann, who came from Lorraine. He is said to have made drawings for the illustrations in Winckelmann's '*Monumenti antichi inediti*', which appeared in two volumes in Rome in 1767. The collection of drawings in the Accademia di San Luca in Rome contains a study by Mosmann among the academic life drawings of 1757 (Noack I, p.324). The *Sibyl* shown here was engraved by him (see cat.no.23). During Mengs's absence he appears to have been in close contact with his pupil, Anton von Maron, as he included some of Maron's works in his volumes. They also contain a portrait of him by Maron.

This contact explains how Mosmann was able to enter Mengs's studio in his absence, since it continued to operate under Maron. This must also be the only reason why he sometimes copied cartoons or drawings in the studio instead of the finished paintings. The drawing shown here of the *Holy Family*, which William Weddell purchased from Jenkins after 1764 (see cat.no.19), is an example of this. Mosmann knew that a version of this painting had been sold to Weddell. However, the picture which he copied was the second version, which Mengs was painting for the original client, the Elector of Saxony. It had not been finished, probably owing to the Seven Years' War, and was still in his studio in Rome. After Mengs's death the picture, together with its cartoon, was sold to Catherine the Great of Russia. A comparison between the picture, which is now in Pavlovsk, and the drawing, and a comparison with the version exhibited here from the Weddell collection confirm this (see cat.no.19). The quality and precision of the copies clearly show that the artist had studied under Mengs. The dense and plastic modelling of the surface, achieved by rubbing the soft chalk, is characteristic of Mengs's work.

Mosmann's drawings from the works of his master have been of immense importance for the reconstruction of the works by Mengs which have been scattered and forgotten over the years. Many of the paintings that have reappeared in recent years, and others that are still believed to be lost, can be identified from Mosmann's drawings.

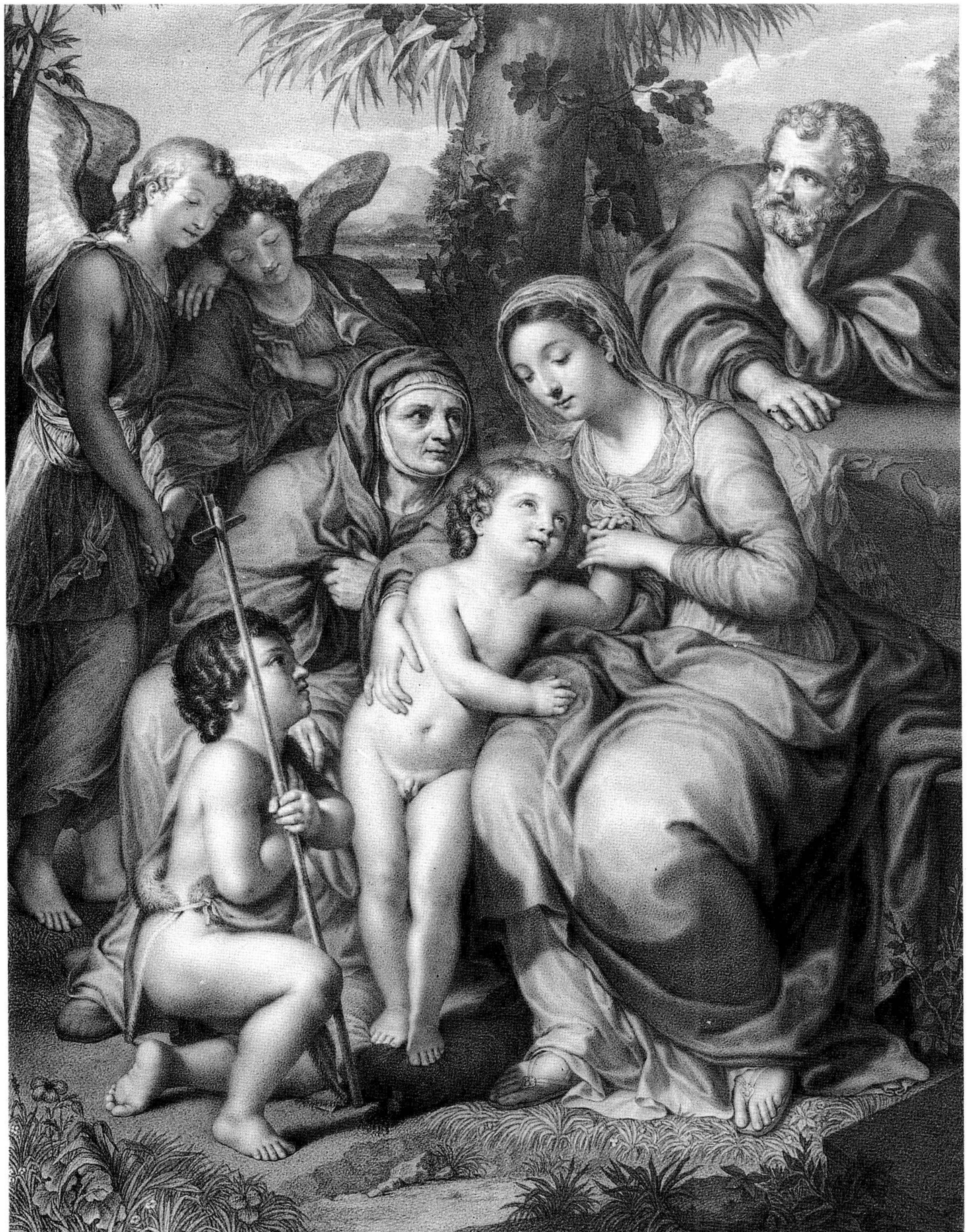

47
John Dean (around 1750-98?) after A. R. Mengs
Augustus and Cleopatra

Mezzotint, 58.2 × 46.8 cm
Inscribed: Engraved by John Dean/Augustus and Cleopatra/ From the Painting of Raphael Mengs/10 Feet high by 7 Feet in the Collection of Henry Hoare Esq.
The Hon. Christopher Lennox-Boyd

John Dean was one of the best engravers in London after 1780, with Richard Earlom, and he was particularly celebrated for his portrait engravings in mezzotint. This print appeared in 1786, that is, not until two years after the print by Earlom, which presumably shows the first version of the painting for Stourhead (cat.no.48).

At this time the artistic reception of the composition of the painting in Stourhead House was already evident. Benjamin West's *Paetus and Arrias* (New Haven, Yale Center for British Art), was made in 1766, and Angelika Kauffmann's painting of *Augustus and Cleopatra* (Kansas University Museum), also based on Mengs's composition, was painted in 1783. Both artists must have seen the original at Stourhead. It is known that Benjamin West was there in 1763.

Although there is an unusually large amount of archive material available on this major commission, the history of the ordering and the creation of the painting have not been clarified in every detail as yet.

48
Richard Earlom (1742/3-1822), after A. R. Mengs Augustus and Cleopatra

Mezzotint, 68.2 × 45.7 cm
Inscribed: Le Chevallier Antoine Raphael Mengs pinxit./ Dessiné par Seydelmann/ Richard Earlom sculpsit/ John Boydell excudit. London/ The Interview of Augustus and Cleopatra. After the original Picture of the same size at Dresden. In the Collection of D.A.R. Charles Comte de Callenberg. Lieut. General of the Saxon Cavalry. Published Aug. 16th 1784 by John Boydell Engraver in Cheapside, London.
Hon. Christopher Lennox-Boyd

LITERATURE: Nagler, IX, 1840, p.121; Saabye (1976), pp.12-13; Roettgen (1977), pp.148-156.

This is a print of a small painting that has been in the Städtische Kunstsammlungen in Augsburg for some years. In subject and period it is related to the commission which Mengs received for Stourhead House in 1758 or 1759 (see cat.nos.34, 47, 52, 53).

It is possible that this version was the artist's first treatment of the subject, for we know from a letter by Mengs that he was only given the dimensions of the picture, which were fixed by the fact that it was to match a work by Carlo Maratti, a long time after the fee had been agreed (see cat. no.34). Hoare had already sealed his purchase of the work by Maratti at the beginning of June 1758 (information kindly provided by Stella Rudolph). He may have given the commission to Mengs at about the same time, so that the artist was already working on the subject without having the exact information on the size it was to be. The proportions of the Augsburg picture differ so markedly from those of the work at Stourhead that it certainly cannot be a second version of that painting, although there might have been occasion for a reworking by Mengs owing to the criticism he received from Hoare of the Stourhead painting (see cat.no.52).

The depiction differs from the painting in Stourhead mainly in the choice of the moment in time. This is not the first moment of the encounter, but the subsequent dialogue, in the course of which Cleopatra attempts to justify her life and deeds to Augustus, while he refutes each of her arguments (see Plutarch, *Life of Mark Antony*, LXXXIII). The dialogue between the two antagonists is hostile and full of mistrust, and this is made plain by the distance between the two gesticulating figures and the formality of their poses. Cleopatra is pointing to the statue of Cæsar in the background and repeatedly referring to him in her defence. Her treacherous servant Seleukos is just emerging from behind the screen decorated with Egyptian motifs, bringing the inventory of her possessions, while she is still trying to conceal some of these. Augustus's moral victory over the Queen was, however, of only short duration, as she had already made preparations for her death before the dialogue commenced and despite strict supervision in her prison preferred death to public humiliation as the vanquished in Rome.

Unlike the Stourhead painting, the Augsburg version shows Cleopatra's sovereign equanimity and calm in the face of the unyielding severity of Augustus. Presumably Hoare would have objected less to this version of the subject than he did to the picture he received. The composition looks back to Poussin and classical reliefs of funeral repasts and it had a deep influence on French Neo-classical painting (see Roettgen, 1977). The engraving by Earlom appeared in 1784, that is, at a time when the architectural severity of the composition and the classical and Egyptian motifs of the setting were particularly in vogue. Possibly the enthusiastic reaction of French artists to the work was partly due to the engraving, for the picture was in a private collection in Dresden and not easily accessible. How Earlom came into the possession of the drawing by Jacob Kreszenz Seydelmann which he used for his engraving is not known. Seydelmann was a pupil of Mengs in Rome from 1772 to 1779, where he also copied other works by his tutor. In 1808 a second print of the painting by J. Pleikart Bittheueser appeared in Nuremberg. It is known in a small version (14.2 × 8.8 cm) and a larger version, exhibited here ex-catalogue (57 × 44.5 cm).

There are preliminary drawings for the painting in Düsseldorf and Copenhagen, where there may possibly also be copies of the painting by Peder Als. An unfinished version of the painting, with life-size figures, appears to have been in Mengs's estate after his death, and was sold to Catherine the Great of Russia.

Angelo Campanella (1746-1811), after A. R. Mengs

49
I. Venus shaking a Tree from which Cupids are falling into a Pool

50
III. Venus and a Nymph by a Pool with Cupids

49. Copper engraving with original gouache hand colour, 57 × 65 cm
Inscribed: Art. Raph. Mengs delin / Ang. Campanella sculp.

50. Copper engraving with original gouache hand colour, 56 × 64.5 cm.
Inscribed: Equi. Ant. Raph. Mengs delin./Ang. Campanella sculp.
London, Trustees of Sir John Soane's Museum

PROVENANCE: George Dance, junior (1741-1825)

LITERATURE: Azara-Fea (1787), p.xxxii; Vittorio Massimo, *Notizie istoriche della Villa Massimo alle Terme Diocleziane*, Rome (1836), p.214-5; T. Ashby, 'Un mecenate inglese della fine del Settecento a Roma, *Roma*', V, 19127, p.52ff; C. Pietrangeli, *Scavi e Scoperte di antichità sotto il Pontificato di Pio VI*, Rome (1958), pp.45-6; exhibition catalogue, *Österreichische Künstler und Rom*, Rome, Vienna, (1972), pp.174-5; Hetty Joyce,' The Ancient Frescoes from the Villa Negroni and their Influence in the Eighteenth and Nineteenth Centuries', *The Art Bulletin* (1983), LXV, 3, pp.423-440.

In June and July 1777 the remains of an antique house were found in the extensive grounds of the former Villa Montalto-Peretti, near the baths of Diocletian. The villa was then owned by the Negroni family of Genoa. In its rooms well-preserved frescos were discovered, showing mythological figures in an elaborate architectural framework. Such paintings had only been seen before in the excavations of Herculaneum and Pompeii, and the excellent quality and pleasing subjects of the large new frescos caused great excitement.

By 19 July 1777 the Diario Ordinario, the Rome weekly, had reported that a certain English dealer was having the frescos removed. This was Henry Tresham, whose visit to the excavations the landscape painter Thomas Jones recorded in his memoirs. Jones made a sketch of the excavation work, and commented that the decorations were 'much in the Chinese taste' (Oppé, p.62). Tresham acquired the frescos and sold them the same year to Frederick Hervey, Bishop of Derry, who had only arrived in Rome on 9 November 1777. Hervey wrote to his daughter on 24 December 1777: ''Tis likewise difficult to say wh. pleases me most the magnificence of ancient or the elegance of modern Rome, for my own part I have been singularly fortunate – several ancient rooms have been unearthed since my arrival – the ptgs were in fresco & almost as perfect as at first – the secret was soon found of detaching the old stucco from the wall, & I have bought three complete rooms with wch I purpose to adorne the Downhill & le rendre un morceau unique' (Joyce (1983), p.426).

The frescos never reached Downhill, and, as Brinsley Ford suspects, they may never have left Italy (Joyce (1983), p.426). Their fame is due to the copperplate engravings made from them. The first three (there were twelve altogether) were based on drawings by Mengs, who had returned to Rome at the beginning of March 1777. Mengs drew the first frescos that were uncovered and also made coloured miniatures of them; these later came into the possession of Azara, but are now regarded as lost. The reason why he used a technique he had not used for years was the astonishing freshness of the colours in the frescos, which Lord Bristol also commented on with admiration. Presumably, however, the miniatures only showed the figurative parts of the frescos. The drawings from which the engravings were made 1778 showed all the painted decoration; this covered the entire wall and ended in a semicircular lunette, as most of the rooms were vaulted. At the same time as Mengs was making his copies, the walls were being sketched by the British artist Thomas Hardwick (London, RIBA, see Joyce, p.433). Hardwick, however, paid less attention to the pictorial appearance of the frescos, aiming to document in his drawings the state of preservation and the architectural situation as well.

The excavations in the Villa Negroni were initiated by Nicolas José de Azara, who was a great expert on and enthusiastic collector of antiquities (his collection is now in the Palacio Real at Aránjuez). Presumably he also bore the costs of the excavation, which aroused so much interest in Rome that it was actually visited by Pope Pius VI.

Mengs drew the paintings in the same sequence as the rooms were discovered. The first picture showing Venus with Cupids (Plate I) was in the first room to be uncovered, a kind of vestibule. It was found before 5 July 1777. The second painting of the same tree, initially described as 'Venus with a Faun', was found before 19 July 1777, while the third picture which Mengs copied, showing Venus seated on a rock (Plate III), was in the second room in the house. This was uncovered shortly before 9 August and it contained altogether three paintings. When the third print from Mengs's drawings was published in 1779, the artist had just died. All the engravings, which could also be purchased as hand-coloured editions, included dedications. Hetty Joyce has compiled the dedications on the various prints, which continued to be re-issued until after 1800. On some that have survived Plate II bears a dedication to Mengs, presumably written by Azara. There are two versions of it, and the earlier reads: 'Antonio Raphaeli Mengs

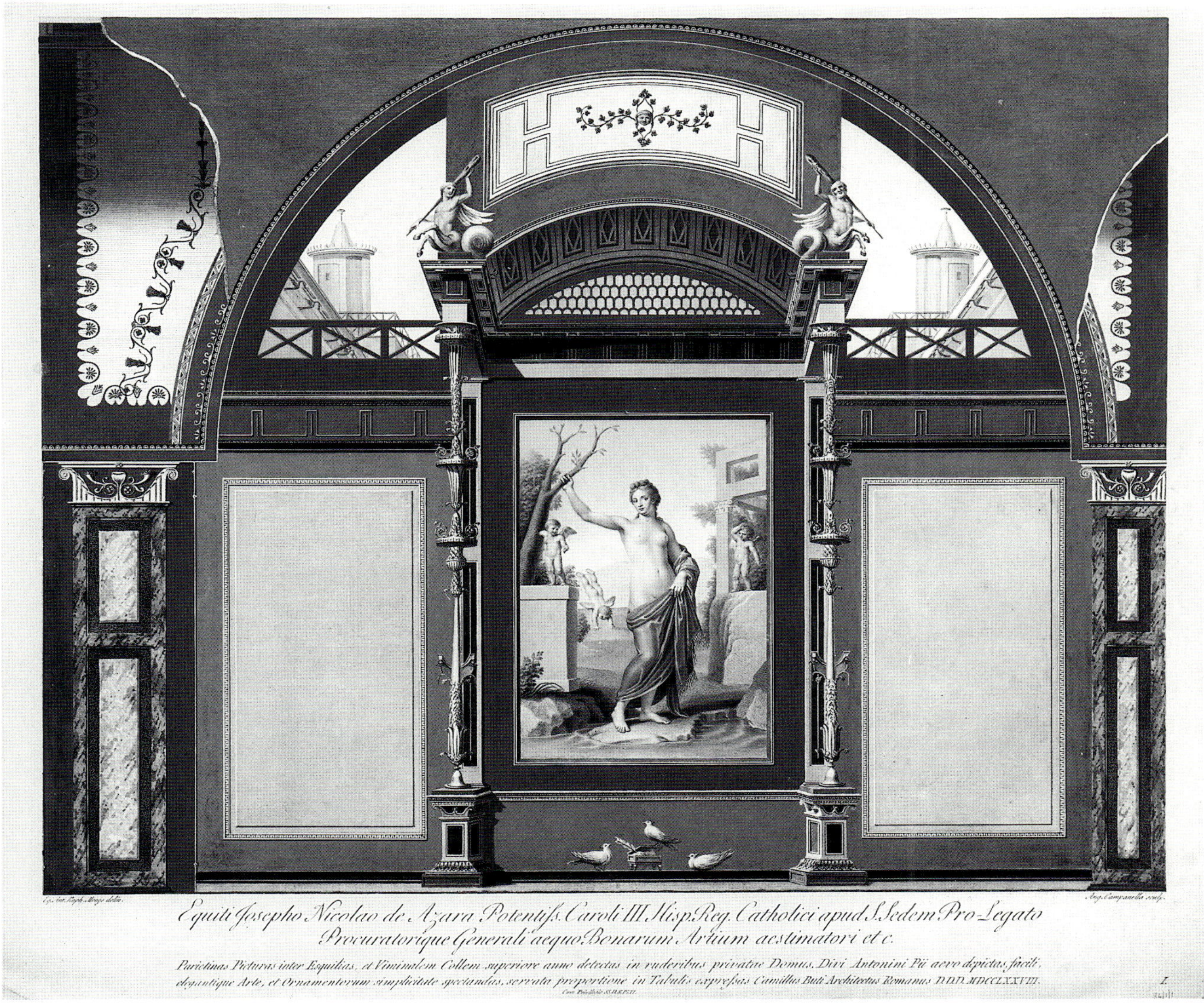

49 *Venus shaking a Tree from which Cupids are falling into a Pool*

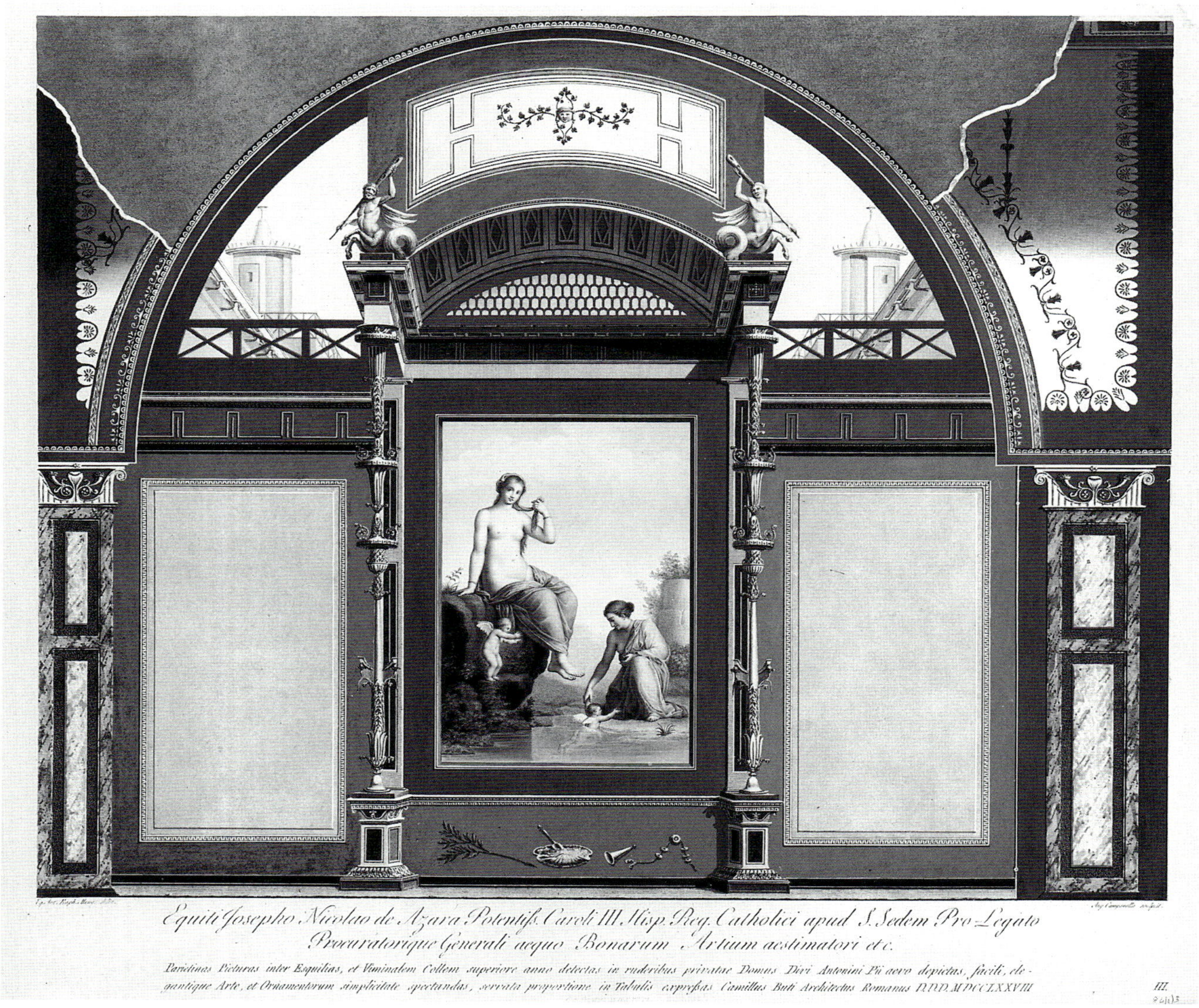

50 *Venus and a Nymph by a Pool with Cupids*

Caroli III Hisp. Reg. ut quondam Alexandri Magni Apelles/ Pictori, Graecorum summis Artificibus comparando; imaginem Adonidis morientis in sinu Venero, nuper/ in exquiliis detectam, in aenea tabula expressam, Amicus D.D.D. MDCCLXXVII.' After Mengs's death this was altered to read as follows: 'Memoriae Antoni Raphaelis Mengs Pictori Philosophi nuper extinctae, exquilinam Adonidis/ Venatoris Picturam in aenea tabula expressam Amicus D.D.D. MDCCLXXIX.' Of the other dedications, most are to Lord Bristol, that is, Frederick Hervey who had bought the paintings, and Azara.

Most of the series that have survived are in British collections. In the Ickworth Rotunda in Bury St Edmunds the engravings were also used as models for a painted wall decoration, probably as the Earl Bishop had intended to install in Downhill. In Sir John Soane's Museum they, with other copies from antiquity, provide the decoration of a room.

51
Letter from Thomas Robinson, later Second Baronet of Grantham (1738-86) to his Father, William Robinson, of 9 August 1760 from Rome

West Yorkshire Archive Service, Lord Grantham Papers, VR6032 (12325)

LITERATURE: Geoffrey Beard, 'Batoni and Mengs', *Leeds Art Calendar*, no.44, 1960, pp.23-4.

This letter is probably the most penetrating, apt and observant account by an impartial visitor to Rome of the rivalry so keenly discussed among art-lovers in the city, between Batoni and Mengs. It is seen with the objectivity of the unprejudiced newcomer. Robinson had enough knowledge of art, and of human nature, to describe the works of both masters so as to give his father and any reader a vivid picture of the strengths and weaknesses of each of the artists.

However, he does not conceal that he likes the works of Mengs better than 'Signore Ettore' and 'Signora Andromache' by Batoni. He mentions several works by Mengs, including his own portrait (fig.12), the portrait of Pope Clement XIII (see cat.no.5), a drawing by Mengs showing Hector and Andromache, which has not survived, the copy of the 'School of Athens' (fig.2) and the painting for Henry Hoare showing Augustus and Cleopatra (see cat.no.34).

52
Letter from Anton Raphael Mengs in Rome to Henry Hoare in London, 27 June 1761

National Trust, Stourhead, records in the Wiltshire Record Office (383/907) (in French)

LITERATURE: Azara-Fea (1787), pp.370-3; *Annals of the Fine Arts*, II (1818), p.492; Woodbridge (1965), pp.106-7; K. Woodbridge, *Landscape and Antiquity: Aspects of English Culture at Stourhead 1718-1838*, Oxford (1970), pp.48ff and 247ff. Dobai (1975), II, p.1312.

The letter, described by Dobai as an 'apologia', was published by Richard Colt Hoare after it had already appeared in Carlo Fea's enlarged edition of the work by Nicolas José de Azara in an Italian translation obtained by Fea.

Mengs writes that Jenkins has translated the letter from Hoare for him, in which Hoare first comments on the painting. The letter from Hoare has not survived, but it was not addressed to Mengs but to Jenkins, who was acting as the agent for the commission. As Mengs could barely speak French, Jenkins wrote his 'apologia' for him. This is clearly evident from the handwriting, which is the same as on the letter which Jenkins himself wrote on 29 July 1761 (cat.no.54).

Mengs's letter must be seen as a kind of programmatic statement on the issues of fidelity to the historical facts and the main problems a painter has to face when handling historical subjects. He discusses the relationship between the painted depiction and literary sources extensively and paradigmatically, and one can see how intensively he had studied the passage in Plutarch on which *Augustus and Cleopatra* is based. Mengs examines practically all the relevant questions – the suitability of the historical setting, the costume, the expression and the degree of fidelity to the source – that can arise in connection with a historical subject. He says he has moved away from the usual approach of a subject painter and is convinced that his Cleopatra, who seems at first glance so subservient, will in time have the emotional effect upon viewers which is appropriate for the historical event depicted. She has borrowed the robe of Venus and not that of Juno or Minerva; for the same reason he has included a ruined temple in the Corinthian order. This detail can no longer be verified from the painting, for apparently Hoare had this part painted over, as he believed that the temple should be in the Doric order.

Above all, Mengs's letter makes it clear that the challenge presented by the picture was an intellectual test for the artist, and that he tackled it with energy and deep thought. This attitude to the picture and to his subject, and the fact that he had to defend himself against criticism based on the literary subject, are significant for our understanding of the artist's approach and standpoint. Imbued with the spirit of the Enlightenment, Mengs saw a painting not only as a technical and aesthetic problem that had to be solved but as a demanding historical interpretation which would have to meet the requirements of the past and their claim to truth.

53
Letter from Henry Hoare in London to Anton Raphael Mengs in Rome, 27 July 1761

National Trust, Stourhead, records in the Wiltshire Record Office (383/907)

LITERATURE: Woodbridge (1965), p.107.

This long letter is the answer to Mengs's letter of 27 June 1761 with his detailed reply to the banker's criticism (cat. no.52). Hoare comments in detail on Mengs's justification of his approach and he is not sparing with the kind of praise which he clearly knows will please the painter. The painter who is fortunate enough to bear the name of Raphael, he says, may justly regard himself as the heir to his fame. The figures of Augustus and that of Cleopatra testify to this. The compliments may easily be called empty phrases, considering the weight of Hoare's objections to the painting, but he does at least attempt to flatter the painter's vanity in his name. Hoare's concealment of his own objections as criticism which another viewer might make is touching. The real nub of Hoare's criticism is that Cleopatra is not majestic enough, and looks more like a Magdalen than a queen. However, and this concludes his letter, he is fully and entirely satisfied with the picture.

Presumably Mengs was no longer in Rome when the letter arrived, for he had left the city on 8 August 1761 to embark for Spain from Naples.

54
Letter from Thomas Jenkins in London to Henry Hoare in London, 25 July 1761

National Trust, Stourhead, records in the Wiltshire Record Office (383/907)

LITERATURE: Leslie Lewis, *Connoisseurs and Secret Agents*, London, 1961, p.188; Woodbridge 1965, p.105.

The letter from Mengs to which Jenkins refers here is presumably the one in which the artist gives a detailed statement on his painting of Augustus and Cleopatra in answer to the criticism from Hoare. Jenkins added a letter by himself to Mengs.

Although he was aware of Hoare's objections to the painting, Jenkins simply ignores these and expresses his satisfaction that the painting has pleased Hoare. To flatter his correspondent, he adds that Mengs was lucky as a painter to have found so understanding a client. Hoare's reaction was in fact flattering to the artist, the subtlety of his criticisms confirmed that Hoare was studying the concept and execution of the work in the way the artist had intended.

We see from other passages in the letter that the landscape painter John Plimmer, who had originally concerned himself with the commission for Mengs's painting, had meantime died in Rome, and that Hoare had apparently made his heirs a present of money.

Jenkins also reports a rather delicate matter connected with the recent purchase of a painting through him by Lord Cowper. This was *Perseus and Andromeda* by Guido Reni, which Jenkins had purchased for 1,500 crowns. The copper engraver Robert Strange had discovered a second version of the painting and was now maintaining that the one which Jenkins had bought was a copy. Thereupon the two pictures were compared, and to the satisfaction of Jenkins and Cowper both proved to be by the artist's hand.

Jenkins tells the story in detail, probably because he was afraid, understandably, that evil tongues might harm his reputation as a dealer with Hoare – he was probably thinking of Strange himself, whom Hoare knew well. So he hastened to inform this important potential customer of his version of the facts.

The episode, on which L. Lewis has commented, also tells us that Jenkins had good business relations with Cowper. So it was probably he who provided the link between Cowper and Mengs which was to lead to some important commissions for the painter later in his career (see Introduction, p.30).

55

Daniel Webb, *Inquiry into the Beauties of Painting and into the Merit of the most celebrated Painters Ancient and Modern*, London 1760

London, The Board and Trustees of the Victoria and Albert Museum, *ex libris* Henry Hoare.

LITERATURE: Dobai II, pp.718ff. (further literature); Finke 1981, p.70ff

The history of the relations between Webb and Mengs is still unclear, and so it is a chapter in the biography of Mengs as a theoretician that has been subject to repeated misinterpretation. The extensive literature on the question of who lifted what from whom, whether Webb's borrowings from Mengs were plagiarisms and how he ultimately utilised Mengs's ideas, is not a matter which we can discuss in detail here.

The facts that are known can be briefly explained as follows: Webb came into such close personal contact with Mengs during his stay in Rome, which has not been exactly dated as yet but was probably in 1756, that Mengs gave him, evidently willingly and with a certain pride, a copy of his essay 'Thoughts on Beauty and Taste in Painting' (*Gedanken über die Schönheit und den Geschmack in der Mahlerey*) which was not yet published. This was not unusual in that several copies of the essay, written between 1757 and 1759, appear to have been circulating at the time, some consisting only of extracts. At that date Mengs does not appear to have considered publishing the work, and as he saw Webb as a man of his own mind in matters of art theory he generously gave him the manuscript. According to Azara, an intensive exchange of ideas had developed between the two men. That they liked each other is also evident from the fact that Mengs painted Webb's portrait, although this painting is lost.

When Webb's essay appeared in 1760, it met with great response in both England and abroad, being reviewed several times and then translated into French in 1765 and German in 1766. Thanks to its wide distribution Winckelmann, who was eager to obtain any literary novelty, very quickly learned of it and acquired a copy. When he read its contents he broke out in a fury as great as if he himself had been Mengs. He announced to all and sundry that Webb was a plagiarist. He was personally affected to a certain extent, in that the rejection of specifically Christian subjects in painting propounded by Webb did derive from his own ideas. If Webb had incurred blame, it was for failing to mention his Roman discussion partner.

Mengs himself, as far as we know, never commented on the affair. His interest in publishing his own essay, which was in German, was not very great, because he had meantime begun another in Italian, in which he hoped to smooth out what he saw as the blemishes of his first attempt at a literary work. However, he never completed this essay, which was published by Azara only in 1780, under the title '*Riflessioni sopra i tre gran pittori*'.

One result of the publication of Webb's 'Inquiry' was that Winckelmann now actively set about ensuring that his friend's work would be published, and did so against the author's will. Mengs's essay appeared in 1762, with a dedication to Winckelmann, but in the first two editions (1762 and 1765) the author's name is not even given.

The third edition of 1771, however, did bear Mengs's name, and it was published, together with the German translation of Webb's essay, by Füssli in Zurich. Diderot and Algarotti, and others interested in art theory who could not speak German, derived their knowledge of Mengs's ideas from Webb's work, which, as explained above, enjoyed a wide distribution throughout Europe. To this extent Winckelmann was right to make known that Mengs's ideas had been incorporated in Webb's work. Great similarities are evident between Webb and Mengs, as Dobai has shown, particularly in the doctrine of selection, in their appreciation of Raphael, Correggio and Titian, and in their views on Antiquity and the concept of grace. On the other hand, both their views have common roots, in the work of Shaftesbury and Richardson. Webb differs from Mengs in one essential point – he sees the role of the 'passions' in artistic depiction as positive (Dobai II, p.726), while Mengs, proceeding from his postulate of beauty, would only accept the depiction of a state of balanced rest. Antiquity offered Webb suitable themes to depict the passions, and this was the most modern element in his article; it explains its great renown.

56

Giovanni Volpato (1735-1803) after Antonio Correggio
Christ on the Mount of Olives

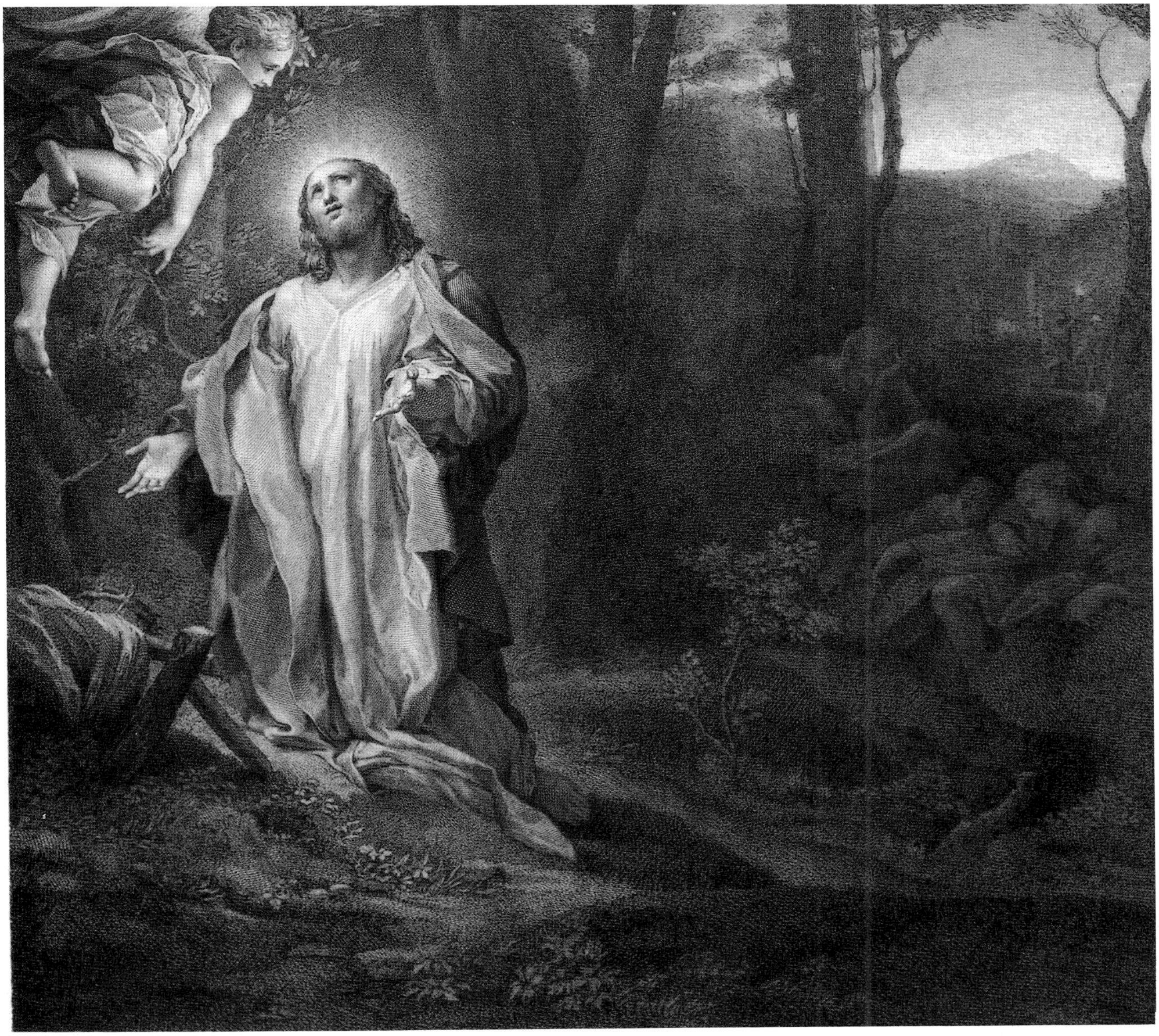

London, Apsley House
31.8 × 34.6 cm
Inscribed: Ant. Allegri da Coreggio pinxit/ Joh. Volpato sculpsit Romae 1773 Cum pervenisset Jesus ad montem Olivarum poitis genibus orabat. Luc. Cap. XII.V.40 / Ex Tabula Madriti in Pinacotheca Regia
Plate 18 in *Schola Italica Picturae/ sive/ selectae quaedam summorum e schola/ italica pictorum tabulae / aere incisae cura et impensio / Gavini Hamilton Pictoris* / Romae MDCCLXXIII
London, Royal Academy of Arts

LITERATURE: Carlo Giuseppe Ratti, *Notizie storiche sincere intorno la vita e le opere del celebre pittore Antonio Allegri da Correggio, scritte da Carlo Giuseppe Ratti.* Finale (Ligure), 1781, pp.121-2; Azara-

Fea 1787, p.XLVI; exhibition catalogue, *Giovanni Volpato 1735-1803*, edited by Giorgio Marini, Bassano del Grappa, 1988, no.168 (with further literature).

According to his own statement (in a letter of 15 August 1772 to Gamba, see exhibition catalogue 1988), Volpato's copperplate was based on a drawing by Mengs, which he in turn had made from the painting by Correggio, then in the collection of the Spanish monarch (now at Apsley House). This does not agree with the information given by Ratti and Azara-Fea, according to which Mengs did not copy the original painting but a very good copy of it by Filippo Lauri, which was then in the Palazzo Falconieri in Rome.

Possibly Volpato was not fully informed, and so believed he was using a copy of the original. Astonishingly, the text on the print makes no mention of the fact that he used a drawing by Mengs.

In 1779 Mengs's estate contained a copy of Correggio's painting which is described as by Mengs himself in the inventory. Mengs admired Correggio's painting, and he recalled the composition in his own painting of the same subject which he produced around 1768 for the bedchamber of Charles III (Madrid, Patrimonio Nacional).

The engraving was included in Gavin Hamilton's *Schola Italica Picturae* of 1773, which was one of the first volumes of prints to be published in Rome. It includes exemplary works of the Italian schools of painting in high-quality reproductions. Hamilton, who spent many years on the publication, had contacted Volpato as early as 1770 to ask him to contribute to the work.

In first place is Michelangelo, whose frescos in the Sistine Chapel also form the frontispiece, in itself a fine example of engraving. He is followed by Raphael and his pupil Polidoro, the Florentines from Leonardo to Andrea del Sarto, while Correggio only comes after Parmigianino. Clearly Hamilton's view of the heirarchy of painters differed from that of Mengs, who would certainly have placed Raphael and Correggio before Michelangelo, although in the last years of his life he developed a very high esteem for the latter's works.

57

Richard Cumberland, *Anecdotes of Eminent Painters in Spain with Cursory Remarks upon the present State of Arts in that Kingdom*, London (1782)

London, Royal Academy of Arts (6515/14.B)

PROVENANCE: Given by the author to the Royal Academy Library.

LITERATURE: Dobai II, (1975) p.1292.

Cumberland (1732-1811) was, with his brother George, one of the first British art critics in the last years of the eighteenth century to see the promotion and improvement of British art as a matter of national concern. This makes it clear why he was so critical and at times even polemical in his views on Mengs's work in Spain. Like Barry (see Introduction p.12), he probably disliked seeing a foreigner produce so many works for English collectors.

Cumberland's sympathies were with Sir Joshua Reynolds, although he does not appear to have cared much about the admiration which Cumberland showed him. The artist to whom Cumberland gave most support was George Romney. He was a member of the next generation, and one of the artists who could most credibly defend the autonomy of English painting against continental trends. Cumberland was strongly resentful of Benjamin West, criticising him mainly for his depictions of little known subjects. The vehicle through which he influenced the London art public for a time was the paper 'The Observer', in which many of his essays appeared in 1785 and 1786.

Cumberland published an autobiography during his lifetime (*Memoirs of Richard Cumberland, written by himself, containing an account of his life and writings*, London, 1806), and he had seen Mengs's work in Spain on a quasi-official visit to that country. His description of the paintings in the royal collections in Madrid, compiled on the same occasion (*An Accurate and Descriptive Catalogue of the Several Paintings in the King of Spain's Palace at Madrid*, London, 1787) is based on the letter from Mengs to Antonio Ponz, which was published in the sixth volume of Ponz's great work *'El viaje de Espana'* of 1776.

Cumberland's verdict on Mengs's Spanish works is clearly influenced by his rejection of academic Italian taste, although chauvinism probably played a part as well. But his observation and comments show a sure and unerring sense of the weaknesses and general problems of a style of painting that devoted itself so exclusively to the ideals of a past epoch. This was also the reason why José Nicolas de Azara, the editor of the writings of Mengs first published in 1780, reacted so furiously to Cumberland's attacks in his second edition. Azara not only saw the fame of his deceased friend Mengs under attack, but the very foundation of his own views on art. Although Cumberland was only four years younger than Mengs, his objections represent a classic 'younger generation' response, that is, they represented the unyielding attitude of young men who need to distance themselves from the ideals of their fathers in order to believe in their own progress. That Cumberland was, on the other hand, fascinated by Mengs, is evident from the fact that he translated Azara's work into English, albeit anonymously (cat.no.61).

58

Des Ritters Anton Raphael Mengs ersten Mahlers Karl III. König in Spanien hinterlaßne Werke. Nach den Originalhandschriften übersetzt und mit ungedruckten Aufsätzen und Anmerkungen vermehrt herausgegeben von M. C. F. Prange. Halle (1786)

Octavo, 3 volumes, Germany, Private collection, ex libris P. M. Ehrenberger

LITERATURE: Lüdecke 1917

The first German translation of the writings of Mengs edited by Azara was published in 1781 and 1782 in extracts in Jagemann's '*Magazin der italienischen Literature und Künste*'. At the same time Wilhelm Gottlieb Becker, a friend of Oeser and Nicolas Guibal, who had lived in Pisa for some years, was working at a German translation, but this was never finished. His material came into the hands of Christian Friedrich Prange, a 'Magister der freyen Künste' who had been teaching in Halle since 1778. The material included two articles by Guibal, which Doray de Longrais had already published as by Mengs (see cat.no.59), and a number of facts on the artist's life, mainly relating to the years 1751 to 1756 and deriving from information which Guibal had given Becker. Prange included this information in the footnotes to Azara's biography, but he also printed the historical eulogy which Gian Ludovico first published in book form in 1780. Prange's catalogue of works combines the data from Azara on the Spanish works with the œuvre catalogue compiled by Mengs's heirs, and which had first appeared in 1780 in Bianconi's '*Elogio storico*'. Prange's edition appeared in 1786, and all three volumes are now very rare. A fourth volume was planned but never appeared. In 1843 and 1844 a two-volume edition appeared in Bonn edited by G. Schilling

59

Oeuvres complètes d'Antoine-Raphael Mengs, premier peintre du Roi d'Espagne contenant différentes traités sur la théorie de la Peinture. Traduit de l'italien. Paris à l'Hôtel de Thon (1786)

Quarto, two volumes, bound in leather, Germany, Private collection, ex libris Holland House.

LITERATURE: Lüdecke (1917); Erhard Preissig, 'Zur Geschichte des deutschen Einflusses in Frankreich, Eine handschriftliche französische Übersetzung der Werke von Raffael Mengs, *Jahresberichte des deutschen Staatsgymnasiums in Prag*, III, (1927/8), pp. 1-9.

The French translation commissioned by the Dutchman Hendrik Jansen follows the Italian edition of 1780 exactly, and that also applies to the division into two volumes made by Azara to suit the contents. Azara had prefaced Mengs's writings with a biography of the painter which he wrote himself, and a list of the works painted in Spain. Jansen used both texts unchanged.

Little is known of how the French translation was made. Jansen had already published a greatly abbreviated French edition of Mengs's writings in 1781, and this met with fierce criticism from Azara. Then in 1782 another French edition of the writings by Mengs that had been published by that date appeared; the editor, J. P. Doray de Longrais, had had some of the work authorised by Mengs himself in 1778. It included a biography which had been compiled by J. P. Hérissant, according to Mengs's pupil Nicolas Guibal, and it included two pieces by Guibal as works by Mengs. Another translation into French, which remained unfinished, was undertaken around 1781 by the French scholar F. J. G. de La Porte du Theil in Rome under the direction of Azara and Milizia. The manuscript of this translation is in the Bibliothèque National in Paris; possibly Jansen used some of this translation for his edition.

60

Opere di Antonio Raffaello Mengs primo Pittore del re Cattolico Carlo III. Pubblicate dal cavaliere D. Giuseppe Niccola d'Azara e in questa edizione corrette ed aumentate dall'Avvocato Carlo Fea. Rome, Pagliarini (1787)

Quarto, in one volume, Germany, Private collection

LITERATURE: *Neuer Deutscher Merkur*, 2 (1796), pp.426-35 (review); Lüdecke (1917); von Einem (1973); Angelo Ciavarella, *De Azara-Bodoni*, Parma, Museo Bodoniano (1979).

Soon after Mengs's death his friend and patron Azara, who was unshakeably convinced that Mengs was unequalled as a painter and art theorist, set about publishing his writings and the many fragments and ideas which Mengs had put on paper in the course of his life. The papers must have been in indescribable chaos after Mengs's death, with repetitions, isolated fragments and ideas jotted down on scraps of paper in a muddle of several languages. Azara was not discouraged by the confusion and he found a patient editor in his friend Francesco Milizia, who was also an enthusiastic admirer of Mengs and had been a close friend of the artist. Milizia could speak German well enough to prepare the fragments and the essays, some of which were finished, for publication within a very short time. He edited all the Italian texts as well, as Azara's Italian was inadequate.

The history of the first Italian edition, which was published by the most renowned and best publisher in Italy, Giovanni Bodoni in Parma, is well documented in the correspondence between Azara and Bodoni, which was published in 1979 by A. Ciavarella. The letters are also important in that they show that the Spanish edition, which appeared soon after the Italian, failed so completely to meet Azara's standards that although he did originally co-edit this, he soon dissociated himself completely from the work. So, although the Spanish edition is occasionally claimed to be authentic, it must be emphasized that only the Italian edition of 1780 and the later ones of 1783 and 1836 are the original editions, edited by Azara and Milizia.

Some of the works in this edition are not by Mengs, as we see from the correspondence between Azara and Bodoni. They are the '*Frammento d'un discorso sopra i mezzi di far fiorire le belle arti nella Spagna*', written by Azara, and some remarks on architecture which closely agree with Milizia's views on architecture published later.

Despite the importance of the Azara edition of 1780 and its bibliographic quality, we are exhibiting the less imposing edition by Carlo Fea here for the following reasons. Fea had already made a name as the editor of the Italian translation of Winckelmann's *History of Ancient Art* (1783-84), and in his edition he included, beside a number of smaller essays and fragments on beauty, the eighteen letters which Winckelmann wrote to Mengs. These provide an insight of inestimable value into Winckelmann's character. The originals of the letters have never been found, but they are a major source of information and Goethe drew on them for his famous account of Winckelmann. The intellectual and human range of the friendship between Mengs and Winckelmann is one of the most interesting aspects of the biographies of both, not least because of the mysterious way it was broken off, a mystery that has never been solved. The relationship gains greatly in vividness through these letters.

Fea also published in his edition, which did not appear until the beginning of 1788, thirty-one other interesting letters which Mengs had written to various correspondents. They include the letter to Henry Hoare (cat.no.52). Some of these letters came into Fea's hands from the Mengs family. They were purchased in 1868 by Winckelmann's biographer Carl Justi in Rome and then came from Justi's heirs to the University Library in Bonn.

Much of the information which Fea packs into his footnotes to Azara's text derives from the artist's sister Therese and her husband Anton von Maron. It includes important facts relating to Mengs's biography. Fea also considerably enlarged the list of Mengs's works. Azara, who had planned a separate publication listing Mengs's works, which was also to include prints, had treated this aspect very summarily in his editions. Fea's œuvre catalogue is very precise and includes the works not painted for Spain.

Although Azara did not have a good word to say for Fea's edition, this now rather rare work is an invaluable source. Azara had two justifiable reasons for his objections: the bad quality of the printing, and the fact that he had not authorised the reprinting of the texts he had edited. So at least part of Fea's work is a pirated edition, although it was published by the celebrated Roman publisher Pagliarini.

61

The Works of Anthony Raphael Mengs. First Painter to His Catholic Majesty Charles III By the Chev. Don. J. N. de Azara. Translated from the Italian. London (1796)

Octavo, two volumes, London, Royal Academy of Arts

LITERATURE: Lüdecke (1917); Dobai II (1975), pp.966/7; Finke (1981), p.77.

The English edition, which was translated by Richard Cumberland (see cat.no.57), is chronologically the last of the editions of Mengs's writings to appear in the eighteenth century. That Cumberland used the Italian and not the Spanish edition is confirmation of his sure instinct that this was the better and more reliable edition (see cat.no.60).

In the brief introduction, in which the translator does not identify himself, some works by Mengs in Great Britain are mentioned. Nevertheless, the translator maintains that Mengs painted only copies for Great Britain. As this was factually not correct, it can only be meant as criticism, the term 'copy' being synonymous with lack of originality. Cumberland thus denies Mengs any artistic independence. In fact, by 1796 imitation of Raphael, Correggio and the seventeenth-century Bolognese painters was regarded as slavish and lacking in inspiration; at any rate, it was certainly no longer seen as a means to 'improve the arts'. The preponderance of religious subjects and the untiring but ultimately unsatisfying reworking of canonical models were seen, not only in Britain but in Germany as well just before the end of the eighteenth century, as exactly the opposite of what was expected of a modern and contemporary art. Hence the fame which Mengs still enjoyed in some quarters was held to be not simply inappropriate but annoying as well.

The artist's writings, many of which deal with the problems of artistic beauty and its ideals, and firmly identify these ideals with Raphael, Correggio and Titian, confirmed all the suspicions that his art was too academic and limited in range.

However, Mengs's writings also include passages dealing with the practice and technique of painting, and with paints and their composition. His knowledge of this was profound, and even after his approach to painting was condemned this information continued to be valued and utilised by painters far into the nineteenth century (see Introduction, p.17); to that extent the English translation of his writings certainly had an influence. This may also have been due to the fact that texts written by a painter who had didactic but not literary ambitions may well be more accessible to painters than texts written by scholars or critics.

Bibliography

Parentheses refer to short bibliographical references

ALGAROTTI, FRANCESCO, *Opere.* 10 volumes, Cremona 1779

ASHBY, THOMAS, 'Thomas Jenkins in Rome'. In: *Papers of the British School at Rome,* VI, 1913, No.8, p.487-510

Exhibition Catalogue, *Antonio Rafael Mengs 1728-1779.* Madrid, Museo del Prado June 1980, ed. M Agueda

(AZARA), *Opere di Antonio Raffaello Mengs. Primo Pittore della Maestà di Carlo III. Re di Spagna.* Parma Bodoni 1780

AZARA – FEA, see cat.no.60

AZARA 1796, see cat.no.61

(BIANCONI), *Elogio storico del Cavaliere Anton Raffaele Mengs scritto dal Consiglier Bianconi con un catalogo in fine delle opere da esso fatte.* Milan 1780

(BULL – HARRIS), BULL, DUNCAN AND ENRIQUETA HARRIS, 'The Companion of Velázquez' Rokeby Venus and a Source for Goya's Naked Maya'. In: *The Burlington Magazine* CXXVIII, 1986, pp.647 ff.

(CASSANOVA, Memoires) CASSONOVA, GIACOMO, CHEVALIER DE SEINGALT, *Geschichte meines Lebens.* Erstmals nach der Urfassung ins Deutsche übersetzt von Heinz von Sauter. Berlin 1985, 12 vols

CÉAN Y BERMUDEZ, JUAN AUGUSTIN, *Diccionario historico de los más illustres professores de las bellas artes en Espana,* Vol.II, Madrid 1800

(CLARK – BOWRON) CLARK, ANTHONY M, *Pompeo Batoni. A Complete Catalogue of his Work with an Introductory Text.* Edited and prepared for Publication by Edgar Peters Bowron, Oxford 1985

(CONCA) Y ALVAREZ, ANTONIO, *Descrizione odeporica della Spagna in cui spezialmente si dà notizia delle cose spettanti alle belle arti.* 4 vols. Parma 1793-97

(CRUZ 1812), CRUZ Y BAHAMONDE, NICOLAS DE LA, CONDE DE MAULE, *Viaje de Espana, Francia y Italia.* 14 vols. Madrid und Cadiz 1806-13 (Vol.XII: 1812)

CUMBERLAND 1782, see cat.no.57

DOBAI, JOHANNES, *Die Kunstlitertur des Klassizismus und der Romantik in England.* 4 vols. Berne 1974-84

EINEM, HERBERT VON, 'Anton Raphael Mengs. Briefe an Raimondo Ghelli und Anton Maron'. In: *Abhandlungen der Akademie der Wissenschaften in Göttingen.* Göttingen 1973

(ERFFA/STALEY) ERFFA, HELMUT VON AND ALLEN STALEY, *The Paintings of Benjamin West.* New Haven – London 1986

(FABRE, D. FRANCISCO JOSÉ), *Description de las alegorias pintadas en las bovedas del Real Palacio de Madrid.* Madrid 1829

FINKE, ULRICH, 'Mengs und England.' In: *Sind Briten hier? Relations between British and Continental Art, 1680-1880.* ed. Zentralinistitut für Kunstgeschichte in München. Munich 1981, pp.57-82

(FLEMING 1959) FLEMING, JOHN, 'Some Roman Cicerones and Art Dealers'. In: *English Miscellany 1958,* pp.127-141

(FLEMING 1962) FLEMING, JOHN, *Robert Adam and his Circle.* London 1962

FORD, BRINSLEY, 'English Patrons in Rome'. In: *Apollo,* June 1974: *Thomas Jenkins. Banker, Dealer and Unofficial English Agent in Rome.* pp.416-25; *Sir Watkin Williams-Wynn. A Welsh Maecenas.* pp.435-39; *James Byres. Principal Antiquarian for the English Visitors to Rome.* pp.446-61

(FREDERICKSEN) FREDERICKSEN, BURTON B, *The Index of Paintings Sold in the British Isles during the Nineteenth Century.* Vol.I: 1801-05. Oxford 1988

GUDIOL, JOSÉ, *Goya. 1746-1828. Biografia Estudio analitico y catalogo de sus pinturas.* Barcelona 1970, 4 vols

HOETINK, H. R., *Duitse Tekeningen uit de 18e et 19e eeuw. Catalogus van de versameling in het Museum Boymans-van Beuningen.* Rotterdam 1964

HONISCH, DIETER, *Anton Raphael Mengs und die Bildform des Frühklassizimus.* Recklinghausen 1965

JANSEN, see cat. no.59

JOYCE, HETTY, 'The Ancient Frescoes from the Villa Negroni and their Influence in the Eighteenth and Nineteenth Centuries'. In: *Art Bulletin* LXV, no.3 1983, Sept. pp.423-40

KAUFFMANN, C. M., *Catalogue of the Paintings in the Wellington Museum.* London 1982

(LEGRAND) Exhibition catalogue: *La Rome baroque de Maratti à Piranèse.* ed. Catherine Legrand and Domitilla d'Ormesson. Paris, Musée du Louvre, Nov 1990 – Feb 1991

LIPPOLD, GEORG, *Gemmen und Kameen des Altertums und der Neuzeit.* Stuttgart 1922

NAGLER, GEORG KASPAR, *Neues Allgemeines Künstler – Lexikon.* Vol.IX. Munich 1840

NOACK, FRIEDRICH, *Das Deutschtum in Rom.* Stuttgart – Berlin – Leipzig 1927, 2 vols.

PONZ, ANTONIO, *Viaje de Espana en que se da noticia de las cosas apreciables y dignas de saberse, que hay en ella.* 18 vols. Madrid 1772-94 (VI: 1776, XIV: 1788)

PRANGE, see cat.no.58

RATTI, CARLO GIUSEPPE, *Epilogo della vita del fù Cavalier Mengs.* Genoa 1779

ROETTGEN, STEFFI, 'Mengs sulle orme di Poussin'. In: *Antologia di Belle Arti,* No.2, 1977, pp.148-56

ROETTGEN, STEFFI, 'Mengs, Winckelmann und Alessandro Albani. Idee und Gestalt des Parnaß in der Villa Albani'. In: *Storia dell' Arte,* No.30, 1977, pp.87-156

ROETTGEN, STEFFI, 'Antonio Raffaello Mengs e Raffaello – rendiconto di un rapporto programmato'. In: *Atti del*

Convegno di Studi 'Raffaello e l'Europa'. Rom, Acc. Naz. dei Lincei. Rom 1990, pp.619-53

ROSENBERG, PIERRE, '*Une correspondance de Jullien de Parme (1736-1799).*' In: *Archives de l'Art Française* XXV, 1984, pp.197-245

RUSSELL, FRANCIS, 'The British Portraits of Anton Raphael Mengs'. In: *National Trust Studies 1979*. The National Trust 1978, pp.9-19

SAABYE, MARIANNE, 'Augustus og Cleopatra. Dokumentation omkring et maleri af Anton Raphael Mengs'. In: *Kunstmuseets Aarskrift*, LXIII, 1976, Kopenhagen 1977, pp.12-38

SCHRÖTER, ELISABETH, die Villa albani als Imago Mundi. Das unbekannte Fresken – und Antikenprogramm im Piano Nobile der Villa Albani zu Rom.' In: *Forschungen zur Villa Albani* Hg. von H. Beck und P.C. Bol. Berlin 1982, pp.185- 299

SPARROW, JOHN, 'An Oxford Altar-Piece'. In: *The Burlington Magazine* CII, 1960, Jan. pp.4-7

SPARROW, JOHN, 'Mengs' Altar-Piece. A Further Note'. In: *The Burlington Magazine* CVII, 1965, p.631

WHITLEY, WILLIAM T. *Artists and their Friends in England 1700-1799.* 2 vols. London 1928

(WINCKELMANN, BRIEFE) WINCKELMANN, JOHAN JOACHIM, *Briefe.* In: *Verbindung mit Hans Diepolder* ed. Walter Rehm, 4 vols., Berlin 1952-57

WOODBRIDGE, KENNETH, 'Henry Hoare's Paradise'. In: *The Art Bulletin* XLVII/1, 1965, pp.83-116

Index